In the hands of women

Manchester University Press

PERSPECTIVES ON DEMOCRATIC PRACTICE

With the ebbing away of the 'third wave' of democratisation, democratic practice is unfolding and consolidating in different ways. While state based representative democracy remains central to our understanding of the concept, we are also conscious of the importance of social movements, non-governmental organisations and governance institutions. New mechanisms of accountability are being developed, together with new political vocabularies to address these elements in democratic practice. The books published in this series focus on three aspects of democratic practice: analytical and normative democratic theory, including processes by which democratic practice can be explained and achieved; new social and protest movements, especially work with a comparative and international focus; and institution-building and practice, including transformations in democratic institutions in response to social and democratic forces. Their importance arises from the fact that they are concerned with key questions about how power can be more fairly distributed and how people can be empowered to have a greater influence on decisions that affect their lives.

This series takes forward the intellectual project of the earlier MUP series, *Perspectives on Democratization*.

SHIRIN M. RAI AND WYN GRANT   series editors

In the hands of women
Paradigms of citizenship

edited by
SUSAN BUCKINGHAM
and
GERALDINE LIEVESLEY

Manchester University Press
Manchester and New York
distributed exclusively in the USA by Palgrave

Published by Manchester University Press
Oxford Road, Manchester M13 9NR, UK
and Room 400, 175 Fifth Avenue, New York, NY 10010, USA
www.manchesteruniversitypress.co.uk

Distributed exclusively in the USA by
Palgrave, 175 Fifth Avenue, New York,
NY10010, USA

Distributed exclusively in Canada by
OBC Press, University of British Columbia, 2029 West Mall,
Vancouver, BC, Canada V6T 1Z2

British Library Cataloguing-in-Publication Data
A catalogue record for this book is available from the British Library

Library of Congress Cataloging-in-Publication Data applied for

ISBN   0 7190 6910 6 *hardback*
EAN   978 0 7190 6910 9

First published 2006

15 14 13 12 11 10 09 08 07 06   10 9 8 7 6 5 4 3 2 1

Typeset in Trump Mediaeval 10.12 pt
by Servis Filmsetting Ltd, Manchester
Printed in Great Britain
by Bell & Bain Ltd, Glasgow

Contents

Acknowledgements

We would like to thank: the editors at Manchester University Press for their encouragement and support throughout this project; Brunel University for providing the means for allowing the writing team to formulate the ideas behind this book; Catherine, Karen and Marion for agreeing to participate in this venture and each other for seeing it through.

Contributors

Susan Buckingham is Senior Lecturer in Geography and Environmental Issues at Brunel University. Her main research interest is in the interactions between women, the environment and political action. She has edited and written a number of books including *Gender and Environment*, published by Routledge in 2000. Susan is a board member of the Women's Environmental Network and regularly broadcasts on gender and environmental issues on BBC Radio 4's *Home Planet*.

Catherine Danks is Senior Lecturer in History at Manchester Metropolitan University. Her main research interests are in the areas of Russian history and contemporary politics. In 2001, she co-edited *Globalisation and National Identities: Crisis or Opportunity* for Palgrave, and her *Russian Politics and Society: An Introduction* was published by Pearson. She is a founder member and treasurer of the Global Studies Association.

Geraldine Lievesley is Senior Lecturer in Politics at Manchester Metropolitan University. Her research interests are Latin American and Cuban politics and the politics of social movements, particularly women, in the Third World. Her most recent book is *The Cuban Revolution: Past, Present and Future Perspectives* (Palgrave Macmillan: 2004).

Karen Morrow is Senior Lecturer in Law at the University of Leeds. Her main research interests lie in the broad area of environmental law and in particular concern the nexus of environmental issues with property law, human rights, decision-making and civil society. She is co-author, with Sean Coyle, of *The Philosophical Foundations of Environmental Law*, published by Hart in 2004. Karen is deputy convenor of the Society of Legal Scholars Environment Panel.

Marion Roberts is Professor of Urban Design at the University of Westminster. Gender divisions and the urban environment have been the source of a long-term research interest. Her current projects lie in the areas of mixed-use development and the night-time economy and her most recent book is *Approaching Urban Design: The Design Process* (Longman: 2001, co-edited with Clara Greed).

Introduction

SUSAN BUCKINGHAM AND GERALDINE
LIEVESLEY

The original idea for this book came about from discussions with Judy Matthews, a geographer committed to social and environmental equity who sadly died in 1999, before the ideas had a chance to materialise. The editors' thinking behind the project was that the book should be a dialogue between women working in citizenship discourses from a variety of perspectives and that it should demonstrate how intellectual ideas are shaped and consolidated by conversations we have with each other, with our friends, colleagues and family members. Our understandings of citizenship are not simply formed by our academic-discipline-based readings, but by our personal experiences, our observations of friends, mothers, daughters and other relatives, colleagues, fellow campaigners and students in different situations to ourselves. In particular we wanted to encourage our readers to see these relationships as rich and valid sources of the arguments that we develop during the course of our lives as women/academics. In 2002 the editors explored the potential for making this project happen and were fortunate in persuading colleagues from a variety of disciplines to join us in this enterprise. We make no argument for the particular disciplines chosen – they are mostly serendipitously self-selected by virtue of the writers' commitment to women's access to citizenship and previous connections to the editors. Clearly politics, law and history are central to any understanding of citizenship and geography provides particular ways of spatialising discourses of citizenship, while urban design offers a way of showing how the intellectual concerns of women's citizenship can be planned for (and against). The case studies give a broad, but by no means exhaustive, range of experiences and are designed to capture moments of citizenship practice rather than to present its full range. We would have liked to include contributions from Asia and Africa but the logistics of the book prevented this.

We hope that the book also shows how any understanding of citizenship is enhanced by interdisciplinary conversations and we attempt, in the last chapter, to show how this emerged in this project. We have learnt substantially from each other – both with surprise in our similarities and from our different disciplinary perspectives. We have realised (or, rather, the project has given us the opportunity to reflect upon) how artificial academic boundaries are – a way of containing and ordering knowledge that in many ways is antithetical to feminist scholarship. So, while this book represents, on the one hand, a collection of essays on citizenship from different disciplinary traditions, we hope that the process we have gone through also renders it greater than the sum of its parts. It is notable that, independently, we wrote about similar structures, shared key reference points and found we could understand each others' language. The project has taken us each through an intellectual and personal journey and it is notable that during the course of writing the book we have gone through various transformations which have sometimes made the writing stressful and have delayed the finished product and we would like to acknowledge the tolerance of our editors at MUP in this regard. Some of this process is captured in the conclusion. In particular, it has thrown into relief the pressures facing the woman academic as we have had to struggle through balancing home and personal life, fighting for and dealing with promotion and carving the thinking and writing time out of a myriad of administrative, management and teaching responsibilities, as well as consultancy and other contracted research, which burdens today's academics.

The book opens with a review of some of the significant themes concerning women's citizenship from the perspective of politics. This was very much part of the learning process that the authors went through as it provided us with a perspective core to the concept of citizenship from which we were able to gauge the 'state of the art' of our own disciplines. In Chapter 1, Geraldine Lievesley considers the environment in which women live and the identities they possess and how these characteristics contribute to the nature of their citizenship. Underlying these themes are important questions. Is the experience of citizenship different in the political, social, economic, cultural, legal and physical spheres of life? Can we draw these experiences together to produce a paradigm of female citizenship? Is citizenship second-hand for some women but not for others? How can women confront the structures, institutions, relationships and attitudes which obstruct, and often deny, their citizenship rights? What kinds of engagement do women embrace and how effective can their struggles be? In posing these and other questions, the first chapter sets the scene for the case-study-based chapters which follow.

In Chapter 2, Karen Morrow analyses how its commitment to gender mainstreaming has affected the United Nations' activities, particularly with respect to environmental law. The latter is an interesting site for study in that the integration of innovative laws into a (relatively) new field of law represents a more favourable situation than grafting them on to more established areas. In addition, there are parallels between the exploitation of women and the natural world in the context of patriarchal society that makes this area one which is philosophically interesting and worthy of closer examination and evaluation. While the UN has displayed considerable activism on paper, the impact of such enlightened policies appears, to date, to be somewhat limited in practice.

Chapter 3 addresses the nature of women's access to citizenship in the West through considering both women's unfair exposure to environmental problems (in that it is disproportionately negative compared to men's) and the strategies they adopt to redress this. Since formal decision-making arenas are largely inaccessible to women – particularly in which to take up issues which are most likely to affect women – the informal arena of environmental campaigning is explored for examples of forging citizenship. Susan Buckingham uses several particularly geographical concepts – place, scale and the relationship between the public and private – to examine the nature of women's citizenship, and its variants. The developing discourse of environmental citizenship is also examined to see how far women have been able to make a political space for themselves both within the relationship between the public and private, and within and outside the nation state (the unit at which citizenship was originally conceptualised).

In Chapter 4, Marion Roberts considers active citizenship in the urban landscape. Women's relationship to the physical realm is problematised because, historically, particular groups of women have experienced and in some cases continue to experience constraints on their spatial mobility and hence their ability to engage in civil society, even in developed countries, in conditions of equality and social justice. The chapter examines the idea of planning by neighbourhood that has now come back into vogue with urban designers and planners and in government policy. It traces the history of the neighbourhood unit and its current re-emergence as an ideal template for planning for environmental sustainability. It notes the tensions between the neighbourhood as a space for women's self-organisation and as a bounded entity that perpetuates inequalities of gender and class. Experiences of the neighbourhood have changed as technologies of movement and communication have shifted the boundaries between the public and private, the local and the global and, crucially, between the 'street neighbourhood' and the city region. The chapter concludes by emphasising the emancipatory potential for women of access to these networks of movement and communication in order to pursue an active and activist citizenship.

In Chapter 5, Geraldine Lievesley considers how women's identities have been shaped by political, socio-economic, legal and cultural processes in Latin and Central America and Cuba historically and in the contemporary period. Women have mobilised and organised in response to a variety of circumstances and problems and in defence of their rights to citizenship. In so doing, they have transformed the nature and boundaries of that citizenship, challenging male-dominated discourses and masculine appropriation of what is considered acceptable behaviour.

Catherine Danks examines women's citizenship in post-communist Russia, focusing on the Soldiers' Mothers' committees in Chapter 6. Their existence constitutes an active part of Russia's nascent civil society. The collapse of soviet socialism has had some highly negative consequences for women, including under-representation in political institutions and growing unemployment. Since his election as president in 2000, Putin has sought to create a 'managed democracy' with the aim of co-opting or coercing civil society organisations. Despite this, and the fact that feminist and human rights discourses are quite weak in Russia today, the Soldiers' Mothers' committees continue to grow and have won respect and support.

In the final chapter, the contributors come together to consider what we have learnt about women's experience of citizenship and also what we have learnt from this collaborative project.

1

Women and the experience of citizenship

Geraldine Lievesley

Introduction

The motivation for this book was a desire to explore different conceptions of citizenship and their consequences for women. The contributors come from distinct academic backgrounds and their hope is to compare and contrast how their specific disciplines deal with the question of women's citizenship and to decide if it is possible to transcend the boundaries which have tended to ring-fence academic scholarship. Traditionally in my own discipline – generally called 'political science' although it is not a label I identify with – culture (anthropology, literature and the visual and aural arts), history, sociology, law, urban planning and geography are sometimes taken into consideration, but as often not. It may be said that this belies the undisciplined and dynamic way that life unfolds and hampers the development of useful knowledge, that is knowledge that accepts the complexity of social behaviour and aspires to generate social progress rather than merely attempting to codify such behaviour. It is not my intention to suggest that codification blocks the pursuit of useful knowledge (although it may do); whether it does, depends upon who oversees the codification process, the criteria upon which it is based (including ideological objectives), and which individuals or groups are excluded from or targeted by it. Attitudes towards cross-fertilisation between disciplines have changed over recent decades amongst some within the academic community. Thus, Lynn Spigel argues that varied disciplinary interests

> are beginning to form an interrelated project ... Even if the fields
> still have different research protocols and different theoretical

traditions, recent exchanges between disciplines in the humanities and social sciences have been extremely productive because the transfer of ideas has resulted in greater knowledge of how different industries and social institutions [such as media or housing] interact with one another and collectively affect people.[1]

The gendered nature of citizenship

I wish to introduce several modalities which inform the discussion concerning the relationship between women and citizenship in this and subsequent chapters. The first centres upon universal and particular notions of citizenship and includes a consideration of who is included and who is excluded within these parameters. Citizenship can be understood both as the status ascribed to individuals by states through constitutional formulations and legal conventions and as a set of social norms and practices which affect relations between individual citizens, between individuals and communities and between the latter and government. Put another way, citizenship is both an ideal type and a process towards attainment of that type. The exercise of citizenship is founded upon rights, responsibilities, obligations and expectations on the part of the individual and of the state. Historically, citizenship rights have been regarded as being based upon an abstract and universal conception of the individual citizen but, in practice, many different groups have been prevented from enjoying them.

In the Athenian *demos*, slaves, colonised peoples and women were not regarded as citizens while, in more recent times, both African-Americans and black South Africans were excluded from such rights solely on account of their skin colour (although this prohibition was hedged around by literacy and property qualifications). In these societies, and in many others, the extension of citizenship rights had to be fought for by marginalised groups. In his important body of work on the subject, the political scientist T. H. Marshall argued that the extension of rights throughout the twentieth century was achieved by social and political movements and that, in these processes, the nature of citizenship rights was transformed from the purely political (the right to vote and ancillary partisan activities) to encompass social and economic opportunities (including citizens as workers in the labour market and citizens claiming state benefits under the aegis of national welfare programmes).[2]

One of the major elements of the liberal model of democracy has been an acknowledgement of the division between the public and private spheres of life. In the public arena, which is the site of governance, it predicates that rationality and justice prevail and all citizens are treated equally. In the private sphere, the site of the family, individuals are seen to act as a consequence of their own preferences and prejudices. Rationality has always been understood as a masculine attribute in traditional literature, whereas 'irrational' women were deemed to feel more 'at home' in the private sphere where they would not be able to interfere in the business of government or economic management. Deconstruction of the distinction between the public and private spheres has been at the core of feminism's critique of citizenship theory and the patriarchal structures of power it has underwritten. Implicit in this critique – and intrinsic to the argument of this volume – has been the contention that individuals act as citizens not only through officially sanctioned routes but in many other circumstances and with many diverse motivations and objectives. In this volume, various manifestations of this diversity – women as environmental activists, as leaders of community self-help projects, as campaigners against human rights violations among others – are foregrounded. Citizenship should be seen as being far more complex a phenomenon than conventional (and, historically, male-dominated) perspectives suggest. This is particularly relevant to the ways in which women experience citizenship.

In talking about women's citizenship rights in the United Kingdom, Katherine O'Donovan argues that a universal model of citizenship ignores the existence of differences of race, gender, ethnicity, class, religion, culture and geographical location. Typically, the middle-class heterosexual man 'masquerades as the abstract individual' and he is accorded privileges not only in the legal sphere but also in political, economic and social life. In contrast, women 'continue to be excluded as full legal subjects despite changes in the law from the mid-1970s'.[3] This is not the product of chance but is the consequence of the way that relations between men and women are structured. The belief that because women have been, and in many instances still are, confined to the private sphere (meaning that their lives are controlled and regulated, not that they are kept in purdah – although the latter is literally true in many societies) has resulted in social contract theory ignoring women's lack of freedom and the fact that they are not incorporated as citizens in the same way as men.

This can be demonstrated by any number of examples. Thus, there has been a traditional exclusion of gender-specific violence from discourses around human rights. The high levels of violence directed at women because of their gender 'constitutes a direct denial of women's right to equality' and the fear of such violence inhibits women's enjoyment of other rights.[4] Double standards are applied to battered wives who must prove that they were in immediate danger when they attacked or killed their male partner during moments of crisis; their experience of cumulative violence is not in itself regarded as just cause for homicide or as a reason for self-defence. The 1979 UN Convention on the Elimination of All Forms of Discrimination Against Women placed obligations upon states to prevent discrimination in public life, in education, employment, health and within the family, but it did not give a comprehensive account of women's rights, nor did it address gender-specific violence. The reason for this was that violence against women, and particularly that experienced privately, did not fit within the framework of its understanding of equality, which was based upon liberal theory and its recognition of the public/private divide. In fact, gender-specific violence is not a private matter but is rather a consequence of women's lack of political and socio-economic power and of the roles and identities imposed upon them.

In recent decades, women activists – meeting at various UN and parallel NGO conferences and organising in advocacy networks in the meantime – have sought to highlight gender-specific violence and to lobby for changes in international legal definitions of equality. Some degree of success was achieved with the Declaration Against Violence Against Women made by the UN General Assembly in 1993. This marked a significant advance in that the Declaration rejected religion or culture as excuses to abuse or discriminate against women. Its politicisation of gender-specific violence identified the formal responsibilities of governments but, sadly, did not suggest how such responsibilities could be enforced or regulated. The ubiquity of such violence – ranging from domestic brutality to state-directed repression, from sex tourism to dowry burnings to female genital mutilation – has contributed to dissolving cultural and strategic differences between the women who seek to eradicate it. The issue of violence is also less divisive than the intractable north–south debates upon the centrality of the struggle against patriarchy or the struggle for survival and social justice.[5]

Women have achieved considerable gains from the state in the United Kingdom (although it must be remembered that these achievements have been the result of long campaigns and were wrested from the state rather than being given by it) in the shape of the vote, married women's legislation and anti-discriminatory laws, equal parental rights, divorce on equal terms and, more recently, a degree of control over sexuality and reproduction and legislation against discrimination.[6] Women in other areas of the world are still denied many of these advances and struggle for them in the face of the intransigence of the state and many men. Although the passing of legislation is subject to the criticism that it is often found wanting in terms of effective implementation, the importance of legalism should not be denigrated. The extension and protection of civic rights and entitlements are an essential foundation if the processes of women's empowerment are to be strengthened and deepened.

A second modality is that which links citizenship to the emergence and consolidation of the nation state and to ideas about modernity. The processes of state-building in individual societies proceeded at diverse rates of speed and stages of institutionalisation, and the establishment of the rule of law all but rested upon various categories of exclusion from citizenship. Over time, this deficit was challenged by social, labour and anti-colonial movements and, in a different way, by the expansion of supranational institutions and organisations. In the post-1945 world, the UN Commission on the Status of Women and the International Labour Organisation specifically targeted the attainment of women's rights as citizens. In the European context, processes of simultaneous integration and regional devolution questioned the nature of national identity and the possible loss of citizenship rights as the nation state appeared to be losing its authority. Citizenship is increasingly conceived in global terms, transcending national boundaries with respect to populations and issues with the latter including international human rights and environmental controls (the rights of the 'person' replacing those of the 'citizen' but with no clear answers to how these rights should be regulated and by whom). If citizenship is no longer the preserve of individual states, the rights of acknowledged citizens may be endangered at worst or caught up in a process of change at the least, and groups existing on the margins of civil society and the state may find themselves in ever more difficult circumstances.

Many women fall into the latter category, be they immigrants, emigrants, refugees, guest workers, mail-order brides, domestic servants or sex workers. Women travelling through the states of an enlarged European Union in search of employment or refuge may find that they do not receive equal citizenship rights and entitlements in their new host countries as they might, or more likely not, in their countries of origin. Discrimination against women migrants with respect to employment (but not informal sweatshop production), education and legal status remains significantly high, while asylum seekers are confined to detention centres and receive public opprobrium. Even if the European Convention for Human Rights is applied to their cases (which involves protracted legal proceedings and is a rare and expensive event), its brief deals primarily with civil and political rights rather than economic and social ones. Thus, the Convention still adheres to the belief that there is a distinction between the two which patently there is not. The International Convention for Migrant Workers and their Families was introduced in 1990 but its impact has been more symbolic than substantive and it does not address the specific situation of migrant women (who also have to contend with domestic patriarchy within their own cultural and religious communities). Although employment and other opportunities have expanded for long-term migrants and their daughters, new arrivals still tend to be concentrated in exploitative industries.[7] In other areas of the world, women who belong to ethnic minorities, indigenous communities, lower castes, religious sub-cultures and other sectors also discover that the formal constitutional guarantees of protection accorded them are ignored in practice and, thus, their citizenship rights are abused.

A final modality centres around the discourse which links cultural identity to citizenship. Distinctions between culture and politics became increasingly blurred as post-structuralism and post-modernism entered intellectual and academic debates in the 1980s and 1990s although, in truth, such perspectives borrowed heavily from earlier bodies of work of writers such as Antonio Gramsci. Cultures ceased to be seen as static and hierarchical (the idea of 'high' and 'low' culture) and were now viewed as continuous and ever-changing processes of creating and attributing meaning to everyday practices which themselves shaped the individual's perception of her identity and her role as citizen. Thus, in this new understanding, cultural signifiers are important not just for what they *mean* but also for how they can contribute to transformative political and social strategies. This appears particularly relevant if applied to the mobilisation of the poor and other groups who struggle for very basic human rights on the fringes of what is seen as the legitimate public arena. Obviously valuable in terms of the study of the majority of women in the Third World, such an understanding can also be applied to other women disadvantaged by colour, marginality and geographical exclusion (thus, refugees and migrants; women living in societies which have experienced political transitions; women in inner city neighbourhoods or peripheral housing estates) in the wealthier areas of the world. Contemporary study of cultural and identity politics is a welcome and stimulating addition to the body of knowledge but it is vital that it should not detract from research into other fundamental forms of oppression (which affect men as well) based upon class, caste, ethnicity and sexuality. It is important that women are not burdened with one overriding identity which then determines how they are received and their actions interpreted; cultural signifiers should be used to inform and facilitate the possibilities for varied types of empowering activities which can contribute to women's citizenship.

The linguistic use made of such words as 'woman', 'women', 'feminine' and 'female' is intrinsic to the way that women's identities are formed. Thus, women have been represented as 'mothers of the nation' at the same time as effectively being excluded from the collective 'we' of the body politic. In many states, women enjoy full civic rights but this does not mean that they enjoy citizenship; in others, they are accorded partial, limited rights on the basis of their 'deficiencies' as women. The exercise of their constitutional and legal rights by women has historically been hampered by particular political and socio-economic circumstances and by social mores and cultural and religious practices which inhibit their behaviour. Women have attempted to counter these obstacles by appropriating the very stereotypes long used to repress them. Thus, the imagery of 'motherhood' has been utilised by diverse groups of women as a weapon in processes of resistance, challenges to the political status quo and critiques of state policy (in this volume, Catherine Danks' chapter on the Soldiers' Mothers' Committees in Russia describes how organisations originally founded out of maternal concern for young conscripts have moved to a position of open criticism of government policy in Chechnia). Social feminist or maternalist theorists have questioned liberalism's individualist values by advocating a set of values based on the experience of women as women and specifically as mothers. Writers such as Sara Ruddick have proposed the creation of a new politics guided by the virtues of love, friendship and cooperation.[8] Ruddick does not, however, believe that men are devoid of such virtues, rather that they can be taught them by women. Women are seen as enjoying moral superiority over men who are fundamentally competitive and aggressive. Many feminist writers have attacked this approach for perpetuating stereotypical and one-dimensional images of women and men and for denying the differences between individuals. It has also been criticised for its inability to offer a rationale for linking the social practice of mothering to democratic politics, the former being intrinsically specific and exclusive and the latter needing to be collective and inclusive.

Feminised images have been used to characterise and so subordinate a wide variety of marginalised groups. They were historically bestowed upon colonised societies whose inhabitants – male and female – were categorised as childlike, irrational, passive and incapable of self-improvement (thus justifying the 'masculine' colonial powers taking control and guiding them towards nationhood 'for their own good'). In similar fashion, Jurgen Habermas has defined the public sphere as a realm of rational male discourse which was inextricably linked to the rise of the bourgeoisie in seventeenth- and eighteenth-century Western Europe and which was physically located in the masculine preserves of coffee house, club and parliament. Women, the working class and people of colour were judged to be inherently irrational and were prohibited from entering such spaces.[9] If they had done so, public life (and, hence, progress) would have been endangered. The public sphere only began to be democratised through struggle in the nineteenth and twentieth centuries; further struggles to extend its boundaries would be undertaken later by anti-capitalist, anti-authoritarian and anti-global movements.

The exploitation of women working in sweated labour in the garment trade, as home-workers, on plantations and in export processing zones is justified by reference to the particular skills women are said to bring to 'women's work' (which would include women working in sex industries, whose 'skills' fuel much tourism publicity). Women have been depicted as opponents of war and as peacemakers, although such womanly attitudes have also been construed as cowardly, as in the conceit that going to war would 'make a man out of you' and would 'sort the men from the boys'. Similarly the notion that defeat in Vietnam demasculinised the United States set the agenda for the ugly *machismo* of Reaganite policy in Central America in the 1980s. Women remain highly vulnerable during wartime (for example, the use of mass rape in Rwanda and during the Balkan wars of the 1990s). Women who take up arms – as suicide bombers in Palestine or airline hijackers – are demonised even more than men because their actions are deemed unnatural.

In studying cultural practices and identities and the manner in which they are infused with significance, the triangular relationship between citizenship, the state and civil society becomes relevant. Women's struggles are often said to belong to the sphere of civil society because of their historical exclusion from the masculine sphere of the state and the public arena. In the following sections, I consider women's relationship with the state and their role within civil society; of necessity, this will involve more discussion of the reality of the public/private divide in women's lives.

Women and the state

The models of citizenship which have been promulgated by the liberal, Marxist and feminist schools of thought will be familiar to readers but it may be useful to offer some general comments here. The liberal democratic perspective – long the dominant paradigm – is predicated upon the idea that individuals are related by contracts made in their own rationally conceived interests. People are differentiated by sex, class, age, culture and history, but these differences are not essential features of a person and are not relevant politically, that is in the sense of persons as citizens. Subjective, arbitrary, personal desires should be relegated to the private realm of the family because they endanger commitment to the common good; rationality must permeate its pursuit. Early liberal theorists such as Hobbes and Locke believed that men should inhabit the public sphere while women, who, they argued, were ruled far more by sentiment and emotion than by reason and should, therefore, be considered as children in their relations with men, should properly be confined to the world of domesticity. Later writers such as Mary Wollstonecraft, Harriet Taylor and John Stuart Mill believed that women were rational and should be treated as men provided they received the necessary education.[10] Mill, despite his high regard for women's intellectual capacities, believed that even if they had the same opportunities as men, women would still choose marriage and motherhood over other roles. Taylor argued that many would choose careers in order to obtain a degree of financial independence from fathers and husbands. In taking this view, she demonstrated her naivety in that upper- and middle-class women in nineteenth-century England had little access to education and the professions and were privileged purely because they were dependent upon male family members, as well as being in a position to exploit poor women as their domestic servants and nannies. The fact that only a minority of women could benefit under liberal democracy was central to the Marxist view which held that gender inequality was a product of capitalism as a system of exploitative power relations and the family was an institution whose purpose was capital's need for women's domestic labour in the home. Class rather than gender determined women's social and political identity. Engels argued that the key to women's liberation was their entry into the labour market and their politicisation through participation in the class struggle.[11]

Liberal democracy has presumed the state's neutrality; that is, it is seen to possess no gender identity. Thus, the state and its institutions are as open to women's demands as to those of any other interest group. As the state is not prejudiced against women, women can rise without obstacle in any area of life. The liberal view is that women are disadvantaged because of their lack of education and their family responsibilities which reduce their public participation. However, this disadvantage is not structurally conditioned but the result of social environmental factors which can be remedied through the passage of legislation protecting women's rights. As they improve themselves, women increasingly adopt the masculine attribute of rationality; that is, in order to become empowered they must become more like men. Men will be happy to accept women's reasoned arguments; it is up to women to convince them.

During the second wave of feminism, which can be dated from the 1950s, liberal feminists, such as Betty Friedan, appeared to be saying that women could advance to the ranks of men through sheer effort.[12] The mystique that she wished to debunk was that women could find satisfaction in the traditional roles of wife and mother; rather, she contended, confinement to the domestic sphere alienated women from their true natures and capabilities. Her 'cure' was college education and work (tellingly, her analysis was based on the experience of white, middle-class, suburban women) but she would later retract this, arguing that career women might be more powerful than housewives but certainly were not happier.[13] This debate has continued until the present day with conservative commentators castigating professional women for their unnatural and unwomanly behaviour which was threatening to destroy the institution of the family. The contradictions involved in centring one's life in or outside the home (although, of course, most women do not have a choice in the matter and many of us try to juggle with both) has had many manifestations and consequences for women. Let me take just one example.

In her study of the cultural transitions in post-Second World War US family life, Lynn Spigel investigates the relationship between ideas of domesticity as reflected in the built environment, patterns of life in the suburbs and the iconography of male and female roles as represented in popular culture. Television – which took over from cinema as the major cultural industry in the 1950s – offered a mirror image of the 'good life' (replete with all the consumer goods vital to its achievement) and of the ways that women and men should contribute to it. Television both intruded into private family life and provided a link between it and the public sphere, constituting itself as a window on that world. Middle-class lifestyles shaped public views about family, while African-Americans and other undesirables were physically excluded from the suburbs (concentrated in urban ghettos, they effectively vanished from the public gaze). The nature of this suburban utopia (or dystopia depending on your viewpoint) was shaped by identification of the home as the place where women were able to both express their creativity and satisfy their consumerism, as well as service the needs of their husbands, who worked and governed in the public sphere. Although this gendered division of space was never clear-cut in practice and the boundaries between the two worlds changed over time, women and men who strayed from their appropriate sphere of activity were demonised for challenging traditional gender roles. This domestic ideal privileged men in terms of their ability to inhabit both spheres, made natural the subordinate position occupied by women and excised unacceptable ethnic and social groups from the picture. Popular culture and particularly television legitimised these separate domains and reinforced ideological constructs of femininity and masculinity.[14]

Liberal feminism's demand for equal rights for women was an important step in the process of women's emancipation and its proponents accomplished much in educational and legal reforms and in lobbying for greater political, professional and occupational opportunities. However, it did not tackle the underlying problem, in that the identification of women with the domestic sphere reinforced stereotypical identities and working women still assumed the main responsibility for childcare and housework and did not enjoy parity in public life (both in terms of pay and status and in positions of power). Women's citizenship continued to be restricted in a variety of ways that reflected societal assumptions about their duties as daughters, wives and mothers. The feminist critique was that family, marriage and sexuality should be issues in which gendered power is acknowledged as being exercised and should not, therefore, be subject to the notion of universal citizenship.

Many women do not identify their lives and concerns with what happens in the traditional public sphere and so why should the latter be regarded as absolutely central to the meaning of citizenship? As well as ignoring the significance of gender, the liberal model also failed to consider how issues of class and ethnicity influence definitions of citizenship. The nineteenth-century English discourse on who should be a citizen was motivated by concerns about the rights of property (thus, men were enfranchised in incremental fashion in order to prevent the feared seizure of power by the popular classes, and women and children were regarded as the economic and legal property of their husbands) as well as an underlying racism (white colonial subjects were deemed worthy of citizenship while subjects of colour were not). The question of how 'foreigners' should be treated by the British state remains a contentious one. Thus, for example, until the 1980s, British law did not allow women who married foreigners to pass on their UK citizenship to their children.

The experience of women under socialist regimes revealed that work did not eradicate oppression in the family as the classical Marxists had predicted. Sexual conservatism marked the approach of the early soviet leaders and it was left to a few pioneers such as the Workers' Opposition militant, Alexandra Kollantai (who headed the Women's Department between 1920 and 1921 before her fall from political grace) to bring women to the forefront. She aimed to help them overcome their backwardness through an understanding of revolutionary ideas as well as initiating proactive legislation on their behalf. She was more and more critical of socialist practice and the ways in which women's needs were subsumed by those of the party and the state. Despite Stalin's famous 1929 declaration that 'the woman question' was solved because of the ending of capitalist exploitation, women continued to be regarded primarily as childbearers and sexist attitudes prevailed. In the USSR, women's empowerment was placed on the official agenda and considerable headway was made in increasing women's access to education and employment, in passing legislation pertaining to marriage, divorce and property rights and in ensuring their representation in party and state institutions.

However their domestic responsibilities prevented women from enjoying these opportunities to the same degree as men and no effort was made to transform the gendered division of labour within the household. Soviet women did not possess the domestic appliances and consumer goods that eased the lives of women in the USA, for example, and thus their burden was more severe. Additionally, women in paid employment typically found themselves at the lower end of the wage scale and did not rise to the top in either party or state hierarchies. Although the CPSU managed quotas which ensured the 'representation' of women, nationalities and the less well-educated in these hierarchies, in reality real power continued to rest with the male elite. The absence of an autonomous sphere of women's organisations within soviet society meant that no voices challenged official attitudes and practices (with the exception of a feminist presence within the underground opposition and the samizdat press). The state intruded into women's lives at all levels.[15] Official state organisations, such as the All-China Women's Federation (ACWF) and the Federación de Mujeres Cubanas (FMC - the Federation of Cuban Women), similarly prevented the emergence of independent women's groups in other socialist states. However the rapidity of economic change in China has made it increasingly difficult for the CCP to maintain tight political control and the ACWF has been compelled to engage with new women's organisations.[16]

Women in political transitions

Dramatic political upheavals involving transitions from authoritarian or military rule to democratic government occurred throughout the world from the fall of military regimes in Latin America in the 1980s to the collapse of state socialism in the former Soviet Union and Eastern Europe and the end of apartheid in South Africa in the 1990s. These transformations focused international attention on the meaning of citizenship and how it could be extended to hitherto marginalised and oppressed groups. Feminist scholars were very interested in how women would fare in these new circumstances and argued that women must be intimately involved in the shaping of new forms of democracy. Women figured prominently in a wide range of movements demanding and working for transition to democracy, but once the dust had settled, what roles were ascribed them by post-transition governments and what progress has been made in terms of their empowerment?

The answer is not straightforward but what can be said is that in many different societies, women have been both included in and excluded from citizenship and that in none of them can it be said that *de jure* equality has been translated into *de facto* equality for women. Sonia Alvarez, writing about the participation of Brazilian women in the military-to-civilian transition which culminated with the elections of 1985, linked the parallel processes of democratisation and 'the politicisation of gender'. Gender-specific agendas were drawn into public debate as a consequence of women's physical presence demonstrating and organising in squares, streets and shanty towns. However, post-transition, the objective of what she calls 'the prevailing pacts of domination' was to sideline women and restore male-dominated party politics.[17]

Transition in Germany was not just one within a country but the merger of two unequal (in terms of wealth and influence) societies with very different histories. Although the border between the former Federal Republic and the German Democratic Republic has been physically removed, it remains vital to an understanding of German politics. As East Germans are colonised by the West (although formally citizens of the same state), East German men and women have a lot in common and the affinity between Western and Eastern women is far less demonstrable. East German women, in particular, have been reduced to second-class citizenship. Having lost the socio-economic entitlements they enjoyed under state socialism, their legal rights have also been downgraded in areas such as pensions legislation and access to legal abortion. It may be argued that those other Eastern European states which were included in the latest round of EU enlargement in May 2004 – that is, the Czech Republic, Estonia, Hungary, Latvia, Lithuania, Poland, Slovakia, Slovenia – will also not achieve parity with the established EU states for many years while those which remain outside (Bulgaria and Romania) will be severely disadvantaged. It is likely that women living in these countries will be most affected in terms of declining provision and status.

Since the disintegration of the soviet bloc (1989–92) and the introduction of free elections to the Russian Parliament, women's representation has remained small and has not been able to effectively influence legislation. Russian women have had to contend with difficult economic conditions compounded by growing social ills such as prostitution and pornography and an increase in discriminatory practices and sexual harassment. Nationalist and religious lobbies have been keen to return women to the home. Women who had been accustomed to living under 'an all-powerful and invasive state during the socialist period' now have to deal with the loss of social entitlements and a declining participation in the labour market (as 'female' industries such as textiles have been swamped by the ending of state subsidies and competition from even cheaper female workers in East and Southeast Asia).[18] When the Chinese state initiated a programme of economic liberalisation from the late 1970s and created special economic zones which welcomed the incursion of foreign investment, women workers were concentrated in poorly paid and repetitive light industrial assembly plants. The arrival of foreign capital consolidated the existing sexual divisions of labour. Similarly the decollectivisation of agriculture has led to increasing demand for labour within the household and a corresponding decline in the percentage of girls attending school. The state's 'one child, one family' policy, introduced in 1980, had already ascribed greater value to male babies, with female infants often being murdered.[19]

Since the end of the apartheid regime and the election of the African National Congress (ANC) government led by Nelson Mandela in April 1994, women have been both incorporated into and marginalised from citizenship in South Africa. Under apartheid, poverty was defined by colour and, within that characteristic, by gender. The urban economy was based on migrant male labour and women had to assume responsibility for the survival of the family. This obligation obstructed the entry of many women into urban areas and those who did migrate from the countryside mainly went into unregulated and exploitative domestic service. Women joined the liberation struggle but subsumed their gendered concerns within the general opposition to white rule. The ANC championed women's rights but in day-to-day relations, many males were resistant to sharing power with female militants and held patronising views about 'women's issues'. Despite these negative reactions, women activists insisted upon inserting gender issues into the ongoing debate about what a post-apartheid South African state would be like.

The year 1992 saw the launching of the Women's National Coalition, which subsequently published a Women's Charter outlining proposals for changes in all areas of private and public life. The Charter, which strongly influenced the Bill of Rights adopted by the ANC and prepared the ground for the establishment of the Commission on Gender Equality, 'reflected the diversity of needs among women as well as the specificity of women's needs as opposed to men. It ... raised the need to account for difference in the understanding of citizenship'.[20] Advances in areas such as the election of women to public office and their entry into the labour market have been slow. Although a great deal of legislation has been introduced, its implementation has been piecemeal and in key areas such as control over their own fertility and their position within the family, women continue to be subject to patriarchal power. No matter how frustrated they may feel, McEwan argues that South African women have no alternative but to 'maintain a strong, highly organised, visible, civil society movement' in order to apply pressure both at the level of official politics and through 'everyday resistance in communities and households'.[21]

The South African transition, whilst having features specific to the history of that country, is typical in many ways of women's experience of living in societies undergoing such transformations. In the South African case, the unique nature of apartheid and the question of race were determining factors, while in other countries, religion and ideas about traditional culture have played a significant role in shaping how independence movements and new states have dealt with the issue of women's citizenship. The examples provided by Algeria and Palestine are instructive here. The idea that an Algerian nation was being constructed provided the motivation for the long fight against

French rule which triumphed with the Evian Accords of 1962. However, embedded in this Algerian nationalism were rigid views about gender relations. After independence, the new state committed itself to modernisation and industrialisation but did not wish to challenge traditional views about the respective roles of men and women. The latter were largely excluded from the exercise of political power and economic independence and their behaviour was structured by conservative social practice and mores. Women who demanded greater rights were condemned as undermining the drive towards national development. Women's situation became even more difficult in the 1980s as Algeria's indebtedness forced the government into the adoption of economic restructuring and austerity. This entailed the withdrawal of welfare provision, which particularly affected women in their capacity as homemakers. At the same time, the hitherto secular state was offering concessions to Islamic fundamentalism in order to gain its political support. A process of the institutionalisation of women's subordination was set in motion and those individuals who have dared to criticise have been subject to increasingly violent attacks from militants.[22]

The General Union of Palestinian Women was founded in 1964 at the same time as the Palestine Liberation Organisation. After the 1967 Six Day War, the Jewish occupation of Gaza, the West Bank and East Jerusalem stimulated growing resistance, the emergence of new organisations and the increased politicisation and involvement of women. Initially, their activities focused upon charitable work and the setting up of support networks for male activists. Over time, women's groups, affiliated to male party organisations and under their firm control, were set up. Under the aegis of Islam, women were offered an acceptable, religiously sanctioned way of participating in resistance, but many families objected to such public displays by wives and daughters. These tensions became more manifest as the PLO's authority was increasingly challenged by groups such as Hamas and Islamic Jihad, who subscribed to a more restrictive understanding of what women's roles should be. This has resulted in the imposition of dress and behaviour codes, an escalation of domestic violence and a growing incidence of young women being forced out of education. These factors do not augur well for the prospects for women if a Palestinian state is ever eventually established.[23]

Women and empowering citizenship

Feminist critics argue that neither the liberal nor the Marxist models of citizenship have acknowledged the centrality of patriarchy to social power. Patriarchy is the systematic institutionalisation of male interests and supremacy. It is built upon a network of social structures, practices and stereotypes by means of which men dominate, oppress and exploit women in the family, in paid work, in the state, in sexual relations and through cultural images, legal statuses and economic formations. Gender concepts are socially constructed as are the identities which delineate masculinity and femininity. The former is always endowed with more significance than the latter. Feminists believe that the recognition of difference between the genders is not the same as accepting women's innate inferiority. Sexual difference structures social and political relationships; this is why society has long accepted the false dichotomy between the public and private spheres. The public sphere has been structured so as to favour men by virtue of their being men and not because of any innate superiority they possess. Patriarchal power is exercised in both the most public of political and economic activities and in the most intimate of relationships. The public and private are not distinct realms but are intricately combined. Political theory has justified and concealed the reality of male power and its bases in private life and has contributed (alongside education and social conditioning) to women's subordination appearing to be a natural and acceptable condition.

In its critique of conventional discourse around citizenship, feminism introduced a range of concerns (such as domestic violence and pornography) not previously considered appropriate for public debate. However feminism itself was divided as to how to challenge patriarchy. Whilst some writers and activists attempted to change governmental and social agendas, others despaired, arguing that men and the institutions they controlled were incapable of such change, and chose separatism. Mainstream feminism would also itself be attacked for its exclusion of black, lesbian, disabled, older and migrant women and for attempting to impose one voice and one identity upon 'women'. Western feminists were accused of universalising their experience, making it normative and thus ignoring and marginalising the very different experiences of other women in their own societies and in the Third World. It was clear that no one strategy for empowerment could be adopted by all women but rather that women would have to be involved in different levels and types of activism and would, thus, interact with the patriarchal state in distinct ways depending upon their circumstances and the possibilities offered by different political and socio-economic conjunctures.

In an earlier piece of work on the women's movement in Peru, I contended that women must seek political and governmental office in order to press for legislative reform, and feminist groups should offer independent and critical reviews of their progress, while women in grassroots organisations must, of necessity, continue their daily practices of survival and resistance. None of these forms of activism should be privileged above the others, but rather (and this is a difficult task) they should be recognised as contributing to what, hopefully, will be a cumulative process of empowerment and the exercise of women's citizenship. In conclusion, I noted: 'If one accepts that the state is a complex apparatus and that it organises different types of sustaining and defensive structures within civil society then activities directed at subverting its power must be as equally complex.'[24]

This leads me to consider what role women play in civil society and to evaluate the obstacles which hinder the expression of their citizenship. Civil society is a much debated but ill-defined concept which does not necessarily have the same meaning in the West, in the former soviet bloc states and in the Third World. Despite the fact that real social-economic and political processes are very different in different parts of the world, 'the language used to describe, evaluate and express the experiences of politics are the same everywhere'.[25] The language is embedded in the western liberal tradition.

The liberal view of civil society locates its foundations in the free exchange of the market economy and in individual aspirations for political liberty and equality. Citizens enter into pluralist relations under the protection of the rule of law which it is the state's duty to regulate. Liberal democracy guarantees civil liberties, including those of political and social minorities, respects the rule of law and has a public space – civil society – in which individuals and groups exercise their rights. Civil society is distinct from economic and political society but interacts with them. Within its parameters many different types of voluntary organisations represent a variety of identities and interests of a political, economic, social and cultural nature. Their activities underpin the transmission of democratic values and norms of behaviour. In the early nineteenth century, Alexis de Tocqueville was preoccupied with the need to avoid the danger mass political participation posed to democracy. He believed that it was essential to safeguard individual liberties and prevent the imposition of a conformist society. The involvement of individual citizens in voluntary associations would create social pluralism and controllable and moderate political mobilisation and so prevent despotism.[26] After the Second World War, Robert Dahl and others disputed the claims made by elite theorists such as C. Wright Mills who contended that power was concentrated in political, economic and military hierarchies and pluralist democracy was a façade.[27]

Based upon his study of public life in New Haven, Dahl contended that the existence of such elites was mediated by the fact that no one group dominated office-holding or determined the policy agenda. Furthermore, he explained the relative passivity of the majority of citizens as indicating the health of democracy, not its absence. If citizens were satisfied with the way that government was being conducted, they felt no need to get involved but could go about their daily lives within civil society.[28] In a similar fashion, North American academics working in the area of comparative politics sought to discover how to maintain stability and prevent radicalisation during periods of rapid political and economic change. Their recipe for good governance in modernising Third World states was for them to follow the example of the industrialised West and to create structures and institutions which embraced the ethos of liberal democracy and capitalism. Here again, citizenship was understood as operating best if it existed within carefully set boundaries and was responsive to and controlled by elites rather than being proactive and participatory. Their involvement in a wide range of civil groups and organisations would be sufficient to express the democratic aspirations of individuals.[29]

A contemporary perspective upon civil society is provided by the work of Robert Puttnam.[30] Puttnam has introduced the concept of social capital, which he sees as being generated by civil society and which he views as both a resource for development and as a means of deepening the democratic experience. Social capital grows on the foundations of everyday linkages and relations which are based on trust. Khilnani has described it as 'a set of cultural acquisitions, in historically inherited manners of civility which moderate relations between groups and individuals'.[31] Puttnam's objective is essentially conservative in that, like earlier pluralist theorists, he believes that this social capital can be employed as an instrument in defending the status quo and consolidating a socially responsible capitalism. His model is explicitly anti-statist and has a great deal in common with New Right or neo-liberal thinking. The New Right ascribed a high positive value to a civil society which existed in antagonism to a state which was profligate, unproductive and inefficient and which also inhibited personal liberty. Civil society represented the perfect expression of free-market individualism, the realm where truly private interests rule and where the role of the state was negated at best or dramatically reduced at least. Susan J. Smith explains it thus: 'The structures, markets and institutions are reduced to the uncoordinated actions of individuals, while social and economic order is the spontaneous accumulation of rational choices.'[32]

Howell and Pearce have criticised the proponents of social capital theories for regarding all groups within civil society as promoters of democracy (they reasonably question how organisations such as the Ku Klux Klan could be included in this definition) and also point out that Puttnam does not address the issue of how poor and marginalised groups can hope to influence wealthy, dominant groups and institutions within societies.[33] They contrast this conservative view of civil society with the European radical tradition (following a lineage from Rousseau, through the utopian socialists, anarchists and Marx to Gramsci), which wished to promote new forms of engagement with a participatory democracy which challenged rather than reinforced the status quo, destroyed inequalities and restored citizenship to the excluded. In its most recent manifestation, this would be represented by the anti-globalisation and environmental justice movements. Implicit in this vision of an alternative social order was the belief that individuals are motivated as much by the goal of collective empowerment as by self-interest. For Gramsci, civil society was composed of the 'trench systems', that is the ideological and cultural relations which constituted capitalism's second line of defence against revolution (the first being its economic and political systems of domination). For him, the withering away of the state would be 'equivalent to the progressive absorption of state functions by the voluntary transactions and organizations of civil society'.[34] Gramsci's views on civil society were fragmented and sometimes contradictory but he did inspire a body of radical opinion which argued that global capital's ideological 'fortresses and earthworks' were fractured and could be challenged by counter-hegemonic voices.

Interest in civil society enjoyed a resurgence from the late 1970s when a marked dissatisfaction with the centrality of the state in political practice and economic management became evident. In the rich, industrialised countries many people expressed their disillusionment with partisan politics and what they saw as the dilution of citizenship and looked to issue politics and civil associations to create new forms of engagement. A multitude of social movements were emerging which stressed popular participation and which sought to effect profound social change without seeking to take control of the state (the failures of both post-1945 liberal democratic and authoritarian command economies had pointed to the bankruptcy of state-led development). In the Third World, civil society came to be regarded as the place of resistance to authoritarian regimes, a site where political liberties and human rights could be preserved and nurtured. Added to these conceptions of a dynamic civil society was recognition that citizenship had to be more than the merely political and must encompass all aspects and areas of life and that cultures could no longer be viewed as static but had become 'dynamic social processes operating in contested terrains in which different voices become more or less hegemonic in their offered interpretations of the world'.[35]

Cultural discourses did not produce definite meanings and identities but could offer 'resistance to homogenisation and marginalisation'; they had become 'the ways individuals experience themselves, their collectivities and the world'.[36]

For women, this offered the possibility of their voices being heard and their multiple identities acknowledged. However they have continued to live within a world order over which a dominant (male, white, heterosexual, affluent) presence presides. As its history has been so male-centred, is it possible to rescue the concept of citizenship for the benefit of women? Much of women's activity takes place in what is still regarded by many commentators as a private sphere and much of it remains either ignored or undervalued. The private sphere is a construct but its presumed existence continues to structure the ways in which women's citizenship is received. In fact, women's participation in informal groups, voluntary work and pressure groups is as much about citizenship as party political activism or inhabiting 'public' roles. Women discover many different ways of coping with their predicaments and this involves them in both individual and communal, personal and public responsibilities where the dichotomies between work and politics or between family and activism become blurred. Women draw upon multi-dimensional experiences and the individual and collective knowledge and networks these help create. The practice of citizenship which is based upon the recognition of commonalities and difference is a healthy and vigorous one.

The danger in endorsing a focus upon women being involved in small, incremental changes to their lives is that this will not have an impact upon larger socio-economic and political structures and that it may perpetuate existing gender relations. Thus, women running communal kitchens in Latin American shanty towns could be seen as satisfying male expectations that women's fundamental role is to provide sustenance for the family through their unpaid and undervalued labour. However the impact of the *ollas comúnes* and *comedores populares* (popular dining rooms) has been far more wide-ranging. The organisation of collective consumption has challenged the state's inability to provide cheap food to the poor, has highlighted the highly unequal distribution of resources within the family and has brought the issue of environmental sustainability to the fore (in that women have a high profile in organic farming and fair-trade initiatives in Third World societies; their presence is also fundamental to such movements in Europe and North America). Mobilisation around the principle of locality can help to create a flourishing and inclusive democratic culture but only so long as it is linked internationally with diverse groups having contacts across local, regional and state boundaries. Resistant discourses at the local and regional levels compete for recognition upon a global map of hierarchies and meanings. Although this is a complex and difficult enterprise, everyday resistances can have global consequences. All of the chapters in this book deal with the specific situations women find themselves in but also draw general conclusions and find common connections.

Notes

1 L. Spigel, *Welcome to the Dreamhouse: Popular Media and Post-war Suburbs* (Durham, NC: Duke University Press, 2001), p. 11.

2 His main text was *Citizenship and Social Class* (Cambridge: Cambridge University Press, 1950).

3 K. O'Donovan, 'Gender blindness or justice engendered' in R. Blackburn (ed.), *Rights of Citizenship* (London: Mansell, 1993), pp. 12–13. Ann Stewart discusses the consequences for African women of the dissonance between customary law and the law of the modern state (and the influences upon the latter's policies represented by developments in international law) in 'The African experience' in S. M. Rai and G. Lievesley (eds), *Women and the State: International Perspectives* (London: Taylor & Francis, 1996).

4 C. Chinkin, 'Gender inequality and international human rights law' in A. Hurrell and N. Woods (eds), *Inequality, Globalization and World Politics* (Oxford: Oxford University Press, 1999), p. 117.

5 Regional and country-based advocacy networks which work to promote gender-specific rights and particularly the right to live without violence are discussed by M. E. Keck and K. Sikkink, *Activists Beyond Borders: Advocacy Networks in International Politics* (New York: Cornell, 1998).

6 Here the stereotype of the white heterosexual woman remains the dominant trope. Lesbians and transsexuals are still denied many fundamental freedoms and citizenship is mainly defined in an essentialist way, encompassing only one category of sexuality.

7 E. Kofman, 'Citizenship for some but not for others: spaces of citizenship in contemporary Europe', *Political Geography*, 14 (1995) argues the need for rights to be attributed on the basis of residence and not ethnic origin and for anti-discriminatory legislation to become more interventionist.

8 S. Ruddick, *Maternal Thinking: Towards a Politics of Peace* (London: Women's Press, 1990).

9 J. Habermas, *The Structural Transformation of the Public Sphere* (Cambridge: Polity, 1989).

10 Wollstonecraft's *Vindication of the Rights of Woman* (London: Dent, 1986) presented an early espousal of women's significance. Taylor and Stuart Mill were both personal and intellectual partners. Their key texts are *The Enfranchisement of Women* (London: Virago, 1983) and *The Subjection of Women* (Cambridge, MA: Massachusetts Institute of Technology, 1970)

11 The key text is F. Engels, *The Origin of the Family, Private Property and the State* (London: Lawrence & Wishart, 1972).

12 B. Friedan, *The Feminine Mystique* (London: Gollancz, 1963).

13 B. Friedan, *The Second Stage* (London: Joseph, 1982).

14 Spigel, *Welcome*. She contends that what she describes as 'counter-publics' (those excluded from the hegemonic sphere) have only been made visible through the work of feminist writers working in a number of areas such as critical geography, film and media studies which have explored how the relations of power based upon gender and sexuality have shaped urban planning, industrial and post-industrial cities, the social uses of space and the cultural representations of these configurations.

15 Women's lives under soviet rule are discussed in S. Fitzpatrick, *Everyday Stalinism: Ordinary Lives in Extraordinary Times. Soviet Russia in the 1930s* (Oxford: Oxford University Press, 1999).

16 J. Howell, 'Gender, civil society and the state in China' in V. Randall and G. Waylen (eds), *Politics and the State in the Third World* (London: Routledge, 1998).

17 S. Alvarez, *Engendering Democracy in Brazil: Women's Movements in Transition Politics* (Princeton, NJ: Princeton University Press, 1990), pp. 205–206.

18 B. Einhorn, 'Political participation: some key issues in the context of political transformation in Central and Eastern Europe'. Paper given at the launch workshop of the Network of European Women's Rights, University of Birmingham, Centre for the Study of Global Studies, January 2003, p. 5.

19 For a discussion of the impact of these government policies upon Chinese women, see F. Christiansen and S. M. Rai, *Chinese Politics and Society: An Introduction* (Hemel Hempstead: Prentice Hall, 1996), pp. 249–250.

20 C. McEwan, 'Engendering citizenship: gendered spaces of democracy in South Africa', *Political Geography*, 19 (2000), 635.

21 *Ibid.*, 646.

22 M. Mehdid, 'En-Gendering the nation state: women, patriarchy and politics in Algeria' in Rai and Lievesley (eds), *Women*.

23 K. Glavanis-Grantham, 'The women's movement, feminism and the national struggle in Palestine: unresolved contradictions' in H. Afshar (ed.), *Women and Politics in the Third World* (London: Routledge, 1996).

24 G. Lievesley, 'Stages of growth? Women dealing with the state and each other in Peru' in Rai and Lievesley (eds), *Women*, p. 58.

25 S. Kaviraj and S. Khilnani, 'Introduction: ideas of civil society' in S. Kaviraj and S. Khilnani (eds), *Civil Society: History and Possibilities* (Cambridge: Cambridge University Press, 2001), p. 5.

26 A. de Tocqueville, *Democracy in America* (Oxford: Oxford University Press, 1961).

27 C. Wright Mills, *The Power Elite* (New York: Oxford University Press, 1956).

28 R. Dahl, *Who Governs? Democracy and Power in an American City* (New Haven: Yale University Press, 1961).

29 Two major comparative studies were G. A. Almond and S. Verba, *The Civic Culture: Political Attitudes and Democracy in Five Nations* (London: Sage, 1989) and S. P. Huntington, *Political Order in Changing Societies* (New Haven: Yale University Press, 1968).

30 The best introduction to his work is *Making Democracy Work: Civic Traditions in Modern Italy* (Princeton: Princeton University Press, 1993).

31 S. Khilnani, 'The development of civil society' in Kaviraj and Khilnani (eds), *Civil Society*, p. 14.

32 S. J. Smith, 'Society, space and citizenship: a human geography for the "new times"?', *Transactions of the Institute of British Geographers*, 14 (1989), 145.

33 J. Howell and J. Pearce, *Civil Society and Development: A Critical Exploration* (Boulder, CO: Westview Press, 2001).

34 J. Femia, 'Civil society and the Marxist tradition' in Kaviraj and Khilnani (eds), *Civil Society*, p. 142.

35 N. Yuval-Davis, *Gender and Nation* (London: Sage, 1997), p. 41.

36 *Ibid.*, p. 42.

2

Gender, international law and the emergence of environmental citizenship

KAREN MORROW

As a child of the late twentieth century I have enjoyed the fruits of what feminism has achieved for women in the developed world, particularly in education, employment and political capacity. I have rarely personally experienced the gender-based inequality that is so manifest for the majority of women the world over. As someone educated in the law, I have always tended in my work to present the law as I have been taught to view it, that is, as an objective and value-neutral system. Researching gender and the environment has caused me to look at my specialist subject, environmental law, through a new lens, and to read much more broadly in feminist environmental theory than I have ever done before. It has proved a personally and intellectually testing area to research and has significantly altered how I view my subject, allowing me to bring to my work a degree of emotional engagement that I have previously confined to my extra-curricular environmental activities. As such, involvement in this project has involved me in one of the steepest learning curves of my academic career to date. Indeed this opening section represents the first time that I have strayed outside the conventions of legal scholarship and used the first person in a piece of academic writing in a career stretching over a decade. The effect is for the most part liberating – but not a little alarming.

This chapter looks at how the international community, as expressed by both the UN and international civil society, has engaged with gender issues through an examination of its work on gender mainstreaming, with particular emphasis on how this has played out, to date, in the context of the environment. It goes on to examine the possibilities that may lie in synthesising new ways of thinking about gender and the environment as an aspect of a new paradigm for citizenship.

Introduction

In the context of the United Nations' Special Assembly, 'Women 2000: Gender Equality, Development and Peace for the Twenty-first Century'[1] and its system-wide medium-term plan for the advancement of women 2002–5,[2] with the avowed aim of ensuring 'that gender perspective is applied in the development of legal frameworks, laws and public regulations', it is a profitable time to review progress to date in international law on gender mainstreaming in practical terms.

One of the most vigorous areas of UN activity in recent years has been environmental law and policy, which in many ways represents the cutting edge of the UN's agenda. Legal activism in the development of both 'hard'[3] and 'soft'[4] law in this area therefore provides a useful area to evaluate gender mainstreaming, since arguably the integration of innovative ideas into a (relatively) new field of law represents a more favourable situation than grafting them on to more established areas of competence. In addition, the parallels that exist between the exploitation of women and the environment in the context of what remains a largely patriarchal system of global governance[5] mean that this area provides a good litmus test against which to measure the UN's progress in altering deep and established societal values.

Gender and the environment

Although women in much of the world have a significant role to play with respect to the state of the environment, due to the wide variety of reproductive roles that they play, their environmental concerns have long been drowned out by the 'global capitalist patriarchy'.[6] It is also abundantly clear that, globally, it is the poor who bear the brunt of environmental pressure, and women make up the majority of this group.[7] Thus, although historically the environmental agenda has been presented as value-neutral,[8] it is, as the product of the society that it serves, both capital-driven and profoundly gendered. Women are doubly disadvantaged by this state of affairs.

For a number of highly complex reasons, which space does not allow to be discussed here, women, even in circumstances of ostensible equality with men, tend not to be proportionately active in public political life. For the most part the female sphere of activity inclines to the private or domestic sphere. However, as the environment represents an area where the private blurs into the public sphere, this is one area where women have been driven to develop a public voice to some degree. For a long time this has primarily manifested itself in a local context,[9] as women have become activists through protecting first their family and then community interests.[10] Although this type of activism has not historically led to engagement with more formal national political processes, recent developments in the context of the new global manifestations of civil society have fostered women's engagement with environmental issues at regional, national and even global levels. This process may allow women to leapfrog the national party politics that they find alienating and allow them to 'think globally and act locally' in those areas that motivate their activism.

As mentioned above, women experience an identity with the environment on another less practical but more symbolic level, as nature and women have historically been both identified with one another and have both been exploited by the patriarchal regime.[11] The dualism in which this finds its expression has seen the feminine equated with nature and both being regarded as debased in comparison to the masculine (which is in turn equated with the human).[12] Thus, sharing the perspective of the exploited, feminism and ecology in many ways make ideal partners[13] and have combined to form ecofeminism,[14] which may be defined as 'a movement and current of analysis that attempts to link feminist struggles with ecological struggles'.[15]

Although the theoretical identity between women and nature is strong, their interests do not of course inevitably or fully coincide;[16] nonetheless there is usually a sufficient community of interest between them for practical purposes.[17] On balance, ecofeminism has done much to enrich both the feminist and the environmental movements and it is certainly growing to be more than the sum of its parts.

Early ecofeminist theories were articulated primarily by the women of the developed world.[18] As a result, while these writings were certainly gender-aware, they were also culturally prescriptive, leaning towards a 'West is best' approach,[19] which was decidedly inappropriate to the experience of women in the developing world. As a reaction to this, in more recent times the women of the developing world[20] have been at pains to point out that there women do not and indeed cannot speak with a single voice on environmental issues, given the vast range of issues and perspectives involved.[21] Despite difference, there is however a strong core of shared female experience vis-à-vis nature, and ecofeminism has evolved into a broad-based movement capable of accommodating great diversity.[22] One part of the broader contribution that can be made by ecofeminism is its participative and inclusive approach to furthering its agenda as 'Ecofeminism contains an inherently democratic political vision'.[23]

At the very least ecofeminism offers a new lens through which to view ecological issues, gender issues and perhaps ultimately governance questions.

The UN and gender

Putting gender on the agenda

Although the UN is reliant on the agreement or at least acquiescence of states for its jurisdiction, and for the most part lacks powers to compel societal change, it can, by applying political pressure, slowly exert considerable influence in changing social mores on a global scale. The UN employs hard and soft law as well as policy in order to achieve its ends. In this context the distinction between law and policy is often difficult to draw, as the international legal system lacks the mandatory compulsion that is the hallmark of domestic legal regimes. The absence of traditional forms of enforcement does not, however, mean that international laws are merely agreed and left unenforced, since despite this they are capable of generating profound change. One example of this can be found in human rights law where the UN has enjoyed a significant role in delivering first-generation civil and political rights; developing second-generation social and economic rights; and pioneering the emergence of third-generation rights, including environmental rights. This section will examine the UN's role in developing, first, women's rights, and subsequently a more profoundly gender-conscious approach to its activities and attitudes.

From its genesis in the UN Charter 1945,[24] the United Nations paid lip-service to women's rights, following the issue up (on paper at least) in the Universal Declaration of Human Rights 1948.[25] Indeed, so enthusiastic has the UN's commitment to gender issues become that the range of entities responsible for it within the UN and the mass of provisions concerned with them is nothing short of labyrinthine. It has, however, taken decades for the international community's approach to women's issues to mature into a substantive commitment to address the equality agenda. Initial action manifested itself in somewhat haphazard initiatives, directed specifically at women's issues. But these were at best fragmented and their freestanding status meant that they were also marginalised in the broader UN agenda.

The 1970s saw the profile of women's issues rise socially and politically,[26] not least due to NGO activism.[27] As a result women's issues shifted fairly swiftly from the periphery to the centre of the UN's agenda with the designation of 1975 as International Women's Year and the institution of the UN Decade for Women 1976–85. A series of conferences on women in Mexico City 1975, Copenhagen 1980 and Nairobi 1985 accompanied these developments. The Decade for Women, and the conferences and initiatives that comprised it, served to make women more visible than before particularly within the UN and, to a lesser degree, outside. Key UN initiatives included the creation of gender units, gender focal points on a system-wide basis and the symbolically and practically significant appointment of the Assistant Secretary-General and Special Adviser to the Secretary-General on Gender Issues and the Advancement of Women enjoying a UN-wide mandate. The Office of the Special Adviser on Gender Issues and the Advancement of Women (OSAGI) supports and advances this work.

In addition to prompting these broad cultural changes in the UN, the Decade for Women also served to hasten the implementation of other initiatives, notably providing the impetus to finalise the Convention on the Elimination of All Forms of Discrimination Against Women 1979 (CEDAW),[28] a self-styled 'international bill of rights for women', and set up the Convention's functional Commission. This process did a great deal to strengthen the role of the Division for the Advancement of Women (DAW).[29] The Commission on the Status of Women (CSW),[30] the UN International Research and Training Institute for the Advancement of Women (INSTRAW)[31] and the UN Development Fund for Women (UNIFEM)[32] also came to enjoy an enhanced profile during this period. Broader gender-based institutional developments, for example the establishment of the Inter-Agency Committee on Women and Gender Equality (IACWGE), also augmented the profile of women's issues. While these activities and initiatives achieved a great deal, in more recent times the limits of such a relatively compartmentalised approach have been recognised.[33] Nonetheless, these developments did serve to reinforce the importance and ensure the persistence of gender in the UN's policy agenda. Not least, the Decade for Women also empowered women, by ultimately redefining their status from object to subject, ensuring that their voices were heard more clearly than ever before.

A maturing approach to gender

The UN General Assembly succinctly summarised the realisation that 'Policies that target women only cannot achieve the best results, nor can those which assume that public actions are gender-neutral in their effects.'[34] The ultimate result of such thinking has been the recognition of the need to ground specific initiatives more thoroughly by attending to fundamental contextual concerns. Thus gender issues are no longer to be focused solely on women, but rather geared to recognise inter-gender dynamics. In addition women's issues are no longer to be compartmentalised but to be dealt with in a crosscutting fashion and integrated into all areas of UN activity. It was from these functional priorities that the concept of gender mainstreaming would ultimately be born, of which more below.

In order for an integrated approach to women's issues to be realised, it was necessary to create the political impetus to underpin it. First, proof positive of the pervasive nature of gender inequality was required and to this end the Decade for Women can claim among its greatest achievements the adoption of initiatives at UN level to compile, for the first time, systematically gender-aggregated statistics.[35] This exercise showed very clearly that traditional statistics systems often concealed pervasive gender inequality. The reports generated provided a revolutionary (if flawed and incomplete[36]) baseline of knowledge with which to highlight gender inequity and upon which to ground initiatives to tackle it. Second, a policy platform capitalising on this factually verified evidence of inequality was required in order to contextualise the UN's response. Thus came the pinnacle of the Decade for Women, its culmination in the unanimous adoption of the Nairobi Forward Looking Strategies for the Advancement of Women (FLS).[37] The FLS was crucially important in providing a springboard for concrete action on the position of women geared to an equality agenda. The new role to be played by women was described in paragraph 15 thus: 'The attainment of the goals and of the Decade requires a sharing of this responsibility by men and women and by society as a whole, and requires that women play a central role as intellectuals, policy-makers, decision-makers, planners, and contributors and beneficiaries of development.' This approach recognises women as powerful actors in society rather than as mere victims of social and economic oppression.

Gender mainstreaming

Gender mainstreaming takes two main forms. The first is institutional gender mainstreaming, whereby the concept is recognised as an integral part of the mainstream institutional agenda and institutional initiatives are undertaken in order to bring about any necessary institutional change. This sets the scene for the second form of gender mainstreaming, instrumental gender mainstreaming, whereby gender-informed approaches are brought to bear on subject-specific laws and policies and upon their implementation. Each will now be briefly examined in turn.

The follow-up to the Nairobi conference, the Fourth World Conference on Women in Beijing in 1995, disappointed many, particularly in the NGO sector,[38] by its lack of unanimity among participating states and the adoption of numerous reservations by them. Nonetheless, in the Platform for Action that was agreed, the Conference did see the UN's own commitment to addressing gender inequality achieve a new maturity in its endorsement of the concept of gender mainstreaming. This was little short of revolution-ary. Prior to this point, the UN's discussion of women's issues had either been limited to special conferences or to the CSW, the UN Economic and Social Council (ECOSOC) and the second and third Committees of the General Assembly. Following the adoption of the Beijing Platform for action, women's issues would become mainstream.

Gender mainstreaming is mentioned in each of the twelve Critical Areas for Concern identified in the Beijing Platform. That said, it does not seek to replace gender-specific initiatives by UN entities, but rather to complement them,[39] aiming first at changing the organisation's institutional culture at a general level and then in respect of specific areas of activity. In this regard it arguably represents the most significant development to date in expanding, advancing and perpetuating the equality agenda. At Beijing, incorporating gender issues into all aspects of UN activity was deemed to be a contextual issue, one that was important from the point of view of pursuing the organisation's priority goals of human rights, social justice and sustainable development. This view ultimately seeks to place gender at the heart of specific organisational mandates.

The term gender mainstreaming has been comprehensively defined by ECOSOC as:

> the process of assessing the implications for women and men of any planned action, including legislation, policies or programmes, in all areas and at all levels. It is a strategy for making women's as well as men's concerns and experiences an integral dimension of the design, implementation, monitoring and evaluation of policies and programmes in all political, economic and societal spheres so that women and men benefit equally and inequality is not perpetuated. The ultimate goal is to achieve gender equality.[40]

Subsequent documentation cleared up a popular misapprehension by explicitly emphasising that gender mainstreaming required a great deal more than increasing women's participation in decision-making (this being a necessary but not sufficient component of the whole) extending to 'identifying and addressing the gender perspectives – the linkages between gender and different sector areas – in the work of an organisation'.[41] The Beijing Platform for Action was reinforced by the inauguration of the first System-Wide Medium

Term Plan for the Advancement of Women (SWMTP), drafted in response to ECOSOC Resolution 1985:46. A second SWMTP ran from 1996 to 2001 and the subsequent one from 2002 to 2005. Each plan has in turn picked up the relevant new themes generated by the UN.

The breadth of the aspirations pertaining to the gender mainstreaming process is clear in that it is seen as not merely incorporating women's concerns into the existing policy agenda but rather transforming the agenda itself.[42] The key tool for achieving gender mainstreaming was identified at Beijing as the proactive gender analysis of all initiatives. The UN's goal is that gender issues will no longer be regarded either in isolation, or as a mere add-on to the existing work of UN entities, but rather integrated into the very fabric of all areas of their activities. To this end intergovernmental mandates for gender mainstreaming have been agreed in all of the major areas of competence enjoyed by the UN.[43] The UN further demonstrated its commitment to gender mainstreaming in 1997 when ECOSOC agreed the general principles of gender mainstreaming;[44] this was followed up by the specific directives to the heads of all UN entities contained in the Secretary-General's communication on gender mainstreaming[45] and finally endorsement by the General Assembly itself.[46]

The CSW has also continued to ensure that gender mainstreaming not only remains on the agenda,[47] but is also further developed as in the introduction of the high-level roundtable on institutional mechanisms in 2003. ECOSOC has returned to the gender mainstreaming issue, in 2001 resolving that it be integrated into all of its activities[48] and in 2002 conducting a review of progress to date and placing gender mainstreaming on its regular agenda. Committees of the General Assembly also address gender mainstreaming issues. Thus it is clear that the mainstreaming agenda has attracted a considerable breadth and depth of organisational support within the UN.

Allowing time for institutional gender mainstreaming to make its influence felt, instrumental gender mainstreaming is beginning to be made manifest at a more concrete level in initiatives by its inclusion in UN entities' policies, plans and programme budgets. Examples of the integration of gender mainstreaming include: the UNCHS (United Nations Centre for Human Settlements) Habitat in its Gender Policy Revision;[49] the ODCCP (United Nations Office for Drug Control and Crime Prevention) Field Representatives Seminar;[50] and the 46th Session of the CSW on Disproportionate impact of natural disasters on women.[51] Gender mainstreaming approaches are also finally beginning to percolate into concrete law and policy and this issue will be now examined in relation to environment and sustainable development issues.

In most countries women, as those who do most subsistence work on the ground, tend to bear the brunt of environmental degradation.[52] Despite their vulnerability to adverse environmental impacts and their substantial role as environmental actors, women have not historically had the power to influence the political agenda in this regard (as in many others). [53] To this end there is an obvious need to foster greater female influence in environmental decision-making at all levels. At first this need was characterised as requiring the encouragement of greater participation by women in environmental decision-making. This approach, however, only addressed some aspects of gender inequality and so the more ambitious gender mainstreaming agenda has been forged.

The concept of gender mainstreaming, with its emphasis on a people-centred approach to evaluating the impact of policy initiatives[54] strikes a chord with the rhetoric of sustainable development. This is one area where, on the face of things at least, gender mainstreaming should not face insurmountable obstacles, but rather should find a setting that is highly conducive to its own evolution. In many respects the broader sustainable development and gender mainstreaming agendas exhibit mutually overlapping and reinforcing values and priorities. Indeed, in principle, the gender mainstreaming and sustainable development agendas have considerable potential for symbiosis: 'The emergence of a more holistic framework for poverty eradication and sustainable development, with a strong focus on the environment of all stakeholders, also provides opportunities for greater responsiveness to the integration of gender perspectives.' [55] It is then unsurprising that among the UN entities making active progress on the gender mainstreaming agenda are those dealing, in one way or another, with the environment. Gender issues in this context have principally emerged from the following UN bodies: the UN Development Programme (UNDP), the Food and Agriculture Organisation (FAO) and the UN Environment Programme (UNEP). This is despite the fact that the Nairobi FLS, as a product of its time, while it engaged thoroughly with development issues, had comparatively little to say about the environment. Nonetheless, if in a somewhat minimal fashion, the environment was identified as an area for strategic action at national level. In substantive terms, however, environmental issues had to wait for another few years to make their way on to the centre of the UN's policy agenda. It is only as both the gender mainstreaming and environmental agendas grow to maturity that the full potential of the two agendas to intertwine can begin to be realised.

There is of course a vast range of subject-specific mandates dealing with gender mainstreaming; those most relevant to the environment include energy, sustainable development and water resources management. INSTRAW began to initiate its own action on aspects of women and the environment in the early 1980s. Its work in this area achieved a new maturity when, in 1990, it set up a new, more coherent, programme on Gender, Environment and Sustainable Development to promote women's participation in environmental issues. In many respects the gender and sustainability agendas mesh well together, as discussed above. The central idea in this context is that enabling women to participate in sustainability decisions and activities will reinforce their role as active agents in society more generally and vice versa. Both agendas require profound societal change to achieve their goals, reversing established hierarchical patterns and replacing them with bottom-up approaches.[56] The UN Conference on Environment and Development (UNCED) provided both the impetus and the opportunity to develop the gender and sustainable development debate.

Beyond the UN system, in broader civil society, gender awareness was making its influence manifest in the sphere of the environment. The women's movement put to good use the networks that it had developed and the lobbying experience that had been gained during and subsequent to the Decade for Women in pressing the feminist agenda in the UNCED.[57] To this end, women's NGOs met in preparation for the Conference, the most significant product of which was the 1991 UNEP and WEDO[58] organised World Women's Congress for a Healthy Planet, which thrashed out Women's Action Agenda 21.[59] This effort was necessary because, despite repeated institutional statements of awareness of gender issues, the initial draft of Agenda 21 hardly mentioned women at all, and where it did it reverted to according them victim status. The achievement of consensus by the Women's Congress in response to this, in the face of class, race and geopolitical conflicts, was little short of revolutionary.[60] One result was that environmental crisis was defined as a global and gendered problem. The WEDO agenda challenged dominant capitalist thought and to this end subjected UNEP's draft Agenda 21 to a critical and systematic feminist analysis aimed at influencing the final form of this document. The fruits of this labour were very clear. The role of women gained sufficient profile to be included in Principle 20 of the Rio Declaration: 'Women have a vital role in environmental management and development. Their full participation is therefore essential to achieve sustainable development.'[61]

This aspiration was carried through in more practical form in Section 3 of Agenda 21 by identifying women as a major group whose involvement was to be actively fostered by the Commission on Sustainable Development (CSD). While this falls short of the subsequent gender mainstreaming rationale, it does represent a significant and symbolic development. Further concrete progress was also ultimately made for women's issues in the Agenda 21 process. In contrast to its beginnings, the final version of Agenda 21 is not only extremely gender-literate throughout, it also focuses specifically on women in Chapters 2 and 24. The very active participation of women at the NGO forum running parallel to the UNCED in Rio also ensured that women's issues stayed to the fore in a very crowded agenda. However, despite the UN's willingness to embrace women's issues in the genesis of Agenda 21, the organisation's follow-up has on occasion been less than inspiring. Nonetheless, the legacy of Rio has been hugely significant, not least in the questions that it has raised: 'there is the sense that the tension between the global and the local is in need of some serious consideration in the wake of the recognition that not all people share the same interests in relation to nature.'[62]

Integrating environment and gender – first steps

In addition to fashioning new instrumental arrangements for dealing with gender issues, the UN has also made a number of provisions relating specifically to women and the environment. The potential for cross-fertilisation of the sustainable development and gender agendas soon became apparent. An early example of this type of development was found in paragraph 13/13 and Strategic Objectives G and K of the Beijing Platform of Action, paragraph 254 of which makes specific reference to the incorporation of gender in the work of the CSD. The document thus includes specific environmental credentials in the broader gender mainstreaming agenda. However, as was the case with Agenda 21, commitments on paper do not necessarily amount to change on the ground. Thus even after Beijing +5 supposedly put gender mainstreaming on to the mainstream political agenda, crosscutting coverage of gender issues has not been consistently delivered in practice. In this context the peripheral coverage given to gender in documents such as the five-year appraisal of Agenda 21 makes for dispiriting reading.[63]

Also in 1997 the CSW issued its Agreed Conclusions on the Status of Women and the Environment.[64] This document constituted the bridge between the role of women as a major group as promoted at Rio and the more demanding concept of gender mainstreaming. The CSW's Conclusions took a broad approach to implementing the Beijing Platform's mainstreaming approach through a range of issues ranging from resource management to sustainable development, drawing particular attention to the Agenda 21 programme and the work of the CSD. However, the CSW went further in exhorting all actors (and not just UN entities) to take a holistic approach to integrating gender into the sustainable development agenda. While the UN has displayed considerable activism on paper, the impact of such enlightened policies appears, to date, to be somewhat limited in practice – it remains to be seen whether the twenty-first century will offer opportunities for real progress or simply perpetuate the status quo. The UN has continued to build upon both its gender-sensitive approach to sustainable development and its integrationist agenda on sustainable development post-Rio, not least in its avowed aim to 'view all the implications of sustainable development through a gender lens and provide policy recommendations about environmentally sound patterns of development'.[65]

UNEP has recognised that gender mainstreaming is a key element in pursuing sustainable development: 'Sustainable and effective development can only be achieved in any area of societal activity, including economic development, if the interests and needs of all groups in society – including both women and men – are taken into account and the potential of all groups is released.'[66] It has also made efforts to integrate the gender dimension more fully into its core work. Like sustainable development, gender mainstreaming has a bottom-up element, when it is applied in an environmental context.[67] This is clearly demonstrated in the context of the UN's work on mitigation of natural disasters. UN research has demonstrated that, as women tend to bear the brunt of such catastrophes, failure to consider their role, not only as victims but also as agents with the capacity to respond to problems, has hampered the effectiveness of initiatives geared to respond to them.[68] In order to maximise its own impact, as much as to progress gender equality, UNEP has included gender in its governing Council Agendas since 1993. It has also actively promoted research and writing in the area, notably with its publication in 1995 of *Gender and Environment: A UNEP Perspective*,[69] and its publication in 2000 of *Success Stories: Gender and the Environment*.[70] More recently, UNEP has adopted a more advanced integrationist approach by producing a gender mainstreaming report entitled *Women and the Environment*,[71] which acknowledges the role of women as brokers of essential knowledge and skills pertaining to their environment: 'a gender perspective on environment and development calls for a specific focus on the contributions, needs and visions of women, as their positions have too often been neglected in environmental arenas.'[72] *Women and the Environment* identifies such key issues as looking at how women use resources, how women contribute to environmental knowledge, and how women engage in environmental management and conservation.[73] It argues that 'gender equality and equity are not only a question of fundamental human rights and social justice, but are also instrumental, and a precondition, for environmental conservation, sustainable development and human security.'[74]

Institutionally UNEP set up a gender focal point in 1999. UNEP's current efforts in this area are focused on making gender a crosscutting priority in all of its programmes. UNEP is zealous in employing the language of mainstreaming advocated by the UN across its work. To this end *Women and the Environment* offers 'a strategic model for gender mainstreaming in institutions dealing with the environment and sustainable development'.[75] This endeavours to promote a more consistent application to gender mainstreaming in the sphere of the environment than had previously been the case. It looks broadly at the issue, covering not only UNEP's own activities but also examining its delivery on the ground. To this end UNEP engages in dialogue with institutional stakeholders ranging from IGOs to NGOs on the gender mainstreaming issue. This is a practical strategy, recognising that, in order to deliver change, 'the focus on gender must exist not only on an abstract and global level, but must evolve within a specific local context'.[76]

The approach adopted is a good example of taking the abstract concept of gender mainstreaming and rendering it practical. UNEP identifies seven areas where 'simultaneous steps' are required in order to realise gender mainstreaming:
- knowledge and understanding of the issue and validation of women's contributions to sustainable development;
- at institutional level – adequate political will and concrete actions;
- assurance of women's rights;
- full participation of women;
- improvement of the socio-economic position of women;
- women's empowerment;
- identifying the impact of the macrocontext on women and their environment.[77]

The document then proceeds to provide practical guidance in each of the areas alluded to. The whole approach adopted by *Women and the Environment* stresses the need for application, taking the view that there is little point in adopting elaborate gender mainstreaming policies if they are not followed through in practice. In addition, UNEP seeks to marry gender mainstreaming into its existing initiatives on sustainability. To this end UNEP provides a gender checklist[78] and cross-refers to its existing Gender Sensitivity Guidelines,[79] indicators of gender equality[80] and to CEDAW. This shows an unusual degree of integration both within the UNEP remit and in a broader institutional context, and provides a clear example of the 'joined-up thinking' required to make gender mainstreaming work. However, the UNEP approach also serves to demonstrate the enormity of the effort that is required to render gender mainstreaming a working reality. At least, though, UNEP is beginning to work its way through this process, perhaps because, as a key player in the sustainable development agenda, it is in a better position than most of its counterparts to work towards an aspirational process-based goal. In any event, UNEP is well-versed in the type of creative thinking required to engage with a far-reaching agenda in this regard, as its day-to-day work has long required it to adopt a truly crosscutting approach.

Gender, the Commission for Sustainable Development and civil society

It is not only UNEP that has done much to foster the integration of the gender and environmental agendas. As a direct result of gender mainstreaming requirements, the functional commissions of ECOSOC, including the CSD, report annually to the committee on gender mainstreaming within their remits. The CSD recognises and fosters the role of women as local community activists, following on from the UN's acknowledgement in the Beijing Declaration of the critical role to be played by women in civil society and acting on the commitment to improve their participation in decision-making and empowerment as equal citizens.[81] It is worthy of note that the sustainable development agenda, with its strong ideological focus on bottom-up societal change, requires the CSD to actively canvass the involvement of groups normally excluded from the top-down approach adopted in other areas of international governance. It may be opportune that the sustainability-based approach strikes a chord with the increasing disillusionment with representative democracy exhibited by the anti-capital movement.[82] In this context it is possible that the desire for a more participative approach to democracy championed by both the CSD and civil society has the potential to develop a symbiotic relationship.

In actively encouraging the involvement of civil society in its activities, the CSD stands in stark contrast to the active exclusion of civil society from their activities by other IGOs and the often brutal repression of public protest that their meetings attract. The dissonance in approach between such bodies as the World Trade Organisation (WTO) and the CSD serves to highlight the fact that the economic aspect of sustainable development continues to drive forward the international community's agenda. Integrating the economic with the social and environmental aspects of sustainability remains to be effectively addressed.

It is indeed arguable that the CSD, in its role of developing Agenda 21, has played a vital part in connecting the work of the UN to civil society. This may begin to fashion what may ultimately prove to be a new paradigm for citizenship that fits better the needs of women and the context of the twenty-first century. In developing its approach to major groups, including of course women, the CSD is attempting to co-opt, or at least attempt to harness, the grassroots direct democracy movements that have long existed but which have risen to new prominence in the global anti-capital movement. Women's involvement in civil society, initially engendered by their shouldering of domestic responsibilities, is frequently made manifest in environmental issues.[83] As a result, women have played a significant role in this sphere of established civil society and are also playing a key role in the new emerging pattern of civil society that is making its mark in current world affairs under the banner of anti-capitalism. The anti-capital faction may be more accurately characterised as a network of movements that have opportunistically and periodically coalesced under this standard to confront other international institutions, and in particular the WTO. Women, as a broad class, have long tended to bear the brunt of global capitalism, and women members of particular groups, for example indigenous peoples, have been subject to more pronounced impacts or a double disadvantage. Thus in this context too, women have had a role to play in realising the global potential of the issues.

In many ways, the global anti-capital movement exhibits strongly female characteristics, not least in its expression in structured but non-hierarchal[84] assemblies, its commitment to dialogue and its narrative driven nature.[85] Women have tended to play a prominent role in many manifestations of civil society stretching beyond women's movements as such into broader social, environmental[86] and human rights groups.[87] In the twenty-first century new synergies in civil society are emerging, exploiting both new and traditional global communications systems. The internet[88] in particular has been used across the globe to identify commonalities and to forge new alliances. In this respect the emergence of 'new hybrid'[89] global networks of cooperation and solidarity between diverse groups, including women's groups, trade unions, students, anarchists and indigenous peoples to name but a few, have helped to bypass women's comparative lack of engagement with national political regimes and agendas. Twenty-first-century global activism has tapped straight into the strength and expertise of numerous actors, especially women, working innovatively in local grassroots issues, allowing them to access new levels of interaction. This is particularly the case in respect of environmental issues, where the mismatch between global governance and local reality is particularly stark. 'Emergence' theory takes the view that 'local knowledge is sovereign',[90] and accords an unprecedented degree of recognition to the influence of grassroots experience and insight. Women, in particular, inhabit community activism which occurs in an intermediate arena that represents a fusion of the public and private.[91] The iterative nature of group interaction allows for information and strategy exchange and encourages dialogue and innovation. The idea that there is power in local knowledge is not limited to civil society itself, as the international community not only recognises the contribution of professional expertise,[92] but also its limitations, and comes to accord more influence to the lived expertise of communities.[93] In the environmental sphere, globalisation runs counter to this recognition of the importance of the local, with its tendency to wrest control over vital resources away from communities and place them in the hands of large businesses. The anti-globalisation movement focuses on redressing the broader balance between the global and the local. As a result, civil society has been evolving with an unprecedented degree of rapidity into a complex system that is arguably more than the sum of its parts.[94] Conversely, conventional international political institutions and law have, on the whole, been slow to respond to societal needs. The CSD and the soft law of sustainable development at least aspire to provide an exception to the general top-down approach espoused by the international community and may ultimately serve as a template for a more inclusive model of international governance that strives to integrate not just the social, economic and environmental, but also states, IGOs and civil society, in a more constructive way.

While the civil society response to globalisation is laudable in many respects, it is not unproblematic. It also brings with it the danger of 'depoliticisation'.[95] Although diverse local campaigns and groups may share objectives, it is by no means inevitable that they will do so, though the problems that can emerge from this focus on the local can be circumvented by a more strategic approach to cooperation, focusing on means rather than ends. This type of approach can prevent localism from being equated with parochialism and foster the development of a global perspective that facilitates interaction with IGOs and the international community. In addition, it must be pointed out that, while an intensified role for civil society promises a great deal, it does not represent a global prescription for gender ills. A more pronounced role for civil society does not inevitably amplify the voices of the marginalised, or represent a quick fix for gender issues. In civil society generally and in the context of gender mainstreaming[96] and the environmental[97] in particular, NGOs play a critical role in this context in particular in advocacy and monitoring. Even though looser affiliations of activists are playing a more pronounced role in modern civil society, NGOs remain, for most purposes, the key agents of civil society. Having said this, while women traditionally have played a significant role in the rank and file of NGOs, they have not been well represented at leadership level.[98] In the environmental sphere at least, in recent times a more visible role for women has been emerging. This increased profile has not, however, been the spontaneous product of the growing prominence for civil society; rather it has been the result of a great deal of hard work, not least by IGOs, and NGOs themselves. Broader civil society too needs to set its house in order on gender issues, a fact not lost on women's groups, who advocate gender mainstreaming for all stakeholders including NGOs themselves, as well as states, IGOs and the international community. In addition, recent innovations in civil society, and in particular new forms of networking, have seen the erosion of what were formally perceived as rigid boundaries between public and private[99] – a change that could serve to enhance the role of women in a broader socio-political context in a more organic way than has previously been possible, allowing, of course, for equal access to technology and the training and time to use it.

Gender mainstreaming – progress and problems

In 2000 at the Millennium Summit in New York, the UN agreed the Millennium Declaration, featuring eight Millennium Development Goals, goals 3 and 7 of which reaffirm the UN's commitment to gender equality and environmental sustainability. In addition General Assembly Resolution 56/133 reiterates the importance of gender in following up the Millennium Declaration. However, gender issues are not always accorded such a high profile in broader UN contexts. The Johannesburg Declaration and Plan agreed at the 2002 World Summit on Sustainable Development (WSSD) reveal how much remains to be done – gender (like environmental issues for the most part) is not strongly represented in the outcomes.[100] Although WEDO followed the same vigorous preparatory approach for the WSSD as it had for the UNCED, updating Women's Action Agenda 21 for the WSSD as the Women's Action Agenda for a Healthy and Peaceful Planet 2015, this time the organisation's efforts had less of an impact. The women's movement used the same focused and meticulous approach to pursuing the feminist agenda at the WSSD.[101] The relative paucity of gender-sensitive material contained in the Johannesburg Plan of Implementation is revealed by WEDO's gender analysis.[102] It appears that the women's agenda, which like the environmental agenda had fared well at Rio, shared the latter's fall from prominence as the international community's focus shifted at Johannesburg. That the coverage of the gender issue is so weak in the context of a more development-centred debate is particularly disturbing as, while the conflict between the environment and development is, at least in part, inevitable, the same cannot be said for development and gender. What is revealed is a worrying lack of consistency in the UN's engagement with gender issues. However, post-Johannesburg, developments on both the gender and sustainable development fronts have been rather more encouraging than might have been expected. The CSD, for example, in its twelfth session in 2004 has reopened both the broader sustainability debate and the relevance of gender to it as a crosscutting issue in its first two-year implementation cycle looking at water, sanitation and human settlements.[103]

On the whole, though, while a great deal has been done to progress gender mainstreaming, starting from a relatively low base-line, given the relatively new nature of the concept, it is unsurprising that much remains to be done. As Hannan argues, 'Gender perspectives and the promotion of gender equality are still too often perceived as purely "social" or "soft" issues, and the critical importance of gender perspectives for macro-economic development is overlooked.'[104]

The scale and nature of the UN has necessitated the adoption of an incremental approach to gender mainstreaming, and progress to date has naturally enough been somewhat uneven. Even fairly substantial commitments on paper are not always followed through enthusiastically in practice. A number of factors have been implicated as ongoing impediments to progress, not least organisational inertia within the UN, which can allow gender mainstreaming to be regarded as 'someone else's problem'. In addition, the lack of thoroughgoing political commitment to gender mainstreaming, both at an institutional and on a personal level, has been identified.[105] More fundamentally, there has been widespread conceptual confusion about gender mainstreaming and failure to grasp links between gender and the work of the UN.[106] The term tends to be used very loosely, sometimes due to lack of understanding, at other times due to a lack of commitment where areas are viewed as 'gender-neutral'. There has been a tendency toward viewing gender mainstreaming as a technical rather than a substantive concern. These factors combine to erode the value of the concept of gender mainstreaming.[107] As time has passed, experience has revealed the obstacles that lie in the path of actualising gender mainstreaming and in turn strategies are being developed to tackle them. In short, gender mainstreaming is evolving from a good idea into a demanding institutional imperative. The UN's Principal Officer for Gender Mainstreaming has played a hugely important role in piloting this change, not least in identifying key preconditions for the successful pursuit of gender mainstreaming, including: fostering a gender mainstreaming supportive institutional culture by the provision of guidance and training; high-level management endorsement; specific resource allocation; and monitoring and evaluation of initiatives.[108]

In 2002 the Office of the Special Adviser on Gender Issues and Advancement of Women UN, acting on these conclusions, produced a guide to gender equality entitled *Gender Mainstreaming: An Overview*.[109] This document evaluates progress to date and sets out to answer the key functional questions posed by gender mainstreaming. It begins by identifying how and why gender is relevant to the particular issue under discussion and adopts a step-by-step problem-solving approach to recognising opportunities and developing approaches to tackle the specific inequalities identified. Although at pains to point out that gender mainstreaming is highly individuated in order to address particular circumstances, the *Overview* also identifies a number of core issues that will need to be considered in any given context. These comprise inequalities in political power; inequalities within households; differences in legal status and entitlements; gender division of labour within the economy; inequalities in the domestic/unpaid sector; violence against women; and discriminatory attitudes.[110] The *Overview* then goes on to examine the application of gender mainstreaming to specific contexts. The systematic approach mooted begins with showing the recurrent role to be accorded to the consideration of gender issues in policy analysis and development. Gender must be considered in initial policy formulation; the identification of information requirements; the assessment of options; determining consultation arrangements and the formulation of recommendations for policy choices.[111] The *Overview* also offers step-by-step guidance on gender mainstreaming in research[112] and technical assistance[113] and on institutional development and capacity building.[114]

A significant role in advancing the equality agenda is also being played by the Inter-Agency Network on Women and Gender Equality (IANWGE). In 2003 it produced an information kit (including policy statements such as examples of

best practice) on gender mainstreaming for all UN entities.[115] The same year also saw the Director of the UN
Division of the Advancement of Women present an overview
of the UN's experience in gender mainstreaming.[116] In 2003
DAW organised a panel discussion on gender mainstreaming
in a group of its functional commissions, including the CSD.
This plethora of advice, while laudable in principle, may
be counter-productive, as the information generated by
research on gender mainstreaming is not always effectively
disseminated. Recently there has been a move towards providing a briefer system of guidance notes, including one on
sustainable development, in order to provide a more accessible entry point into the subject.

Conclusion

It is important that gender mainstreaming, wide-ranging as
it is, is not regarded as a universal panacea for society's ills.
The UN itself has recognised that, important as gender
issues are, they are not the only relevant issues to be taken
into account in addressing inequality. A number of other
factors must be included in order to promote the equality
agenda, including (but not confined to) class, religion, age
and ethnicity.[117] Nonetheless, while not sufficient for building a just and equitable society, gender mainstreaming is
undoubtedly necessary to this end. In a broader context,
gender mainstreaming may ultimately provide a model for
addressing other entrenched systemic aspects of social
inequality.

Although gender mainstreaming is an intuitively appealing concept in theory, and one that it is difficult to contest
in principle to boot, it is clear that its application in practice
is decidedly more problematic. Much the same can be said
for the concept of sustainable development. Neither can or
will be brought to fruition unless backed by the requisite
political will to bring them to the fore as substantive considerations, rather than allowing them to languish as procedu-
ral dead letters. To quote Hilary French of the World Watch
Institute:

> Despite ... notable paper achievements, actual on-the-ground
> practices in most countries and communities around the world

have not advanced nearly far enough, reflecting a widely-decried 'implementation gap'. Bridging this divide will require greater efforts to translate international commitments into policy changes at all levels of governance, as well as better mechanisms for bringing wisdom gained through hard-won local experience to the international environmental negotiating table.[118]

The concepts of sustainable development and gender mainstreaming, as things stand in international hard and soft law, promise a great deal, but unless they can be made to deliver, which is ultimately a question of political will rather than jurisprudence, they will quickly become discredited, breeding disillusionment rather than change. Although reams of law and policy have been produced in the name of advancing both sustainability and gender equality, on the whole, practical progress towards realising these mutually supporting goals has at best been slight and at worst illusory. A number of core problems are yet to be overcome. As time passes and experience of what gender mainstreaming and sustainable development are and what they require grows, the oft-repeated claim that a 'lack of understanding' is involved becomes more difficult to justify. It increasingly seems to be arguable that what is involved is not based on the lack of knowledge or comprehension; rather, the true extent of what is required is understood only too well by those who hold power, generally men from the developed world. Those in power are at least passively resisting the sustainability and gender mainstreaming agendas because of the fundamental shift in power that implementing them would necessitate.

One of the ways that the power issue can be addressed in both the gender and sustainability contexts would be to increase the role accorded to civil society, opening up the range of influence more widely than is currently the case. This approach views the active engagement of civil society with existing political institutions as an alternative or additional manifestation of citizenship. Although civil society itself is flawed, it still offers a route to a more plural and sophisticated concept of democracy. In the context of the environment in particular a great deal may potentially be gained from the development of a new more active style of environmental citizenship, one that is not gender-blind but gender-aware and equal for all. At its most radical, this approach could allow citizenship to be reclaimed or at least moulded for all in a way that allows disillusionment with nation-state-based politics to be bypassed, revitalising the political agenda at an international level. This type of more active citizen engagement with issues that can be grasped and identified with on a community and individual level and has the potential to fit well with the new ways that we are defining ourselves in the light of new technology and the global networks that are developing. Even if this radical agenda is not pursued in the long term, then, at the very least in the short term, dialogue and discourse in respect of gender and the environment can enrich the debates that we should be having here and now: 'locally sustainable lifestyles, participatory democracy and recovery of dominated peoples' subjugated knowledge are important contributions to a reconstruction of locally adapted sustainable development styles in both South and North.'[119] While it may not be the case that gender and sustainability issues will ultimately stand or fall together, there is the danger that neglecting one will hamper progress on the other. On the other hand, if they are pursued vigorously and in tandem they have the potential to fundamentally reshape not only the global *polis*, but also the very fabric of our society.

Notes

1 GA/9174, Twenty-Third Special Session, 5 June 2000.

2 E/CN.6/2001/4.

3 This term applies primarily to treaty law, for example, the Climate Change Convention.

4 This term applies to agreements falling short of treaty status, for example Agenda 21.

5 See, for example, J. A. Nelson, 'Feminism, ecology and philosophy of economics', *Ecological Economics*, 20 (1997), 155–162.

6 S. Sittirak, *The Daughters of Development: Women in a Changing Environment* (London: Zed Books, 1998), preface by Maria Mies.

7 See, for example, S. Buckingham-Hatfield, *Gender and the Environment* (London: Routledge, 2000).

8 Women and Geography Study Group, *Feminist Geographies: Explorations in Diversity and Difference* (Harlow: Longman, 1997), p. 59.

9 *Ibid.*, pp. 60 and 82.

10 S. Buckingham-Hatfield, 'Gendering Agenda 21: women's involvement in setting the environmental agenda', *Journal of Environmental Policy and Planning* 1 (1999), 121–132.

11 See C. Merchant, *The Death of Nature: Women, Ecology and the Scientific Revolution* (London: Wildwood House, 1981).

12 See V. Plumwood, 'Nature, self and gender: feminism, environmental philosophy, and the critique of rationalism' in R. Elliot (ed.), *Environmental Ethics* (Oxford: Oxford University Press, 1998).

13 See, C. Sandilands, *The Good-Natured Feminist: Ecofeminism and the Quest for Democracy* (Minneapolis: University of Minnesota Press, 1999).

14 Although ecofeminism manifests itself in a number of forms, notably cultural ecofeminism and social ecofeminism, for the purposes of this paper the term will be used in its broadest and most inclusive sense.

15 Sandilands, *The Good-Natured Feminist*, p. xvi.

16 Sittirak, *The Daughters of Development*.

17 Y. King, 'Feminism and the revolt of Nature', *Hereses*, 4:1 (1981), 12–16.

18 Sandilands, *The Good-Natured Feminist*.

19 Sittirak, *The Daughters of Development*.

20 See, for example, V. Shiva, *Staying Alive: Women, Ecology and Survival* (London: Zed Books, 1988).

21 R. Lister, *Citizenship: Feminist Perspectives* (London: Macmillan, 1997), ch. 3.

22 Sandilands, *The Good-Natured Feminist*, ch. 3.

23 *Ibid.*, p. xvii.

24 Article 55 c.

25 In particular in Articles 1 and 2.

26 The International Year for Women was instituted as the result of NGO pressure: see H. Pietila and J. Vickers, *Making Women Matter: The Role of the United Nations* (London: Zed Books, 1996, 3rd edn), ch. 4.

27 See Pietila and Vickers, *Making Women Matter*, p. viii.

28 Adopted by General Assembly Resolution 34/180, 18 December 1979.

29 A division in the UN Secretariat, within the Department for Policy Coordination and Sustainable Development, supporting the work of the CSW and CEDAW.

30 Established in 1947.

31 INSTRAW is a freestanding UN institute.

32 UNIFEM operates under the auspices of the UNDP.

33 Pietila and Vickers, *Making Women Matter*.

34 Preliminary Version of the 1994 World Survey on the Role of Women in Development, General Assembly, 48th Session. A/48/70, 23 February 1993.

35 Most significantly, the *World Survey on the Role of Women in Development* (New York: United Nations, 1986), A/CONF.116/4/Rev.1; the Report of the Secretary-General, the *Review and appraisal of progress and obstacles encountered at the national level in the realisation of the goals and objectives of the United Nations Decade for Women: Equality, Development and Peace* (New York: United Nations, 1986), A/CONF.116/5; and Addenda 1–14, which were key preparatory documents for the Nairobi Conference, and which marked the begin-

ning of an ongoing new approach to the compilation of gender-aggregated statistics.

36 Pietila and Vickers, *Making Women Matter*, p. 10.

37 *Nairobi Forward Looking Strategies for the Advancement of Women* (New York: UN Department for Public Information, 1985). The focal points are coordinated through the ACC Interagency Meeting on Women and Gender Equality, which employs ad hoc taskforces to disseminate best practice.

38 Pietila and Vickers, *Making Women Matter*, p. xi.

39 United Nations, Office of the Special Adviser on Gender Issues and Advancement of Women UN, *Gender Mainstreaming: An Overview* (New York: United Nations, 2002), p. 2.

40 E.1997.L.O. Para 4. Adopted by ECOSOC as agreed conclusions 1997/2, 17/7/97.

41 C. Hannan, 'The policy context for gender mainstreaming', Presentation to the UNCHS Habitat Workshop on UNCHS Habitat's Gender Policy Revision, New York, 6 June 2001.

42 C. Hannan, 'Gender mainstreaming: some experience from the UN', at the Swiss Agency for Development and Cooperation Conference 'Gender Mainstreaming: A Way towards Equality', Berne, 20 June 2003, p. 2.

43 United Nations, *Gender Mainstreaming*, p. v.

44 ECOSOC, Generic Mandates 1997/2.

45 13 October 1997.

46 United Nations General Assembly, outcome document, 23rd Special Session, 'Women 2000: gender equality, development and peace for the twenty-first century' (Beijing +5), June 2000.

47 See, for example, CSW resolution E/CN.6/2000/1.6rev 1.

48 Resolution 2001/41, on gender mainstreaming, July 2001.

49 UNCHS Habitat Workshop on UNCHS Habitat's Gender Policy Revision, New York, 6 June 2001.

50 New York, 2001.

51 www.un.org/womenwatch/daw/csw/46sess.htm.

52 UNEP, *Women and the Environment* (New York: United Nations, 2004), chs 3, 4 and 5.

53 See Lister, *Citizenship*.

54 United Nations, *Gender Mainstreaming*, p. 10.

55 Hannan, 'Gender mainstreaming', p. 4.

56 R. Braidotti, E. Charkiewicz, S. Hausler and S. Wieringa, *Women, the Environment and Sustainable Development: Towards a Theoretical Synthesis* (London: Zed Books, 1994).

57 Pietila and Vickers, *Making Women Matter*, ch. 9.

58 Women's Environment and Development Organisation.

59 WEDO, *Women's Action Agenda 21* (New York: WEDO, 1991).

60 Braidotti *et al.*, *Women, the Environment and Sustainable Development*, p. 103.

61 www.un.org/documents/ga/conf151/aconf15126-1annex1.htm.

62 Sandilands, *The Good-Natured Feminist*, p. 126.

63 General Assembly Nineteenth Special Session: Overall Review and Appraisal of the Implementation of Agenda 21 A/s-19//29, 27 June 1997.

64 www.un.org/womenwatch/osagi/gmsustdevelop.htm. See, in particular, paragraphs 2, 3, 4, 5, 7, 10 and 21.

65 The Report of the Secretary-General, Development and International Economic Cooperation: Effective Mobilisation of Women in Development, A/48/393, 20 September 1993.

66 C. Hannan, 'The United Nations commitment to gender mainstreaming: a global strategy for promoting equality between women and men', ODCCP Field Representatives Seminar 2001.

67 C. Hannan, 'Mainstreaming gender perspectives in environmental management and mitigation of natural disasters', at the UNDAW and NGO Committee on the Status of Women Roundtable Panel and Discussion on the Disproportionate Impact of Natural Disasters on Women, New York, 17 January 2002.

68 *Ibid.*

69 UNEP, *Gender and the Environment: A UNEP Perspective* (Nairobi: UNEP, 1995).

70 UNEP, *Success Stories: Gender and the Environment* (Nairobi: UNEP, 2000).

71 UNEP, *Women and the Environment.*

72 *Ibid.*, p. 5.

73 *Ibid.*, p. 8.

74 *Ibid.*, p. 11.

75 *Ibid.*, p. 84.

76 Drawn from Davids and Van Driel, 2000, in UNEP, *Women and the Environment*, p. 84.

77 *Ibid.*, p. 85.

78 *Ibid.*, p. 88.

79 www.unep.org/Project_Manual/5 1.asp.

80 *UNEP Project Manual: Formulation, Approval, Monitoring and Evaluation* (Nairobi: UNEP, 1997).

81 Beijing Declaration, paragraph 20.

82 See, for example, 'Autonomy: creating space for freedom', from Notes from Nowhere (eds), *We are Everywhere: The Irresistible Rise of Global Anticaptialism* (London: Verso, 2003), p. 108.

83 See, for example, C. Pye-Smith and G. Borrini Feyerabend, 'What Next?' in J. Kirkby, P. O'Keefe and L. Timberlake (eds), *The Earthscan Reader in Sustainable Development* (London: Earthscan, 1995).

84 Subcomandante Insurgente Marcos, 'Tomorrow Begins Today: invitation to an insurrection' from Notes from Nowhere (eds), *We are Everywhere*, p. 37.

85 *Ibid.*, p. 14.

86 T. Kaplan, 'Uncommon women and the common good: women and environmental protest' in S. Rowbotham and S. Linkogle (eds), *Women Resist Globalisation: Mobilising for Livelihood and Rights* (London: Zed Books, 2001).

87 Lister, *Citizenship*.

88 Notes from Nowhere (eds), *We are Everywhere*.

89 'Networks: the ecology of the movements' in Notes from Nowhere (eds), *We are Everywhere*, p. 66.

90 *Ibid.*, p. 71.

91 Buckingham-Hatfield, 'Gendering Agenda 21'.

92 J. Black, 'Regulatory conversations', *Journal of Law and Society*, 29:1 (2002), 163–196, and P. Haas, 'Obtaining international environmental protection through epistemic consensus' in I. Rowlands and M. Greene (eds), *Global Environmental Change and International Relations* (Basingstoke: Macmillan, 1991).

93 As, for example in the work of UNEP and the CSD.

94 Notes from Nowhere (eds), *We are Everywhere*, pp. 67 and 71.

95 C. Boggs, 'The new world order and social movements', *Society and Nature*, 2:2 (1994).

96 C. Hannan, 'The policy context for gender mainstreaming', Presentation to the UNCHS Habitat Workshop on UNCHS Habitat's Gender Policy Revision, New York, 6 June 2001.

97 See, for example, UNEP, *Women and the Environment*, p. 92 and Hannan, 'Gender mainstreaming', p. 11.

98 Buckingham-Hatfield, *Gender and the Environment*, p. 92.

99 See, for example, S. Picciotto, 'Reconceptualising regulation in the era of globalisation', *Journal of Law and Society*, 29:1 (2002), 1–12.

100 Hannan, 'Gender mainstreaming', p. 5.

101 Pietila and Vickers, *Making Women Matter*, ch. 10.

102 WEDO, *Gender Analysis of the Johannesburg Plan of Implementation*, at www.wedo.org.

103 www.un.org/esa/sustdev/csd/csd12/

104 Hannan, 'Gender mainstreaming', p. 10.

105 Hannan, 'The United Nations commitment to gender mainstreaming'.

106 Hannan, 'Gender mainstreaming', p. vi.

107 *Ibid.*

108 *Ibid.*

109 *Ibid.*

110 *Ibid.*, pp. 5–7.

111 *Ibid.*, pp. 13–14.

112 *Ibid.*, pp. 16–18.

113 *Ibid.*, pp. 17–20.

114 *Ibid.*, pp. 25–26.

115 See www.un.org/womenwatch/ianwge/gm_facts/

116 Hannan, 'Gender mainstreaming'.

117 United Nations, *Gender Mainstreaming*, p. 4.

118 UNEP, *Women and the Environment*, p. 101.

119 Braidotti *et al.*, *Women, the Environment and Sustainable Development*, p. 170.

3

Environmental action as a space for developing women's citizenship

SUSAN BUCKINGHAM

Introduction

I write as a geographer and an environmental feminist (or a feminist environmentalist?) on a concept that has relatively recently been incorporated into geographical scholarship and, more problematically, into environmental discourses. I write 'problematically' because, traditionally, 'citizenship' has been defined by its relationship to the nation state, whilst environmental concerns are increasingly being seen as transcending national frontiers. While Morrow's preceding chapter has considered the ways in which women's and environmental discourses and activity are leapfrogging from the local, over the national, to the global, the national is arguably still a critical dimension of citizenship.

The nexus between women, the environment and citizenship is also problematic for a number of potentially overlapping reasons:

1 Women often get involved in the politics of environmental concerns *because* they are disproportionately affected by the issues (for example, as prime carers of family members' health), or because they feel that these concerns are not adequately addressed by existing political structures or mainstream environmental campaigns.

2 The environmental concerns with which women generally get involved (or more specifically, the angle which they take on these concerns) is often intimately linked with their social roles as mothers, carers, domestic workers, and this involvement can ossify these roles just as much as it can liberate women from them.

3 Women tend to be more vulnerable to environmental pollution in that their body mass and body chemistry differ from men's, on whom chemical loadings have traditionally been measured. Potentially this could be seen as illustrating an, albeit problematic, biologically essentialist relationship with the environment, but could, perhaps, more usefully be conceived as a social model of vulnerability, in which a society which privileges the male (as the 'norm' for measuring chemical exposure), bears responsibility.

All three of these reasons are predicated on the uneven relationship between men and women, which Chapter 1 has already illustrated. It is therefore paradoxical that it is precisely this unevenness which renders women unequal citizens that propels some women into an arena and activities in which their status as citizens becomes better defined, thereby challenging dominant decision-making (though not necessarily the underlying decision-making structures). This chapter seeks to explore a number of areas where women have thereby tested and developed their rights to citizenship and, by extension, the reality of citizenship itself. It does so through an analysis of women's involvement in environmental action and their relationship to environmental problems.

Aspects of citizenship that have been found to be useful over the past decade and a half in the geography and environmental literature will be used to contextualise the work that women have been doing to combat environmental problems. Specifically attention will be focused on the concept of environmental citizenship and on the importance of space, place and geographic scale in forging women's identity as citizens with reference to the environment.

'Environmental issues' are a useful way of exploring both the strength and dynamism of women's citizenship status, and of the potential for representative and participative democracy at a variety of scales to incorporate this.[1] It is useful here, also, to reflect on Karen Morrow's point in Chapter 2 that while the two campaigning movements of environmentalism and feminism are separate, each stands to gain substantially from mutually beneficial prosecution. Women's environmental activities range all the way from local campaigning to prevent, for example, the construction of a local incinerator, to lobbying international organisations for greater sensitivity to gender differences; at all scales these activities bring women face to face with gendered structures of power. These campaigns attract or galvanise women's involvement in large part because they affect their roles as mothers, carers, domestic workers and consumers, and in the process can either reinforce these roles or be profoundly disruptive of them – as this chapter will later show in presenting the activities of women in environmental campaigning.

It is, however, important not to equate being a woman with being a mother. There are issues around women's exposure to environmental pollution, gendered occupational and pay structures, and gendered access to political power that affect women regardless of whether or not they have children. It is also important to note, as Reed points out, that motherhood and environmental concern can also be falsely conflated and that these are not mutually contingent factors, even though most surveys of environmental attitudes and behaviour reveal women with children to be the group most concerned about environmental issues.[2]

Despite a widespread increase in environmental campaigning – and a growing institutionalisation of a large sector of the environmental movement – citizenship is not a concept that necessarily informs much of this activity. Many environmental non-governmental organisations (hereafter ENGOs) are undemocratic in that they are funded, but not defined, by a subscription membership, and decisions are not always arrived at consensually or collectively. They also tend to replicate gendered (and racialised) hierarchies found in many for-profit companies and government organisations, and tend to be driven by issues rather than process. Joni Seager's review of the North American environmental movement in the early 1990s demonstrated this clearly, and most UK environmental groups in the early 2000s are still characterised by this structure.[3] In the EU, a review of ENGOs which are members of the 'Civil Society Contact Group' established that 43 per cent of the heads of these groups were women, while only 24 per cent of members of their highest decision-making bodies were women. Contact Group members have agreed as a condition of their membership to promote gender parity, so it is reasonable to assume that ENGOs not part of this group are unlikely to have better women's representation in senior management levels.[4] If, as Morrow suggests, NGOs are the 'key agents of civil society', there is clearly work to be done in creating more representative civic organisations.

The environmental justice movement has begun to address some of the inequalities of environmental exposure, particularly with regard to race and poverty. For example, Friends of the Earth (FoE) Scotland's campaign for environmental justice, sparked by concerns that higher incidences of environmental damage are found close to communities with higher levels of poverty and social disadvantage, demands 'no less than a decent environment for all; no more than our fair share of the Earth's resources.'[5] In the US, in 1987, the Commission for Racial Justice collected evidence that strongly suggested that race was found to be the most potent variable in predicting where a factory would be located, and reinforced a popular movement that resulted in an Executive Order being passed in 1994 to ensure that Federal Actions were taken 'to address environmental justice in minority populations and low income populations'.[6] However, gender inequalities, are not yet a prominent feature in either environmental justice campaigns or their academic analyses, although there are exceptions, such as Wickramasinghe's work in South Asia.[7] Overwhelmingly, the environmental movement can often be characterised as macho and its campaigns do not always best serve women.

Joni Seager[8] regrets that a mainly male-led environmental movement in North America ignores the more social- and urban-focused environmental justice issues, which she believes preoccupy women, confining their interests to 'hyper-events' and the large scale. In the UK, the Women's Environmental Network (WEN) was formed as a breakaway group from Friends of the Earth in 1988 because WEN's founders did not feel that these more localised concerns were being addressed by the mainstream environmental movement – a point developed later in this chapter.

One of the reasons that women are disproportionately negatively affected by environmental degradation is poverty and whilst this is, of course, not unique to women, they are far more likely to be poor than men, as will be demonstrated later in this chapter. In the 1950s, T. H. Marshall, in developing a social dimension to citizenship, argued that it was insufficient for citizenship to be legally defined and defended if the mechanisms for translating it into a fully functioning citizenship were weak (see also Lievesley's discussion in Chapter 1). Ruth Lister develops this by arguing that women's lack of access to adequately paid work, childcare and so on in effect renders them second-class citizens.[9] This argument can be extended by considering that an added exposure to environmental problems that poorer women cannot buy their way out of (such as the link between poorer environmental quality and low-cost housing, cheap genetically modified food compared to more expensive organically guaranteed quality) compounds this secondary status. This thread of women's relative poverty has been pulled through the feminist geography literature in the 1980s and 1990s and has been shown to work against women, and especially marginalised women such as refugees, immigrant women and those seeking asylum.[10] Geography has a well-developed literature on gender inequalities, and while not all is explicitly linked to citizenship, the connections can clearly be made.

The next section of this chapter will look at some of the concepts referred to above in more detail – particularly that of environmental citizenship and the link between citizenship and the places (from private to public – one of the defining aspects of Chapter 1's first modality: universal and particular notions of citizenship) in which this is expressed. Following this, the chapter will explore a number of overlapping relationships: between women and poverty; between gender and social roles; and between gender and political power (contained within Lievesley's second modality), which limit women's access to full citizenship. In the light of these relationships, I will examine the implications for women's entitlement to environmental justice – an entitlement not to be disproportionately negatively affected by environmental degradation, relative to men, and in their own right. Women's involvement in various forms of environmental campaigning is then considered: both its empowering dimension and its ability to confine women to the social roles to which society habituates them (us?). This analysis will explore the gendered nature of the environmental movement, women's place in it, its 'safeness'/'acceptability' as a forum in which women can test citizenship rights and responsibilities, and what happens when women transgress what is considered 'acceptable'. (An example from the UK is the Greenham Common women, who left their homes to camp out – in some cases for months and years – in protest against American nuclear warheads being housed in Britain. Much of the popular press castigated these women for 'abandoning' their homes and families.)

Finally, the chapter will explore ways in which political identities (Lievesley's third modality) have been developed through environmental action, and how the ways in which this has been achieved may challenge dominant notions of citizenship. There are different scales at which this political process takes place and the chapter will consider its development at the international and transnational scale, and, at the other end of the spectrum, at how women are making the links between the intensely local – or even bodily – scale and the trans- and inter-national. Without the nation state can this be understood as citizenship? Does the concept need further adaptation? Seager recognises citizenship as a dynamic process – how far are women involved in its reformulations? Feminism, like environmentalism is, of course, also an international and transnational movement, both historically and contemporarily, with much equal opportunities legislation originating at the inter- and trans-national scale (see Morrow in Chapter 2).

These strands, then, will be drawn together in the conclusion, where I will consider how concepts of citizenship used in Geography and environmental discourses are applicable to an understanding of the social relationship between women and the environment.

Environmental citizenship and its spaces

Most of the environmental movement, and increasingly environmental legislation, is predicated on a rights-based approach – for example, the UN Subcommission on the Prevention of Discrimination and Protection of Minorities (also known as the Ksentini Report) provides for the 'universal right to a secure, healthy and ecologically sound environment'.[11] Perhaps because a 'rights'-based approach does not necessarily involve real 'equality' this has not served women well up to now, with regard to social justice, and it is therefore questionable how far a rights-based approach to social-environment relations will achieve this. Simply securing a right does not necessarily enable that right to be exercised or realised. Continuing with the example of the Ksentini Report, it identified the following rights :

- to information concerning the environment;
- to receive and disseminate ideas and information;
- to participate in planning and decision-making processes, including prior environmental impact assessment;
- to freedom of association for the purpose of protecting the environment or the rights of persons affected by environmental harm;
- to effective remedies and redress for environmental harm in administrative or judicial proceedings.

Clearly, in order for these rights to be realised, there has to be universal literacy (including environmental and legal literacy – everyone needs to be aware of these rights). People also have to be able to organise their time in order to effectively participate, which implies an equality within the family so no family member is prohibited or dissuaded from attending meetings or getting involved in participation exercises. As sections later in this chapter will show, and as is shown elsewhere in this book, this situation is far from being obtained for women in the West, let alone the world as a whole.

The environmental justice movement has come to the fore at a time when human rights discourses have become more prominent. With this comes a universalist assumption that is challenged in some quarters by arguments to recognise diversity and difference, but which may sit more easily within a rights-based than an equalities-based regime. There may be an argument for separating out rights from equality as far as women (and sub-groups of women) are concerned, in order to enable them/us to 'catch up' with our male counterparts. For example, an argument could be made for women to be accorded greater rights than men, or children than adults, or the more vulnerable than the strong, although there has been prohibitive resistance to this in many countries where equal rights legislation has resolutely stopped short of quotas as a form of positive discrimination. The Treaty of Amsterdam, which came into effect for the European Union and its member states in 1999, requires that the organisation 'must aim to eliminate inequalities, and to promote equality, between men and women'. 'Active measures' are expected to ensure that 'the principle of equal treatment is applied … [and] Member States may maintain or adopt measures providing for specific advantages in order to make it easier for the under-represented sex to pursue a vocational activity or to prevent or compensate for disadvantages in professional careers.' The European Court of Justice, however, has, to date, ruled against 'strict quotas'. [12]

Environmentalists are concerned about the most appropriate form of democracy to deliver environmental equalities and rights. Participatory democracy is often favoured as being a more community-based and direct form of decision-making. On the face of it, since this is likely to thrive in more localised communities in which women have historically had a more active part to play, it is likely to have greater potential to secure environmental rights and equalities for women. The community, as a site in which citizenship can be exercised, received momentum through Marshall's thesis of social citizenship and Peled has proposed a two-tier system of citizenship in which the community provides the context for the most developed form of 'strong' citizenship. While this might benefit particular groups of women who are well embedded in their local community, as Yuval-Davis points out, this could work against minority ethnic women and others considered outsiders.[13] Marion Roberts develops this argument in Chapter 4, and also cautions against the neighbourhood being assumed always to serve women well. Both forms of democracy, then, are problematic in how they provide women with opportunities for expressing their rights and responsibilities as citizens. Since both human rights and participatory democracy have emerged from and are shaped by patriarchal political systems that have privileged the male over the female, and the human over the non-human, the degree to which it is capable of an internal transformation has to be raised, as it is by Seager, Emel and Plumwood, among others.[14]

Environmental citizenship is additionally problematic, particularly so for women. Its origins in the international political arena challenge the nation-state boundedness of citizenship. The international agreements which have emphasised the universal right to a clean, healthy and viable environment are frequently at odds with national, regional and local realities. Mason, arguing the case for an environmental democracy, observes links between the strength of a national environmental policy and inclusive political practice, and optimistically suggests that a regard for environmental citizenship can help to 'wean democratic identities away from self-interest, nationality and consumerism'.[15] Whilst this observance favours a move towards more open, transparent and participative governance, it also reinforces the point that international agreements still need to be nationally brokered and implemented, which accounts for national variations in achieving environmental citizenship. The relationship between the transnational and the national is dialectical and iterative in that as well as transnational agreements and decisions affecting the locally grounded situation of citizens, 'being an environmental citizen … means exercising rights and responsibilities that have a transnational scope'.[16] Environmental citizenship can, therefore potentially be seen as a contemporary development of political identity away from the nation state. As such, it may be useful to consider this alongside feminist calls to transnationalise citizenship from Werbner and Yuval-Davis.[17] With regard to women, as other chapters in this book also show, the state is a grossly limiting factor for equality of citizenship. Moreover, much of the rights-based literature on environmental citizenship ignores the fact that a rights-based practice has been severely restrictive for women (as a body, or differentiated by race, class, income and so on). Grounding new forms of citizenship in a historically divisive system is, then, not without its problems.

Mason uses the 'political opportunity structure' to analyse the profile and impact of non-institutional political mobilisation and its subsequent integration within the political system and in particular, how non-institutional political actors shape the nature of the political opportunities they encounter.[18] Since political structures and systems reflect existing unequal gender relations, it is arguable that the opportunities and the shape of non-institutional political mobilisation will also reflect these, and so subsequently shape them. However, it is within these gendered structures and systems that, as Fincher and Panelli suggest, 'activists make political space for themselves in the light of strategic assessments of their geographical, historical and institutional contexts'.[19] Elsewhere, Gibson-Graham is optimistic that both the women's and environmental movements 'have generated new discourses of social and ecological identity' that have challenged pre-existing forms of exploitation. She argues that these 'alternative rights discourses' have challenged masculine hegemonies sufficiently to create new claims on resources.[20] These analyses provide a context in which, while recognising broader constraining structures and processes which limit women's exercise of citizenship, suggest some room in which women can manoeuvre the environmental agenda. While these manoeuvres may be small, subtle and disconnected, they create 'micro-ruptures' which Lipietz has optimistically suggested have the potential to, cumulatively, disrupt broader structures.[21]

Carter draws on 'discursive democracy' or 'the power of argument' as a more effective way to change people's attitudes and behaviour than the rights-based approach of representative democracy. Participatory democracy, he argues, has greater scope to yield better ecological outcomes as citizens are more likely to develop a stronger understanding of social-ecological relationships, and through which public institutions may become more open and transparent. Arguably, participatory democracy thrives in smaller-scale political units, and Carter here looks to the work of advocates such as Kropotkin, Schumacher, Sale and Bookchin, who have all extolled the virtues of the region/locality to provide more sensitive environmental and social governance.[22] However, Carter is concerned about the potential dangers of homogeneity and small-mindedness such a form of governance may generate, as this chapter's earlier use of Peled's two-tier construction of citizenship cautions. Feminist geographers such as Liz Bondi have written about the liberating nature of city living for women, just as Roberts discusses the potentially limiting nature of 'the neighbourhood' for women.[23] However, there has recently been some interesting work on bioregional solutions[24] which rest on the appropriateness of scale. An *appropriate* focus on the regional and local may also, potentially, work in the favour of women who customarily have had a stronger profile at the community level in informal political activity, as this chapter will later develop. Nevertheless, it is important to keep in sight the connectivity of the local/particular and the global/universal. John

Lechte's proposal that the private (or local) constitutes the material reality of the universal is useful here. This conceptualisation offers environmental citizenship the potential to move between scales and helps to define it as something broader than the parochialism of the NIMBY (not in my back yard) movement.[25]

Public and private spaces

The public–private dichotomy can be useful in conceptualising citizenship and in understanding women's partial incorporation into citizenship and political activity. It is also a profoundly geographical and spatial concept, which defines particular *spaces* by activities and consequently has been of some interest to feminist geographers. Ultimately, however, this is too crude and un-nuanced a division and does not satisfactorily explain ways in which the most intimately private spaces, for example, are bound to processes operating at much broader scales. For example, Margaret Walton-Roberts demonstrates the imbrication of the public and private through her analysis of Indian immigration to Canada in which global migration patterns are linked to the micro domestic and family politics of arranged marriages.[26] In an environmental context, this imbrication can be seen in how, for example, the development and marketing practices of transnational chemical and pharmaceutical companies have a particular impact on the bodies of women. Martin argues that this dichotomy of the private and public atomises lives into discrete components, which do not adequately reflect women's lives as they are lived, although she values the dichotomy as an 'illustrative analytical construct'.[27] Likewise, Yuval-Davis argues against dichotomising the public and private, arguing that all geographic spaces are subject to state intervention. Her review of different attempts to categorise spaces and activities as private reveals the problems of doing so; indeed, she suggests that constructing the boundary between the public and the private is a political act in itself.[28]

There is a subtle balance to be achieved in recognising, valuing and politicising women's activities in the private sphere and in also recognising, securing and promoting the role women can play in the public realm. Moreover, there is a need to recognise and explore the intersection of the public and private which environmental concerns are well placed to expose and articulate. There have been various conceptions of an intervening space between the public and the private variously described as a 'community public sphere' (Martin), a 'third sphere' or 'neighbourhood sphere' (Milroy and Wismer) and an 'intermediate sphere' (Horelli and Vepsa).[29] This occupies a physical and an activity space which grows out of the private but is not fully public and in which women are predominantly active. An interesting Venezuelan example illustrates how, soon after the most local scale of government was reclassified from community and voluntary to more formal, professional and salaried status the same unit moved from being predominantly women-led to being dominated by men.[30]

This community public sphere is an important political space for environmental activity, which is both closely bound to community space and place as a generator or manifester of concerns, and as a site for protest, as will be developed below. While this combination of the content of the concern and the site of its protest is often well-connected in environmental activity, the two are not necessarily contingently or causally linked and Staeheli emphasises the need to recognise this and uncouple these where necessary.[31] These discussions raise the importance of place – another quintessentially geographical concept – in constructing citizenship. Fincher and Panelli focus on the strategic use of spaces, places and various spatial scales at which activist protest is constituted. Places at which daily practices are enacted can be symbolic and imbued with significance, factors which can be potent in constructing informal political action. These places also materialise and spatialise broader environmental concerns, as suggested earlier. Despite her caution above, Staeheli writes about how 'material sites/places are helpful in the formation of political action'.[32]

This section, then has attempted to understand what environmental citizenship represents for women – not a consideration which features in the literature on environmental citizenship itself – and how geographies of citizenship (the public to private, the local to international) may be useful in this understanding. The following section will consider the environmental implications and results of women's relative poverty, embodied vulnerability, political powerlessness and social position and will argue that there is a clear case to argue for an equality of both treatment and outcome for women which requires a different set of 'norms' to that which currently obtain.

Distributions of social, economic and political power: a case for environmental justice

Women and poverty

A survey of poverty and social exclusion published by the UK Equal Opportunities Commission reported that 36 per cent of women, compared to 30 per cent of men, lived in households with incomes less than 60 per cent of the median. In addition, women were more likely to be poor on all four dimensions of poverty used by the UK Government.[33] Even when controlling for other factors such as labour-market status, number and age of children, household composition, and age, there was still a clear gender dimension to poverty. In addition, women who are single pensioners, unemployed, of Pakistani or Bangladeshi origin, a teenage householder, or tenant, are more likely to be poor than men with the same characteristics. Those likely to experience the greatest degree of poverty are lone mothers and older single women.

Women in full-time paid work in the UK will, on average, earn 81 per cent of the hourly wage earned by men in full-time work. Although this gap is currently closing, the hourly pay rate gap between women in part-time work and men in full-time work is widening such that these women earn 61 per cent of the hourly rate of men in full-time work.[34] The EOC report also suggests that there is unequal poverty within the household with some women having unequal access to household earnings, where the male partner is the main earner, and that mothers sometimes forgo consumption in order to meet the demands of the rest of their family. The situation is worse in the USA, where the National Commission on Pay Equity has reported that in 2004 the relative median earnings of full-time, year-round workers had worsened for women, who earned 76 per cent of the equivalent men's wage ($30,724 compared to $40,668). This had reached an all-time high of 77 per cent in 2003. Many ethnic minority women's share was significantly less, with African-American women earning 60 per cent of the average male (all ethnic groups) earnings, and latinas earning 55 per cent. The Institute for Women's Policy Research has established that 90 per cent of long-term low earners among prime age adults are women and that this, together with time off for childrearing, results in women's average earnings over a fifteen-year period being $273,592 compared to $722,693 for men. This has significant implications for women's long-term independent financial security.[35]

Since links between poverty and poor environmental quality are well documented (FoE Scotland), the above suggests that women are, consequently, on average, more likely (because they are women) to experience poorer environmental quality than men. Those with low income will be exposed to higher rates of traffic and industrial pollution, as they do not have the resources to buy themselves out of the most environmentally degraded areas. They are more likely to experience fuel and food poverty by living in draughty, poorly insulated and damp accommodation, and having to be less discriminating with regard to food quality.

Around 1.2 billion people currently live below the UN-defined poverty line of $1 a day, while a further 2.8 billion earn less than $2 a day. Seventy per cent of these people in poverty are women.[36] The education gap between girls and boys in the developing world is still sufficiently wide to ensure that gender inequalities will persist into the next adult generation with girl/boy secondary school enrolment ratios standing at 0.96 in North Africa, 0.79 in sub-Saharan Africa, 0.79 in West Asia and 0.77 in South Asia. Only in Latin America (1.07, but a decline since a high 1.09 in 1998/99) is this reversed.[37] The percentage of women in paid non-agricultural employment is 46.1 per cent in developed regions, 18.2 per cent in South Asia, 19.2 per cent in West Asia, 20.5 per cent in North Africa, 28.9 per cent in Oceania, 38.5 per cent in South-East Asia, 38.9 per cent in East Asia, 42.9 per cent in Latin America and 48.9 per cent in CIS and transition countries.[38] These figures suggest a lack of independent income for more than half, rising to around 80 per cent, of all women of some global regions. These concerns are articulated as some of the UN Millennium Goals, which are far from being met and raise the issue of the effectiveness of international legislation and agreements.

Impact of environmental damage on women's social roles

Despite the alleged rise of the 'New Man' in the 1990s, surveys, such as the UK's Social Trends, continue to demonstrate that women do the majority of grocery shopping, cooking, cleaning, childcare and care of other vulnerable family members. This is not unique to the UK, and studies from across the EU and in places as far apart as Colombia and Sri Lanka confirm that this is a global pattern.[39] Such activities bring the participant into closer contact with environmental concerns and problems, whether this is the woman who has to walk an extra hour to collect water for cooking, drinking and cleaning because of groundwater depletion, the woman whose daily journey to collect firewood is lengthened due to deforestation, or the woman who is checking food or toiletries in the supermarket to ensure that it is organic, not tested on animals, is GM-free and otherwise free of chemicals likely to cause allergic reactions in her family members. Surveys consistently show that women are more concerned about environmental issues then men and are more likely to take action to mitigate these (such as recycling, cutting down water use or buying 'environmentally friendly' products).[40] Disturbing reports from some CIS countries highlight the impact that deteriorating environmental conditions are having on women's reproductive health, and the burden that deficits in electric power and water-quality issues are putting on women's domestic activities.[41] Problems associated with this political transition such as reduced employment and education opportunities, health problems, poverty and violence disproportionately affect women, with 60 per cent of those now registered unemployed being women. All the domestic work made increasingly burdensome by economic and environmental problems is unpaid and, as such, greatly undervalued by society.

In the past twenty-five years there has been some interesting work undertaken by women to attempt to quantify the monetary value of housework and caring in order to expose its real value and encourage governments to add this value to national accounting systems. This has included Marilyn Waring's work on challenging the United Nations' approved system of national accounting which is used to judge the financial salience of all countries.[42] UNEP has estimated the global figure that women's unpaid work produces in terms of output to be $11 trillion, compared to a global GDP of about $23 trillion. This includes subsistence production (such as growing food and making clothes for family members), informal sector employment (where women work, unpaid, to support family businesses), domestic and reproductive work (such as cleaning, cooking, shopping or collecting material for the home and caring for children and other dependents) and voluntary community work.[43] Clearly much of this work is both affected by the environment and is involved in managing it in some respect.

Women's embodied vulnerability

It is becoming better recognised in environmental policy-making circles that pregnant women are particularly vulnerable, for example to environmental toxins, along with children, the elderly, some ethnic groups and those with pre-existing health problems. The new European Registration and Evaluation Authority for the Restriction of Chemicals (REACH) has stated that DNELs (derived no-effect levels) may be needed to be identified separately for different human populations (such as workers, consumers) and sub-groups (such as pregnant women). However, there is very little mention of women in the REACH documentation or the European Environment Agency 2003 Environmental Assessment Report, which, incidentally, cautions that there remain a number of instances where target levels for chemicals are exceeded and which necessitate particular food recommendations for pregnant women, such as dioxins and mercury in fish. The UK Royal Commission on Environmental Pollution's 24th *Report on Chemicals in Products: Safeguarding the Environment and Human Health*, published in 2003, carried only three references to women. Nor are pregnancy and old age the only vulnerable periods in a woman's life: according to Dr Lilian Corra, (Vice President of the International Society of Doctors for the Environment), anatomical and physiological changes during puberty and the menopause affect the way in which the body absorbs and gets rid of toxins, circulation, fat distribution and metabolism.[44] Women's particular susceptibility to chemical pollution has resulted in women's health, particularly reproductive health, becoming an 'indicator of environmental pollution'.[45]

Kathleen Jones has claimed that 'the body is a significant dimension in the definition of citizenship'. Whilst her argument centres on the right some women claim to represent the state in armed struggle, nonetheless it is a useful organising concept to understand how women's bodies are sites in which environmental citizenship is worked through. As well as the gendered body responding differently to environmental pollutants, decisions regarding the calculation of 'safe' levels of pollutants and the norm on which these are calculated are also profoundly gendered. Other environmental impacts on the body can include the increased incidence of male physical violence against women in times of environmental stress.[46]

Women's political role

As Catherine Danks' chapter on women in Russia demonstrates later in this book, women are usually in a minority in governments worldwide: in the European Parliament, around 25 per cent of elected representatives are women, in the UK 19 per cent of Members of Parliament are women – with just over 25 per cent of the UK cabinet being women. Half of the Welsh Assembly is now composed of women, with four women in its nine-member Cabinet; 39 per cent of Members of the Scottish Parliament are women, but only 28 per cent of the Scottish Cabinet.[47] In the USA in 2005, 14 per cent of senators and 16 per cent of state governors were women. Table 3.1 shows the low participation of women in formal political activity in parts of Europe, while Table 3.2 illustrates a similar pattern in selected commonwealth countries.

Worldwide there are few political forums, then, where women are able to form a critical mass, which Bhattar argues is necessary for women to support each other in policy initiatives, to be a catalyst for other women to become involved and to be in a position to allocate and control resources.[48] The proportion generally agreed to constitute this critical mass is 30 to 35 per cent. Of course, such a proportion of itself is only a proxy for the degree of change – simply having women in power is no guarantee that attitudes towards anything, and particularly gender equality or environmental policy, will change, but it does represent the potential for change which, as will be illustrated below, can make a difference. A recent

Table 3.1 Positions held by women and men in European institutions, and in Ireland and UK

Role/institution	% Women	% Men
Members of European Parliament	28	72
Senior Ministerial Positions – Ireland	14	86
Senior Ministerial Positions – UK	21	79
Junior Ministerial Positions – Ireland	12	88
Junior Ministerial Positions – UK	31	69
Senior Ministerial Positions – EU average	25	75
Junior Ministerial Positions – EU average	22	78
Members of Parliament – Ireland	12	88
Members of Parliament – UK	18	82
Members of Parliament – EU Average	23	77
Members of Upper House – Ireland	17	83
Members of Upper House – UK	16	84
Members of Upper House – EU Average	21	79

Source: European Commission, Employment and Social Affairs, 2004.

Table 3.2 Women in politics in selected Commonwealth case-studies

Country/date of election	% women in upper house	% women in lower house	% women in cabinet
Australia/1996	30.7	15.5	13.3
Canada/1996	23.3	17.6	26.5
Bangladesh/1996	–	11.2	8.0
Dominica/1995	–	10.0	22.2
Guyana/1996	–	19.4	11.1
India/1994	8.0	7.4	2.9
Malaysia/1995	17.4	6.8	8.0
Seychelles/1993	–	27.3	25.0
South Africa/1994	17.8	26.5	28.0
Uganda/1994	–	20.6	11.1

Source: Commonwealth Secretariat, 1998.

Commonwealth Secretariat document suggests that 'even a few women in the corridors of power lead to a more participatory, less autocratic style of government'.[49]

National power structures are generally characterised by an inverse relationship between degrees of power on the one hand and degrees of localness and higher proportions of women, on the other. Women are generally more prominent in local government (in England and Wales, for example, around 30 per cent of local councillors are women), and most notably women are most active in grassroots community action, which is often the only forum in which women feel they can express their concerns. This chapter has already raised the issue of affirmative action and quotas within the European context. Sweden was the first country worldwide to introduce a quota system to increase the number of women in parliament, and is the first country to have reached gender parity in its representation. The ANC, in its first elections in post-apartheid South Africa, set a quota for 30 per cent of women candidates, resulting in women taking 26.5 per cent of the lower house of representatives in 1994. Similar quotas have been used by the FRELIMO party in Mozambique, the Canadian Liberal Party and the Australian Labor Party. If, indeed, there is a likelihood that more women elected representatives lead to more participatory government, and that more participatory government benefits both women's citizenship status as well as being more environmentally sensitive, as this chapter has already suggested, then this must be a significant step towards both full citizenship for women and environmental citizenship. Having explored issues of poverty, social role, embodiment and representation that limit women's full access to environmental (as well as other forms of) citizenship, the next section will consider the campaigning that women have engaged in, have been successful in, and the implications of this.

Women's environmental campaigning: exercising citizenship

Women's environmental campaigning frequently moves between different spatial scales and locations. Notable and well-documented campaigns include the formal lobbying of the United Nations through preparatory committees for the 1992 Conference on Environment and Development, the 1995 Fourth Women's Conference at Beijing and the World Summit on Sustainable Development in 2002. These formal engagements in the international policy-setting arena are time-consuming and expensive and the resources available to women's groups limit this involvement, although significant publicity coups and some groundbreaking work has been achieved.[50]

Many of the concerns brought together at these events relate to the domestic and the community – safe waste disposal, access to clean drinking water and sewage disposal, exposure to environmental pollution and the health consequences of these exposures. Women's groups internationally have derived strength from a common purpose and a recognition that on some issues women's concerns are shared in many different places and circumstances. At the same time, there is concern that better resourced, more powerful women's groups from the North outbid those from the South.

Results of women's specific involvement in international policy-making, through preparatory committees and through direct lobbying at the conferences, include Chapter 24 on Women for Agenda 21, a programme for environmental action which was agreed at the UN Conference on Environment and Development in 1992. This argues that women need to be involved in environmental decision-making as equal partners as they have at least an equal stake in environmental outcomes, have a particularly valuable perspective on environmental issues through their roles as mothers, cooks, provisioners and subsistence farmers, and have been previously excluded from decision-making. Moreover, the eleventh session of the UN Commission on Sustainable Development (CSD) recognised gender as a key crosscutting issue in its ten-year work plan. The commitment to 'gender mainstreaming' emanated from the Beijing Conference on Women in 1995, which requires signatories to 'mainstream a gender perspective into all policies and programmes, so that, before decisions are taken, an analysis is made of the effects on women and men respectively'.[51] In 2002, the World Summit on Sustainable Development arguably moved the agreements of the 1990s forward from specific chapters on women, with little inclusion of women in proposals beyond these chapters, to a much broader inclusion of women and gendered concerns throughout the agreement. This has drawn a mixed response from the cautious optimism of the Women in Environment and Development Organisation (WEDO) to the more sceptical analysis by the Women's Environmental Network (WEN). In contrast to its cautious optimism regarding the WSSD, WEDO is critical of the CSD's reports for its reviews on water, sanitation and human settlements which, WEDO accuses, lack:

1 the identification of gender differences and an integration of practical and strategic gender needs;
2 disaggregated data on gender which undermines informed policies and decision-making procedures;
3 a recognition of the contributions and involvement of women in maintaining and providing resources;
4 an analysis of the harmful social and economic effects on women caused by privatisation policies;
5 an estimation of economic and social burdens, including increasing insecurity and neglect of women's dignity, carried by female-headed households impacted by poor environmental and sanitary conditions;
6 a recognition of the need to systematically bring women's expertise to decision-making at all levels of policy-making, political administration and management;
7 any concrete recommendations to benefit women such as guaranteeing land and resources tenure, targeting poor women with subsidies to ensure housing, water and sanitation provision, supporting women's efforts in water management, mainstreaming gender through all plans and procedures and guaranteeing gender balance in advisory, planning and decision-making bodies.[52]

That WEDO is raising these issues eight years after the Beijing conference indicates the scale of the problem of operationalising gender, a point to which this chapter will return. Transnational lobbying activity by women on environmental issues is also evident in the European Union, which has incorporated a number of these international directives, and this chapter will shortly examine the extent to which these are challenging the EU's and member states' practice of citizenship and environmental governance.

In the political pyramid that characterises environmental decision-making (and most other kinds of decision-making), however, women only feature significantly at the foundation. This is often women's only resort to raising their concerns about how the environment may be negatively affecting the health of their own bodies, their children, other family members and neighbours, and the environment more widely. Although many women feel frustrated at their lack of influence, and angry at how decisions insensitive to gender (and poverty, and race) are made, there are a number of campaigns that exemplify what women can bring to the policy table – sometimes with a humour, grace and camaraderie not evident elsewhere. Three examples are presented here – contributing to Lipietz's 'micro-ruptures' referred to earlier – which illustrate what can be achieved at different scales of informal political activity: the Women's Environmental Network, a UK-based environmental campaigning organisation; Love Canal, an internationally known example of grassroots women's political action which has entered the environmental campaigning / environmental justice vocabulary; and lastly, an example from South Wales which illustrates that even if an individual battle is felt to be lost, the politicisation and empowerment that women have acquired as a result of their involvement is likely to make a real difference in the future.

The Women's Environmental Network

The Women's Environmental Network (WEN) was formed in 1988 by some women campaigners from Friends of the Earth, which, WEN founder-members felt, was not sufficiently engaged with the concerns and situation of 'ordinary women'. Their work from the late 1980s until now combines a pragmatic, practical attitude to getting things changed with a feminine/feminist flamboyance, which attracts headlines. Their pragmatism has led to significant inputs into central and local government policy including women's health, local food production, and waste prevention. The promotion of real nappies to replace disposables has been one of WEN's highest-profile campaigns, in which they have fought off complaints by manufacturers of disposable nappies, concerned about their loss of market share.[53] WEN is particularly keen to raise awareness on issues considered 'taboo' (e.g. sanitary and incontinence protection) and issues that other environmental groups do not or will not take on. There have been several instances where WEN has developed campaigns which were not popular elsewhere at the time (real nappies being a good case in point) only to see other environmental organisations embrace these at a later date, often without acknowledgement. WEN is also concerned with the process of developing projects that involve the subject (whether Bangladeshi women in community gardening projects, or women diagnosed with breast cancer in mapping cancer 'hot spots'), with the hope that women will become empowered through this experience (as the example of Theresa Brzoza below will show). WEN is aware that its emphasis on women can attract prurient, as well as increasingly serious, press coverage and occasionally puts this to use. For example, part of their 'Putting Breast Cancer on the Map' project involved Toxic Tours of Westminster and Wrexham; on the Westminster tour, a performance artist 'Monique Toxique' led the tour with a provocatively revealed left breast cut out of her pin-striped suit, which guaranteed high press coverage.

Other campaigns have included an Easter egg hunt in local high streets to highlight the perils of lindane-laced non-organic chocolate, which persist despite the 2002 ban on lindane in Europe. One of WEN's latest campaigns – as this chapter was being written – 'Getting Lippy', highlights the presence of toxic chemicals in cosmetics and toiletries and challenges manufacturers to list these to enable women to use their consumer power to lobby for a ban on such chemicals in cosmetics. The focus on women as consumers is potentially controversial in that it can reify social roles, although the problems of so categorising women needs to be balanced against the benefits of appealing to what power women do hold in their ascribed social roles. As a campaigning group promoting women's power as consumers, as well as inequality with regard to environmental issues, which takes on a number of high-profile manufacturers (for example, of disposable nappies, sanitary protection, cosmetics and toiletries, flooring, food products, and packaging), WEN is unable to accept donations from commercial organisations, and is reliant on a relatively small membership compared to many other ENGOs, grants from charitable foundations and some limited government grants for research and capacity/social capital building. As such, it is in a state of permanent financial insecurity incommensurate with its now quite high national profile.[54] This raises real issues concerning the salience of small, highly principled environmental campaigning groups and, clearly, by focusing on women, WEN halves the support available to other, non-gender-specific groups. Nevertheless, WEN is offered here as an example of a women's environmental NGO which achieves its success despite these limiting factors and which has built up cross-party political support amongst women MPs and MEPs representing UK constituencies. This illustrates the advantages for women of mobilising at a range of scales and contexts, noted by Lievesley in Chapter 1 as essential for securing any advancement in women's citizenship status.

Lois Gibbs and Love Canal

In the 1970s, Lois Gibbs lived in what she described as a lower-middle-class blue-collar neighbourhood in a town in upper New York state, where she began to notice a rise in miscarriages, perinatal deaths and cancers in her local neighbourhood, which coincided with the construction of a local primary school on a disused chemical waste dump (Love Canal). After a years-long campaign using meticulously collected primary data (famously dismissed as 'housewives' data' by local and State politicians), during which time houses became unsaleable, marriages broke up, and people became ill and died, the state eventually agreed that residents had been affected (though by the 'mental anguish' rather than by the more incriminating chemical poisoning), and paid compensation. This was only a partial victory, in that the land was later used to build public housing. Lois Gibbs went on to found the Center for Health, Environment and Justice and has written and spoken about how the experience 'opened her eyes to ... how corporate power and influence had more influence and rights than tax paying citizens'.[55] Central to the way in which the Love Canal campaign has been taken up as emblematic for the women's environmental/justice movement is the fact that Lois Gibbs was (and is) a woman, lacked a higher education and came from a moderate-income neighbourhood. These were undoubtedly contributing factors to the extreme length of time it took for any decision to be reached on the community, the dismissal of research that did not fit the 'expert' mould, and the contingency of the campaign's limited 'success' on political expediency. Arguably, the successes achieved by the campaign exploited political opportunities opened up by elections at the State and Federal level. The feminist environmental movement also sees in Lois Gibbs a woman who has transcended her domestic role to take a leading political stance in her community, a role she was ill-prepared for either scientifically or politically. This led to considerable personal cost (strained friendships, divorce, stress), although as Gibbs herself also points out, it also resulted in a degree of empowerment which has led her to become an enduring national figure in the US environmental justice movement.[56]

Anti-incineration campaign in Wales

There are echoes on a smaller scale of Love Canal and Lois Gibbs in Theresa Brzoza's story. Prompted by health concerns arising out of her role as a mother, Brzoza had campaigned against the incinerator proposed for Neath/Port Talbot, an old industrial area in South Wales. Although the campaign was unsuccessful in that the incinerator has been built (though not commissioned as this chapter was written), Theresa says that the campaign changed her: it questioned her political values and attitudes, caused her to join the Green Party, for which she stood as a candidate for councillor in 2004, and raised her sights from an individual, localised campaign to environmental inequalities more widely (a good example of the local expressing the materiality of wider environmental processes and concerns). Brzoza set up a campaigning organisation, PAIN (Parents Against the Incinerator), in her words 'set up with a bunch of mums over cups of tea'. This was her second transformation – the first was having a baby – which, Theresa said, changed her life, previously not much concerned with environmental problems. Brzoza, then, is another women politically empowered through community environmental action, which has acted as a step from immediate community concerns to more broadly based environment concerns. This demonstrates the potentially powerful role that environmental campaigning, mobilised around core concerns such as health, can perform.[57]

Challenging contemporary forms of citizenship and governance

Campaigning of the type reviewed above is both an oppositional activity and an activity of 'last resort'. It emerges after the failure of other democratic avenues, whether representative (voting for a candidate who will pursue congruent lines) or participative (in which women would be involved in the original decision-making). Does the emergent politicisation of women through campaigning provide an alternative route to representative or participatory democracy for women? If so, this suggests that women have to claim rights and equalities to be heard, and to have issues that they consider to be important taken seriously – they will not be offered to them. This might, indeed, provide the strength behind this mobilisation, which Gibson-Graham argues is creating those new discourses and alternative rights referred to earlier in this chapter, and behind what Lipietz suggests is accumulating as a series of 'micro-ruptures' to challenge hegemonic discourse. The problem with this, despite the power of the experience, is that single-issue politics and campaigns have a notoriously short life and carry a high burnout rate, so it is crucially important that women's environmental activities are not confined to the grassroots level – this is unfair on the women and their lives – which makes lasting structural changes more difficult to achieve. These grassroots campaigns, necessary as they are, must have a way of being incorporated into the wider policy context, if they are not constantly to be reinvented, and the gender (and other) inequalities they reveal must also be redressed. By the same token, national and international campaigning on environmental issues which are considered priorities by women, and which have hitherto largely been ignored, need adequate support if they are not to be casualties of inadequate funding (a problem that dogs many women's organisations, not just environmental).

I argue that not only must more women get involved, and be supported in doing so, in environmental politics and decision-making, but that they must do so in enough numbers to create cooperative and sensitive ways of doing business which keeps gender (and other) concerns in the picture, and not to get sidetracked into 'political business as usual'. Potential ways of achieving this may be through gender mainstreaming and through positive discrimination, which are strategies that the European Union has taken seriously at the strategy development level, as have the Commonwealth Secretariat, the United Nations and the World Bank. The European Treaty of Amsterdam permits/encourages the use of positive discrimination, although stops short of quotas, to bring more women into decision-making. The European

Commission Communication on [Gender] Mainstreaming, which came into force in 1996, specifies that

> All general policies and measures [be mobilised] specifically for the purpose of achieving equality by actively and openly taking into account at the planning stage their possible effects on the respective situation of men and women. This means systematically examining measures and policies and taking into account such possible effects when defining and implementing them.[58]

The problem with gender mainstreaming, and similar policies, is that there are no effective mechanisms for cascading this down the policy chain. Research undertaken for the EU (DG-Environment) to examine how far gender mainstreaming had been incorporated in municipal waste management revealed that while national policies had developed policy statements in their 'women's units', the strictures these contained did not easily penetrate either horizontally to other central government departments (although this was less so in Ireland which had applied a gender critique to all central government policies, including environment), or vertically through to local government. In the UK it proved impossible to find out just how gender mainstreaming could be monitored, and its application in municipal waste management, central government monitoring (via the Environmental Agency) and central government environmental policy-making was patchy to say the least.[59] With regard to environmental governance, then, women's involvement in formal or informal political decision-making is tenuous.

This may be of less concern if, as Morrow suggests in Chapter 2, the nation state is becoming less important and NGOs are increasingly able to leapfrog the national level of government to the transnational and global. However, although the demise of the nation state has been much debated, particularly in Europe, it is a risky strategy or default position if this is not certain. John Gray has recently written, with, to my mind, disturbing persuasiveness, of the 'comeback' of the nation state. His evidence for this mostly relates to the USA and cites its readiness to impose trade barriers and ignore international agreements – a trend exacerbated since 9/11. In the light of such concerns, it is important that women continue to focus their attention at the national level and attempt to claim a much greater share of its decision-making power.[60]

Conclusions

Citizenship through environmental action

Women continue to be second-class citizens in terms of how their voices are heard, their concerns marginalised, their bodies considered 'abnormal', and their social roles persistently undervalued, and in how they are subject to unequal treatment through greater likelihood of poverty. It is unsurprising, therefore, that a study of environmental activism and women's position in environmental decision-making as ways of examining women's access to citizenship in the West reveals it to be partial, claimed rather than easily accessible, and problematic.

Any empowerment that women achieve tends to be through opposition, rather than through spontaneous invitations into decision-making fora. Such an oppositional challenge can be galvanising – as well as exhausting. The drawing up of alliances with sympathetic NGOs can be productive and help to combat 'campaign fatigue', but women's groups need to be constantly alert to the potential for their achievements and goals to be captured to serve the campaigns of these potential partners. But, while there is synergy between environmentalism and feminism, it is by no means automatic or inevitable and can actively be counter-productive, as the discussion on environmental justice at the beginning of this chapter revealed.

Mechanisms for trying to incorporate women more into environmental decision-making, thereby enabling conditions for full citizenship, are lamentably rare and are most prolific at international levels where it is much spoken of. This writer's research indicates that the centrality of women and women's concerns become less evident further away from the department which originates gender mainstreaming policy. For example, tracking gender-sensitive policy developed by the UK's Women and Equality Unit through the Department of the Environment, Food, and Rural Affairs to local authority departments charged with implementing environmental policy shows a distinct leakage along the way.[61]

This chapter began with questioning how the concepts of citizenship used in geography and environmental discourses are applicable to understanding the relationship between women and the environment. Two particularly geographical continuums, public/private space and global/local scale, are intersected by a third continuum of power, which reduces in magnitude towards the local and the private. Women's lives are more likely than men's to be played out in spaces and places where power is less accessible and yet, the often sub-altern political activity which brings to the foreground women's concerns also has the capacity to forge an active and engaged citizen practice. Through this women may use and hone these citizenship skills which enable them to fulfil a civic role beyond the parameters of the state. This begs the question of why, given this developed 'social capital' which governments and development agencies are at pains to point out needs to be developed to pursue the course of western democracy, there remains such a gap between women's con-siderable activity in grassroots civic engagement and the lack of women in the majority of governments worldwide. We might also be drawn to question the necessary link between civic engagement and positions of power both in terms of 'career progression' and of issue adoption. A third question raised is how women-rich campaigns have been able to leapfrog the nation state to engage with issues at the international level, and to affect the international environ-mental and social policy agenda. However, this is only ulti-mately meaningful if there are mechanisms to translate these arguments into policies and actions which materially improve women's lives.

As long as the nation state remains the most powerful leg-islator, the concerns expressed by women at the community, civic and international level can more easily be marginal-ised. However, where power is genuinely devolved to the local, there is a possibility that the claims women have wrought from the state have a chance to be embedded in a more enduring way, (although a perceptible gender bias in civil society – including the mainstream environmental movement – also needs to be taken on). There may, then, be an argument to extending Mason's claim to a contingent link between strong environmental policy and inclusive political practice to include the activity of women in the local envi-ronment, which, indeed, 'goes beyond self-interest, national-ity and consumerism'.[62]

Notes

1 By 'representative democracy' I refer to the practice of electing representatives to take decisions on our behalf, whereas I use 'participative
   democracy' to describe a practice of citizens' direct involvement in governing and decision-making.

2 See M. G. Reed, 'Taking stands: a feminist perspective on "other"
   women's activism in forestry communities of Northern Vancouver
   Island', *Gender, Place and Culture*, 7:4 (2000), 363–387.

3 J. Seager, *Earth Follies: Coming to Feminist Terms with the Global
   Environmental Crisis* (London: Routledge, 1993). Information on how
   the UK environmental lobby and campaigning groups are structured
   comes from personal communications with these groups.

4 Data from a European Commission for Employment and Social Affairs
   report entitled 'Women and men in decision-making'. Database: Social
   and Economic Domain Decision Making in the European non-governmental organisations, http://europa.eu.int/comm/employment_social_
   women_men_stats/out/measures_out43 (accessed 25.1.2005).

5 In J. Agyeman, R. Bullard and B. Evans (eds), *Just Sustainabilities:
   Development in an Unequal World* (London/Cambridge, MA:
   Earthscan/MIT Press, 2003), p. 312.

6 R. D. Bullard, 'Dismantling environmental racism in the USA', *Local
   Environment*, 4:1 (1999), 5–19, at 13. See also J. Agyeman,
   Environmental Justice (London: TCPA, 2000).

7 A. Wickramasinghe, 'Women and environmental justice in South Asia'
   in Agyeman *et al.*, *Just Sustainabilities*.

8 J. Seager, 'Rachel Carson died of breast cancer: the coming of age of feminist environmentalism', *Signs: Journal of Women in Culture and
   Society*, 28:3 (2003), 945–972.

9 T. H. Marshall, *Citizenship and Social Class* (Cambridge: CUP, 1950);
   R. Lister, *Citizenship: Feminist Perspectives* (London: Macmillan,
   1997).

10 E. Kofman, 'Contemporary European migrations: civic stratification and
   citizenship', *Political Geography*, 21 (2002), 1035–1054.

11 UN Subcommission on the Prevention of Discrimination and
   Protection of Minorities, 1994, also known as the Ksentini Report, is
   drawn on by M. Mason, *The New Accountability: Environmental
   Responsibility Across Borders* (London: Earthscan, 1999), p. 34.

12 The legal framework following the Treaty of Amsterdam, signed by
   Heads of State or Government in 1997, and entered into force on 1
   May 1999, can be found at: http://europa.eu.int/scadplus/leg/en/chc/
   c10101.htm (accessed 10.2.2004).

13 See Y. Peled (1992) in N. Yuval-Davis, 'Women, citizenship and difference', *Feminist Review*, 57 (1997), 4–27.

14 Joni Seager, Jody Emel and Val Plumwood all write about inequalities
   within the environmental context with regard to gender and to the non-
   human.

15 Mason, *Environmental Democracy*, p. 234.

16 *Ibid.*, p. 235.

17 P. Werbner and N. Yuval-Davis, 'Women and the new discourse of

citizenship' in N. Yuval-Davis and P. Werbner (eds), *Women, Citizenship and Difference* (London: Zed Press, 1999).

18 Mason, *Environmental Democracy*, p. 88.

19 R. Fincher and R. Panelli in 'Making space: women's urban and rural activism and the Australian state', *Gender, Place and Culture*, 8:2 (2001), 129–148, at p. 129.

20 J. K. Gibson-Graham, *The End of Capitalism (as we knew it): A Feminist Critique of Political Economy* (Cambridge, MA: Blackwell Publishers, 1995), pp. 71 and 205.

21 See A. Lipietz, 'Political ecology and the future of Marxism', *Capitalism, Nature, Socialism*, 11:1 (2000).

22 N. Carter, *The Politics of the Environment: Ideas, Activism, Policy* (Cambridge: Cambridge University Press, 2001), p. 53.

23 L. Bondi, 'Class and gentrification: enriching the debate', *Environment and Planning D: Society and Space*, 17 (1999), 253–255.

24 Such work is being done by the Bioregional Development Group, a not-for-profit consultancy which seeks to localise the production of low-order goods such as food, while enabling producer economies to specialise in higher order and higher value goods such as IT.

25 See John Lechte's argument summarised by Yuval-Davis, 'Women, citizenship and difference'. NIMBY movements (Not In My Back Yard) are defined by their objection to environmental pollution of various forms in particular spaces rather than opposing the activity in general.

26 M. Walton-Roberts, 'Rescaling citizenship: gendering Canadian immigration policy', *Political Geography*, 23 (2004), 265–281.

27 D. Martin, 'Constructing the "Neighborhood Sphere" ': gender and community organizing', *Gender, Place and Culture*, 9:4 (2002), 333–350, at 338.

28 Yuval-Davis, 'Women, citizenship and difference'. Yuval-Davis's review of attempts to categorise what constitutes the private include the family, that which is not financed or controlled by the state, including religious institutions, leisure and the spiritual, and 'where the person is autonomous'.

29 Martin, 'Constructing the "Neighborhood Sphere", 336; B. M. Milroy and S. Wismer, 'Work and public/private sphere models', *Gender, Place and Culture*, 1 (1994), 71–91; L. Horelli and K. Vepsa, 'In search of supportive structures for everyday life' in I. Altman and A. Churchman (eds), *Women and the Environment* (New York: Plenum, 1994).

30 M. P. Garcia Guadilla, '*ECOLOGIA*: Women, environment and politics in Venezuela' in S. A. Radcliffe and S. Westwood (eds), '*Viva*': *Women and Popular Protest in Latin America* (London: Routledge, 1993).

31 L. Staeheli, 'Publicity, privacy and women's political action', *Environment and Planning D: Society and Space*, 14 (1996), 601–619, quoted in Fincher and Panelli, 'Making space'.

32 *Ibid.*

33 These are: lacking two or more perceived necessities; earning less than 60 per cent of the median income; subjective poverty; receiving income support. For details of the survey, see J. Bradshaw, N. Finch, P. A. Kemp, E. Mayhew and J. Williams, *Gender and Poverty in Britain* (Manchester: Equal Opportunities Commission, 2003).

34 D. Kingsmill, *Kingsmill Report on Women's Employment and Pay* (London: DTI, 2001).

35 See The National Commission on Pay Equity, www.pay-equity.org/index.html (accessed 18.4.2005) and S. J. Rose and H. I. Hartman, *Still a Man's Labor Market: the long term earnings gap* (Washington DC: Institute for Women's Policy Research, 2004).

36 I. Dankleman, 'Poverty eradication as a challenge for sustainable development' in Women in Europe for a Common Future, *Why Women are Essential for Sustainable Development: Results of the European Women's Conference for a Sustainable Future*, Celakovice (Prague), 14–17 March 2002.

37 United Nations General Assembly, *Implementation of the United Nations Millennium Declaration, Report of the Secretary-General* A/59/282, New York, 59th Session, 2004. www.unstats.org/unsd/mi/pdf/MDG%20Book.pdf (accessed 15.11.04).

38 *Ibid.*

39 For the UK see HMSO, *Social Trends*, (London: HMSO, 1998); for France, J. Fagnani, 'Family policies and working mothers: a comparison of France and West Germany' in M. D. García-Ramon and J. Monk (eds), *Women of the European Union: The Politics of Work and Daily Life* (London: Routledge, 1996); for Sri Lanka, Wickramasinghe, 'Women and environmental justice'; and for Colombia, J. Townsend, 'Gender and the life course on the frontiers of settlement in Colombia' in C. Katz and J. Monk (eds), *Full Circles: Geographies of Women over the Life Course* (London: Routledge, 1993).

40 *The Digest of Environmental Statistics 20*, (London: The Stationery Office, 1998) showed that women were more concerned than men on twenty-six out of thirty-two environmental issues; surveys accessed from DEFRA reveal that women claimed to be 'more worried' than men on eighteen out of twenty environmental issues, http://defra.gov.uk/environment/statistics/pubatt/download/csv/pa01tbl4b.csv (accessed 19.1.2005).

41 Women in Europe for a Common Future, *Why Women are Essential for Sustainable Development*, p. 148.

42 M. Waring, *Counting for Nothing: What Men Value, and What Women are Worth* (Wellington, New Zealand: Allen and Unwin, 1988); S. James, *The Global Kitchen: The Case for Governments Measuring and Valuing Unwaged Work* (London: Crossroads Books, 1995).

43 Commonwealth Secretariat, *Gender Mainstreaming: Commonwealth Strategies on Politics, Macroeconmics and Human Rights* (London: Commonwealth Secretariat, 1998) pp. 42–43.

44 REACH is the single integrated system for the 'registration, evaluation and authorisation of chemicals' which the EU is proposing to establish (http://europa.eu.int/scadplus/leg/en/lvb/l21282.htm); EEA 2003 Environmental Assessment Report; UK RCEP, *24th Report on Chemicals in Products, Safeguarding the Environment and Human Health* (2003); Dr Lilian Corra's speech was reported in *WEN News* (London: Women's Environmental Network, Autumn 2003), p. 5.

45 Women in Europe for a Common Future, *Why Women are Essential*, p. 134.

46 For a discussion of Kathleen Jones on women in the military, see Yuval-Davis, 'Women, citizenship and difference'. For information on violence against women in times of environmental stress, see Women in Europe

for a Common Future, *Why Women are Essential*. See also S. Krupp, 'Environmental hazards: assessing the risks to women', *Fordham Law Journal*, 111 (2000) for a wide-ranging discussion on how women's bodies are disproportionately exposed to environmental pollutants.

47 All data downloaded on 22 July 2005 from respective government websites.

48 G. Bhattar, 'Of geese and ganders: mainstreaming gender in the context of sustainable human development', *Journal of Gender Studies*, 10:1 (2001).

49 Commonwealth Secretariat, *Gender Mainstreaming*.

50 See Women in Europe for a Common Future, *Why Women are Essential*, and Karen Morrow in Chapter 2 of this volume.

51 See the UN Beijing Declaration and Platform for Action, strategic objective H: Institutional mechanisms for the advancement of women (www.un.org/womenwatch/daw/beijing/platform/institu.htm# object2).

52 From WEDO 2004 Women's Recommendations for 12th Session of the Commission on Sustainable Development, p. 222.

53 As this chapter was being revised the Environment Agency had just brought out its highly controversial report on the relative environmental impacts of disposable and reusable nappies: Environment Agency, *Life Cycle Assessment of Disposable and Reusable Nappies in the UK* (Bristol: Environment Agency, 2005), which concluded that there was no significant difference between the two. The report and the methodology the commissioned researchers used is currently contested by at least two of its Advisory Board members and more widely.

54 For details about the Women's Environmental Network and its campaigns, see www.wen.org.uk. Please note that the author of this chapter is a Board Member of WEN and that some information reported here has been made available through personal communications.

55 L. Gibbs, *Love Canal: The Story Continues* (Gabriola Island, British Columbia: New Society Press, 1996), p. 222.

56 Many discussions of environmental movements and environmental feminism refer to Lois Gibbs and the Love Canal protests, often inaccurately, depending on the purpose to which the case-study is being put. For example, since Love Canal is often seen as an achievement by women campaigners (which it undoubtedly is in many respects), its lack of a satisfactory resolution is often glossed over or omitted. For a rich and full account of the years-long campaign, Lois Gibbs's own account is valuable: Gibbs, *Love Canal*.

57 Material from personal communication with Theresa Brzoza.

58 European Commission Communication on Mainstreaming 2/1999.

59 For a detailed discussion of this, see S. Buckingham, D. Reeves, The Women's Environmental Network, A. Batchelor and S. Colucas, *Research into Gender Differentiated Impacts of Municipal Planning in the European Union*, Report to the European Commission DG-Environment (2004).

60 J. Gray, *Al Qaeda and What it Means to be Modern* (London: Faber and Faber, 2003).

61 Buckingham *et al.*, *Research into Gender Differentiated Impacts*.

62 Mason, *Environmental Democracy*, p. 234.

4

A place for citizenship? Women, urban design and neighbourhood planning

MARION ROBERTS

Introduction

The design of the public sphere has received welcome attention in Britain in the last decade. Once the effects of the market-led planning of the 1980s became apparent, in the 'private affluence and public squalor'[1] of town centres, in the production of a new urban landscape of out-of-town shopping centres and business parks, of suburban housing estates and decentralised leisure zones, a reappraisal of quality in towns and cities emerged.[2] The physical setting for public life, which has an intertwined and complex relationship with civic engagement and hence citizenship, has increasingly become a focus for government-sponsored policy, research and action.[3]

Urban design is the field of study and arena of professional practice that is most concerned with the physical aspects of the public realm. The easiest way to describe urban design to those outside the built environment professions is to use Cowan's shorthand formulation that urban design is akin to three-dimensional town planning. It is concerned with the configuration of space and place, the arrangements of activities, buildings, landscape features and infrastructure across all scales of development, from the civic square to the disposition of the city region.[4] In short, it deals with aspects of 'life between buildings'.[5] While its focus lies in the visually observed, 'concrete' dimensions of physical space, it also has social, perceptual, functional and temporal dimensions.[6]

In a commentary on New Labour's urban policy, Holden and Iveson[7] argue that urban design provides new grounds for a discussion of citizenship and the space of the urban because of its emphasis on public space as a common good. They suggest that the participation of urban design professionals in the practical processes of regeneration is opening up a new 'public space' in which visions of the 'good city' may be debated. This chapter examines one aspect of the vision for the 'good city' that has re-emerged in urban design theory and practice in the last decade. Planning by neighbourhood is now being reasserted in the physical planning agenda in both Britain and North America. For those with an interest in the history of urban design, the resurrection of the neighbourhood as a unit for spatial organisation is somewhat surprising. The 'neighbourhood unit' was a popular concept in the planning of post-war Britain, but was dropped during the decades that followed the 1960s. Women, particularly, in their roles as wives and mothers, played an important part in the original concept, in producing social cohesion through neighbourly relations and their supposed appropriation of the public space of the unit. This chapter teases out some of the links between the actualities and mythologies of women's role in this subdivision of urban space and suggests that this has been a missing dimension to the debate on the constitution of a 'good city'. The argument is proposed that the concept for the self-contained neighbourhood unit was shaped by women's experiences in poor working-class districts in the nineteenth and early twentieth centuries, experiences that are no longer relevant to contemporary circumstances.[8] The resurrection of the self-contained 'neighbourhood' therefore requires careful examination with regard to its context and potential disbenefits for particular groups of women, despite its current championing as a strategy for environmental sustainability.

Urban design and civic engagement

This chapter is not written from the point of view of environmental determinism, that is the now discredited idea that physical settings have a direct, causal effect upon social relationships. This is not to say that physical arrangements have no implications for society. There are many ways in which urban design and civic engagement, in a broad sense, are interconnected. In terms of the neighbourhood these ways might be summarised as lying between the opposite poles of bolstering and hindering social contact.

Leaving aside the most dystopian of fantasies regarding the impact of cyberspace, social relationships are, in the main, still dependent upon people moving around and meeting each other. The configuration of movement, that is the physical layout of streets, roads, railways, houses, shops, offices and other urban artefacts and the ease with which different groups of people can progress through the different arteries of movement, has a direct relationship to the ability of people to engage with each other. Puttnam, for example, argues that urban sprawl in the USA has made a contribution of approximately 10 per cent to Americans' disengagement from public life.[9] With reference to Lievesley's comments in Chapter 1, this is the argument in his book that most clearly challenges the status quo. In simple terms, 'active citizenship' relies on association between people, and where that is made difficult such connections are diminished. For example, there is a strong body of evidence to demonstrate that fear of crime deters many older women – and older men – from going out at night despite the fact that it is young men who are most at risk from personal assault by a stranger.[10] The difficulties of making changes from one mode of transport to another, or even of crossing a busy road, can impede both the disabled and the able-bodied from certain types of essential journeys.[11]

Density of development and the interconnectedness of the route system, pedestrian and vehicular, also influences how many people are on a street. This has an impact on the types of casual encounter that are possible, as well as on feelings of safety. Hillier and Hanson have characterised some modernist housing estates as being in a state of 'perpetual night'. They demonstrated that the pedestrian and vehicular route system in these estates discourages anyone but the residents from walking through the estate. This means that even during the day, the chance of meeting any other person outside of the dwelling is comparable to the chance of meeting strangers in a different, more 'integrated', area late at night.[12] Encountering others, in different ways that may range from the most casual to the most intense of exchanges, is an important component of public life in society. Indeed Sennett argues that encounters that are unstructured and that hold the possibility of conflict as well as agreement, provide the richness and fulfilment of an active civic life.[13]

The physical design of neighbourhoods – the extent to which they provide easy connections to a wider urban area, or the extent to which they are inward-looking and exclusive – makes a significant contribution to civic life and to the everyday encounters and life chances of citizens. For women, whose involvement with the domestic sphere of home and whose responsibilities for childcare are more intense, issues of neighbourhood connectivity and services are more critical. In Chapter 1 it was suggested that much of women's active citizenship takes place around the private sphere. If mobility is limited to within walking distance of the home, as it was historically for much of the population, then the neighbourhood formed the horizon of her personal world. Personal networks of friendship and obligation became confined to a few streets, as did work opportunities and membership of civic organisations such as the church.

Bell[14] has introduced the concept of 'activist citizenship', that is a citizenship in which people are actively engaged in transgression. In a traditional reading of the splits, public/ private and male/female, male activism has been associated with the workplace and female activism with the home. Of course, these splits are conceptual and the public/ private divisions not so clearly cut. Susan Buckingham in Chapter 3 describes some examples of women's engagement as citizen activists in the environmental movement. Nevertheless women's organisation within the 'private' sphere of the home has been an important component of British social history, with a significant example being provided by the Scottish women's rent strikes in 1915 that eventually led to the introduction of council housing as a national service in 1919.[15] Geraldine Lievesley in Chapter 1 also points to the home and neighbourhood as a key locus for activism in developing countries. This chapter will argue that since the nineteenth century the significance of the neighbourhood has changed, as the diffusion of technologies of mobility and communication have impacted upon everyday life.

Personal mobility has changed dramatically, as have personal communications with the advent of the telephone. These transformations have not been even for both genders and different social classes. The penetration of the home by global telecommunications and media networks has played a role in the shifting boundaries between public and private. This chapter will begin its review of the relationship between women, class, communication and neighbourhood in the late nineteenth century before proceeding chronologically.

Women and neighbourhoods: 'the communal life of the poor'

The idea for the neighbourhood unit gained ground within the UK and the US as a response to what was perceived as a breakdown in 'community' at different points in the twentieth century.[16] The experiences of poor working-class neighbourhoods in the nineteenth and very early twentieth centuries provided a measure of how such social cohesion might be practised. Britain's rapid industrialisation had encouraged a dramatic growth in high-density housing, mainly in the form of by-law terraced housing.[17] Landlords further exploited an overwhelming demand for housing by renting out properties to two or more households.[18] In these circumstances, many women were forced to live in close proximity, sharing some intimate aspects of their lives. Accounts of lives in working-class neighbourhoods stress the hard, unremitting nature of domestic work in circumstances without modern conveniences such as running hot water, central heating, refrigerators and other appliances. Poverty and poor health for both women and children created further burdens that were, on occasion, life-threatening.[19]

In her perceptive study of women's social networks in these types of communities, Tebbutt elaborates how working-class women forged networks of neighbourliness.[20] The 'sociability of gossip' was the medium through which women were able to provide support, maintain or break relationships and to create and extend local mores. Confidences could be shared, experiences exchanged and practical help provided. It was women in the neighbourhood who were the principal protagonists in the informal social interactions that took place around the houses. Her respondents recorded how their menfolk regarded these interactions as being outside their frame of reference and, in some cases, actively distanced themselves, not liking their wives even to take tea with each other. This is not to suggest a nostalgic, idealised view of these networks of friendship and mutual support. In the cramped living conditions of poor working-class housing, conflicts frequently broke out between neighbours, over for example, issues such as the sharing of the yard to hang out washing.

The place for this sociability was located in the public life of the street as well as in the more exclusive recesses of the home. Men's gossip tended to be removed from the 'life of the street' and was located in the pub and the workplace. Many men felt resentful of the invasive nature of women's networks and misinterpreted them as an invasion into a privatised notion of family life. Tebbutt points out that in the nineteenth and early twentieth centuries, in poor urban localities, it is perpetuating stereotypes of women's behaviour to suggest that women were 'confined' to the private sphere. Women had 'possession of the public territory' in street life.[21] Oral testimony provides a record of women sitting out on the street, greeting neighbours, observing behaviour and storing such observation for later comment and judgement.

The strengths of such personal networks were that they provided support mechanisms to deal with many of life's vicissitudes such as poverty, illness and bereavement. However receiving help was an acknowledgement of weakness, a weakness that, in the gender-segregated role system of industrialised society, suggested that a man was an inadequate husband and provider. The audible expression of women's views, on the street, also posed a challenge to privatised notions of family life. Loud arguments, either between female neighbours, or acting as a commentary on marital life, became a marker of the 'rough' working class. 'Respectability' was associated with privacy – 'keeping yourself to yourself' – and orderly and demure comportment. A further negative aspect of neighbourhood gossip was its role in supporting social mores. Such gossip could act as a strong arbiter of morality for the young, with young girls in particular facing censorship for what was observed to be unseemly behaviour.

Women's neighbourly networks provided an invaluable contribution to the public life of poorer urban areas. While some feminists, such as Dale Spender, have regretted the lack of place for 'women's talk'[22] it would be an over-simplification to suggest that this contribution has not been recognised in British town planning. The 'neighbourhood unit' formed a significant component of British town planning in the years between the end of the Second World War and the early 1960s and the next section will consider the place of women's networks in that context.

Neighbourhood planning 1945–60

The American town planner Clarence Perry first proposed the idea for the neighbourhood unit in 1929. Perry drew on ideas developed in the US and the UK that combined enhancing social cohesion through providing social centres with physical housing improvements of the type made in Hampstead Garden Suburb. Perry sought to reduce the anonymity of life in the age of mass production and promote the cause of neighbourliness. Perry's neighbourhood unit was envisioned to be primarily residential, accommodating approximately 5,000 people. It was to be centred around a primary school and the shops would be dispersed to arterial routes that bounded it. The intention was that traffic would be discouraged from crossing it, so that it would form a relatively self-contained entity, with its own parks and playgrounds.[23]

Perry's ideas were taken into the mainstream of British town planning at the local level in the County of London Plan (1943) and nationally in the Dudley Report of 1944. Neighbourhood units were given immediate physical expression in the construction of eleven of the post-war New Towns.[24] The essential elements of the neighbourhood unit in design terms incorporated and enlarged Perry's concept. The primary school was still to form the nucleus, but now its catchment population was increased to up to 10,000. Local shops and community buildings would be provided within the unit together with parks and open spaces. Whereas Perry had argued for socially homogeneous neighbourhoods, with the controversial idea of the unit preventing the encroachment of poor households upon the rich, the more egalitarian post-war Labour government proposed the idea of 'balanced communities' with a mixture of income groups. The unit would be buffered from the rest of the town through the provision of open space or a natural 'edge' such as a railway line.

In one interpretation, the concept of the neighbourhood unit could be seen as benignly women- and children-centred, with its notion of local shops and a primary school within walking distance helping to support face-to-face contact and neighbourly connection. A less optimistic reading would suggest a reliance on stereotypes of a typical household consisting of a male breadwinner with dependent wife and children, with neighbourhood facilities being planned around the idea of a mother who lives and works locally.[25] The provision of local facilities could also be read not so much as a provision for need but as a reduction in choice, particularly as the buffer zone would impede access to shops and facilities in other neighbourhoods.[26]

The neighbourhood unit policy was adopted without detailed research. Key politicians and civil servants championed the idea because it appeared to offer both social and physical improvements in terms of a better residential environment and greater social cohesion.[27] The idea was dropped in the mid-1950s because once the key figures had departed, no one was left to champion the idea. From the point of view of young married women, a ground-breaking piece of research undermined claims that the New Towns helped to promote social ties. Young and Wilmott's classic study *Family and Kinship in East London*,[28] found that a majority of young mothers among their sample suffered from isolation, which later became popularly dubbed 'New Town blues'. Young and Wilmott emphasised the importance of kinship and especially the mother–daughter relationship. In the absence of easy access to transport these relationships were disrupted and young women became isolated at a crucial point in their lives. Although there has been debate about the significance of this study's findings with regard to family structure,[29] a contemporary re-reading would suggest that, had the importance of kinship and social ties been given importance and facilitated with adequate transport links, these young mothers' lives would have been much improved. From the other side of the Atlantic, criticisms of the neighbourhood unit came from Jane Jacobs, who has been described as the first commentator on planning to provide a woman's point of view.[30] Jacobs did not provide an explicitly feminist critique of the neighbourhood unit, but straightforwardly characterised it in its ideal form as an inward-turned unit supporting a population of 7,000, sufficient to support an elementary school, convenience shopping and a community centre. There is an implicit criticism of a patronising attitude towards women in her comments that 'This unit is then further rationalized into smaller groupings of a size scaled to the play and supposed management of children and the chitchat of housewives.'[31]

Noting the prevalence of the idea, in that in 1959 more than half a million people in the USA were living in adaptations of planned neighbourhoods, she explained why she thought the 'ideal' of the unit was 'silly and even harmful for cities'. Jacobs regarded the neighbourhood as too large a unit to form a point of identification for city dwellers. She emphasised the fluidity and cosmopolitan nature of city life, with its richness of contacts, and ability to provide work and leisure opportunities across the entire city. She pointed out that in contrast to a small town of 5,000–10,000, where residents were quite likely to have come across workmates or other casual contacts, friends, professional acquaintances or neighbours as they moved around the town, the chances of a city dweller meeting someone that they knew in an equivalent area was much more remote. The notion of creating a cohesive community out of this kind of unit was, she argued, unrealistic. Jacobs did not oppose the idea that urban dwellers needed to form a feeling of identity with the area that they lived in. Her observation was that identity worked at three levels: at the level of the city as a whole, at the level of the street neighbourhood and, in terms of self-governance, at the level of the district. By 'street neighbourhood' Jacobs meant precisely that, the neighbourhood that was formed around a street or a section of the street and its immediate hinterland.

Jacobs' account of the street neighbourhood has become renowned. Her observations were based on her work as a resident, architectural journalist and community activist in New York's Manhattan, but also drew on her experiences of other North American cities of a similar era, such as Chicago, Boston and Philadelphia. The streets that Jacobs so illuminatingly described were formed from mixed-use urban blocks, which typically rose to between five and seven stories and whose ground and/or basement floors were frequently given over to commercial uses such as individual shops, small workshops, small bars and local restaurants, pool halls, art galleries, and the other myriad service and social facilities that made up the life of a big city. Jacobs elaborated and dissected the intricate social solidarities that bound together the strongest street neighbourhoods. She recounted the 'ballet of Hudson Street' and described how the life of the street was enacted over an eighteen-hour period, from the time the first early morning shop opened to the early hours of the following morning when the last printworker and bar owner retired to bed. Her observation of her own street led to a formulation of how these diverse activities could form a web of 'natural' surveillance, 'eyes on the street', [32] where residents and business owners looked out for each others' children and properties, preventing accidents, mishaps and minor crimes. The civilising qualities that Jacobs ascribed to these 'sidewalk' neighbourhoods included socialising children to behave in public places by means of individual 'stakeholders', residents and business owners and some more responsible passers-by taking responsibility for admonition and encouragement.

In Jacobs' world, the types of gender demarcations described earlier in this chapter in the context of British industrial cities were not evident. It was not the women who 'controlled' neighbourhood life while men worked in factories and workshops elsewhere. In Jacobs' streets there existed a greater equality and reciprocity, with descriptions of male store-keepers playing a significant part through looking after property such as keys, imparting information selectively and sensitively and combating anti-social behaviour. There is a further contrast in that Jacobs celebrated social distance rather than intimacy and gossip. She argued that such distance is crucial to city relations, such that people can keep their privacy while retaining the civilities and trust that are essential to citizenship. Moreover, she argued that the types of social contact made possible through casual and chance relationships formed on the street could enhance an activist form of citizenship. She described how she herself was able to organise an effective petition to oppose a highway improvement by leaving copies in local shops and businesses. Linkages were made with other neighbourhoods by word-of-mouth contact and through key 'self-appointed public characters',[33] male and female, who were able, collectively, to mount an effective opposition.

Jacobs painted an attractive picture not only of how real cities worked in practice, but of a social and physical environment where differences between people could be respected, yet civility and engagement could be allowed to flourish. The strength of her observations resided not only in their acuity, but also in the way in which she was able to pinpoint precise physical and land-use characteristics of flourishing neighbourhoods. Her prescriptions were clear and could be summarised by her chapter headings: sufficient density of development to ensure adequate footfall along the street throughout the day and into the evening and night, a diversity of uses, a diversity of age of buildings and therefore rents and prices, short blocks to allow a variety of routes, key 'magnets' or primary uses and usable open space in the form of 'pocket parks' or similar.

Jacobs' book, *The Death and Life of Great American Cities*, was published in 1961. It ran through several editions in the English-speaking world and its initial impact contributed to the mounting tide of criticism of modernist town planning. Although Jacobs' ideas were controversial, the salience of her analysis was borne out by the gentrification of central and inner city areas that took place during the following three decades whereby new generations of city dwellers recolonised inner and central city districts. Gentrification is a diverse process undertaken for a variety of reasons, but the impact of a reclamation of nineteenth-century urban form for end-of-twentieth-century living reasserted the attraction of living at higher densities, in formal arrangements of streets that are in close proximity to streets which accommodate a mix and diversity of uses. While many British inner city areas lack the intensity of their North American counterparts, they nevertheless could support the type of public culture of a strong street neighbourhood as set out by Jacobs. From a US perspective, Appleton has concluded that these types of inner city areas provide a 'gender regime' that offers a wide range of alternative lifestyles supported by a series of informal and formal networks. Dual earner families, lone mothers, gay and lesbian households and unmarried adults, often without children, receive support.[34] Bondi's research on gentrification also found evidence that couples who were striving to achieve a greater gender equality were drawn to these inner city districts with traditional street layouts and mixed use.[35]

In Britain, it was not until the 1990s that Jacobs' prescriptions for street neighbourhoods could be incorporated into new development. In the intervening decades a free-market approach to urban design had been imposed. This, combined with technological and social change, contributed to new forms of urban landscape that were at the opposite end of the planning spectrum to the closely packed urbanism of the nineteenth and early twentieth centuries.

Technological changes

The rationale for self-contained neighbourhood planning was developed in the early part of the twentieth century. Since its implementation in Britain in the years following the Second World War there have been significant changes in employment structure, the size and formation of households and technologies of mobility and communication that are shaping place-bound identities at many scales. Worpole comments that Jane Jacobs was writing 'before the modern media made such an intrusive encroachment into the modern home'.[36] In particular, technological change has extended the possibilities for social interaction, not only through a greater diffusion of the 'old' technologies of the car and phone, but also through the rapid assimilation of the 'new' technologies of mobile (cell) phones and the internet. Not only does the phone (terrestrial and satellite) provide an additional means of communication, but the use of the private car permits increased possibilities for informal meetings without the constraints of mass transportation systems. Visits are not limited by timetables and considerations of safety, but by the mutual convenience of the participants. The combination of old and new technologies of mobility and communication have had profound impacts on city structure with regard to the world hierarchy of cities and the growth of the city region.[37] It would seem logical that the take-up of the car, phone and cyberspace communication would also have an impact on the relationships between women, the neighbourhood and the wider city.

The latest bulletin of transport statistics based on a UK national travel survey of 9,000 respondents found that the number of women holding driving licences has doubled in the last twenty years, such that now 59 per cent of women hold driving licences in comparison to 82 per cent of men. Women under the age of fifty make more trips than men, but men travel 40 per cent further than women. The report notes that between the periods of 1985 and 1986, and 1997 and 1999 the average length of educational, commuting and leisure trips increased by over 33 per cent. Moreover, people are choosing to travel further to visit friends, both in their homes (with trips averaging over 8 miles) and in other places such as pubs and restaurants, with an average trip length of six miles. In general, the number of trips made between five and twenty-five miles increased between 1985 and 1986, and 1997 and 1999, whereas short walking trips of under one mile decreased.[38] A study of car drivers found that women have a different relationship to cars than do men; while both women and men derive feelings of control over their lives from car driving, as well as a sense of security, men are more likely to derive a sense of satisfaction from the type of car that they drive.[39]

Even in a metropolitan area as well-served by public transport as London[40] women's car use has increased dramatically.[41] A study based on discussion groups held in 1996–97 found a 50 per cent increase in women's driving trips between 1981 and 1991. By contrast, male driving trips had not risen at all in the same period. The report argued that women use cars because of the nature of the trips that they do, for example women do 60 per cent of all shopping trips and 70 per cent of all escort trips. Women tend to make shorter trips than men, although this is changing, and they also tend to make more short journeys on local roads.[42] The national survey found that 40 per cent of car mileage is for leisure uses and 13 per cent for shopping. There is also the phenomenon of 'trip chaining', that is, making journeys with more than one purpose. Evidence from the US suggests that this is more prevalent among women than men,[43] but a UK survey[44] suggested that this was equal between the sexes. Both studies agreed that the purposes for which the 'chains' are constructed differ, with women more likely to visit shops on their way home and men more likely to chain two education escort stops and in the US case to visit a bar or a restaurant.

Since the mid-1970s there has been a dramatic increase in household ownership of terrestrial phones in Britain. In 1970 only 35 per cent of households had a home telephone. By 2000, diffusion was almost complete with 95 per cent of households having a phone. The figures for mobile phone possession display an even steeper progression. Public data has only been collected since 1996–97, when only 16 per cent of households had at least one mobile phone. By 1999–2000 this had increased to 44 per cent.[45] A recent figure of individual ownership by 65 per cent of the population has been cited in the national media.[46] Internet access has also shown a sharp increase in take-up with 48 per cent of households in the UK in the second quarter of 2003 having access to the internet.[47]

The evidence suggests that women, in general, are becoming increasingly mobile. Feminist critiques that date from the 1970s and 1980s that pointed out that women as a gender were more limited in transport terms than men[48] are becoming less relevant to women as a whole. This is not to deny that there are still important and significant differences between women. Older women and women with a low income are less likely either to hold a driving licence or to have access to a car.[49] There are also significant differences between the ways in which women and men use cars. On average women still walk more than men, with 30 per cent of their journeys being made on foot compared to 25 per cent of men's.[50]

It can be speculated that the impact of increased mobility and the dramatic rise in interpersonal communications has been to extend social networks across a wider area. The evidence cited above suggests that people in general are communicating more than ever, travelling more by car and making longer journeys. A further inference would be, given the preponderance of leisure trips as a percentage of total trips made, that trips to see friends and relatives are being extended well beyond the confines of the neighbourhood. There is a layering of activities between physical and virtual communications. Here, the concept developed by Mitchell, in what Graham and Marvin dub the 'city of bits' hypothesis, is useful. Mitchell contends that there is a spectrum of urban typologies, extending from the face-to-face interaction and traditional transportation of the early twentieth-century neighbourhood to fully virtual communities, which extend between physical places linked by virtual connections. In between these two extremes, new hybrids are formed, with a combination formed from aspects of the two typologies.[51] In the emerging urban landscape, personal networks are formed, stretching well beyond the confines of the traditional neighbourhood. In denser urban areas it is possible to maintain a plurality of identities and to participate in many aspects of citizenship provided that there is access to the means of communication.[52] For example, a woman could be an active member of a professional association or trade union, a member of a gay club or network and a governor at a local primary school. Even the seemingly most place-bound women, such as recently arrived immigrants who are also mothers of young children, can have access to global personal networks through the advent of cheap internet cafes.

It may seem idealistic to argue that barriers between the global and the local are being broken down for everyone through wider use of the internet. Nevertheless the flourishing of independent internet cafes in developing countries[53] and in the more deprived neighbourhoods of British cities suggests that connections are being made between those who have least on different continents. Information technology can also support active citizenship through the supply of information, top-down, from central and local government. Although the 'digital divide' between those with access to ICTs is still a barrier with regard to the ownership and access to PCs, the relatively low cost of mobile phone use is eroding stark divisions in access to personal contacts and certain types of public information. Mobile phone technology, by definition, breaks down the divisions between public and private. Certain types of organisation that require precision, such as meeting another person in a public place, are facilitated. In particular, the practice of 'activist citizenship' is made easier and safer. Agitational and organisational activities such as going on a march, leafleting an area and going from door to door are made less threatening and more communal through the ready contact that a mobile phone provides. When mobile phones are allied to the older technology of the car, concerns for security and safety are diminished. The take-up of the technology has been so rapid that it is difficult to assess the changes that will happen in the use and hence the configuration of public space. What does seem clear, however, is that traditional divisions between localities and a wider area are changing and that women are particular beneficiaries of the increased sense of security that mobile phone ownership and car driving can produce. It is in this context that an idealisation of walkable, face-to-face communities seems surprising.

The re-emergence of neighbourhood as a component of urban structure

The idea of the neighbourhood unit was dropped, after which no more were explicitly built after the 1960s. Nevertheless, a diluted form of the ideal continued and formed part of the culture of planning, frequently made manifest in an aspiration for many housing estates to have their own local centres and some degree of self-containment. Criticism of the self-contained neighbourhood came not only from Jane Jacobs but also from other Anglo-American sources in the 1960s and 1970s.[54] Similar arguments were made about the size of neighbourhood being too large for meaningful encounter and a lack of realism in expecting only local facilities to be used in urban areas. A debate opened up between scholars who propounded the virtues of physically based neighbourhood and community and those who argued that communication technologies and increased mobility were producing 'non-place-based' forms of community.[55] It was somewhat disconcerting, therefore, following this intellectual disengagement and a gradual acceptance of the values of more traditional forms of urban living[56] on the part of urban design professionals to find the notion of the neighbourhood as a designed entity reappearing on the agenda of government.

The background to the re-emergence of the idea of the neighbourhood into contemporary policy after four decades echoes its adoption in the 1940s. As Madanipour comments, each new generation seems to rediscover for itself the need for community building and the physical shape that it takes.[57] Furthermore there is a school of thought among urban scholars that has been called 'community lost',[58] which regrets the fragmentation of contemporary western societies. The theme of building social cohesion has been included in the social programmes set up by the New Labour government, which are specifically targeted at areas of deprivation and decline.[59] Contemporary design propositions, by contrast, have been given a wider applicability, to higher as well as low-income areas. Their resurgence in the UK may be attributed to a desire to incorporate ideas about environmental sustainability in the sense of reducing car use and creating a more compact and efficient urban structure. There are also underlying themes of the promotion of active citizenship and social cohesion that are implicit in the North American versions of these proposals.

Ideas about environmental sustainability had been explored, first in theory and then in practice in the USA. A group of urbanists, amongst whom Peter Calthorpe, Andrés Duany and Elizabeth Plater-Zyberk are key protagonists, came together to form the Congress for New Urbanism (CNU).[60] The CNU has proved to be an influential organisation in promoting the idea of sustainable settlements. Its premise is that the contemporary sprawl that characterises much of the North American landscape with its low-density housing and excessive car use is environmentally wasteful and socially degrading. The CNU programme includes the reconfiguration of neighbourhoods and downtown areas and regional planning policies, coining the term 'smart growth'. There are different strands within the CNU movement[61] but the common ingredients of their ideas are for many of the design features that Jacobs proposed to increase activity on the street. These include clearly defined streets, a hierarchy of streets and squares, a mixture of land-uses, with higher densities around transit stops, and a diminution of private space in favour of the public domain. In contrast to Jacobs, however, the proposals are for a small-town density of development with distinct well-defined neighbourhoods. In fact, Duany suggests that the principles of Clarence Perry's neighbourhood unit are embodied in a number of design prototypes that are endorsed by the CNU. These comprise Urban Villages, Traditional Neighbourhood Developments, Liveable Neighbourhoods and Leon Krier's Quarters.[62] Leon Krier, an architect who originated from Luxembourg, has also been most influential in the British Urban Villages movement. Although most of the developments that have come under the umbrella of the CNU have been middle-to upper-income, the national public housing body in the US, the Department of Housing and Urban Development, has taken up their ideas in a multi-million dollar programme.

The distinguished British town planner, Sir Peter Hall, who helped the British government formulate its proposals for urban extensions along the Thames Gateway, is of the opinion that the built results of the CNU's work do not achieve their stated goals of sustainability. He comments that 'with a few exceptions, such as Peter Calthorpe's work in San Jose, it is disappointing that most actual examples of New Urbanism are either new suburbs on greenfield land such as Laguna West in California and Kentlands in Maryland, or resort/retirement communities typified by Seaside, Florida.'[63]

The Urban Villages Forum in Britain is promoting similar ideas. Their ideal size of settlement is between 3,000 and 5,000 people but their proposals share many of the same features as the CNU designs in terms of self-sufficiency, mixed use and a clear hierarchy of streets and spaces. The Forum acts as a lobby group supported by the Prince of Wales and his Prince's Trust Foundation.[64] The government has given endorsement to their ideas in national planning policy guidance,[65] and has 'badged' particular new developments as 'urban villages'. The Prince provided support and publicity to the idea through the development of an extension to Dorchester, Poundbury, on his own lands. The first stages of Poundbury to be completed caused controversy, because in common with the New Urbanist developments in the USA, they were targeted at middle- to high-income owner-occupiers. There has also been criticism of the traditional appearance of the architecture and, despite the professed aims of environmental sustainability, the need for car use. More social housing, workplaces and a greater variety of facilities are being introduced in subsequent phases, but the predominance of higher income housing is such that it will take many years before the development can migrate from being a well-provided residential suburb to becoming an authentic part of a town.

The most coherent design guidance that reasserts the neighbourhood unit to be endorsed by the British Government is contained in a report produced in 1999, *Towards an Urban Renaissance*, under the authorship of the Urban Taskforce headed by the architect Lord Rogers. In contrast to the neighbourhood unit proposed in the 1940s, the diagrams setting out the design propositions suggest that rather than being self-contained, the neighbourhood should be well connected to the district and the city as a whole. Its size remains approximately at the traditional 7,000 population and its proposed facilities could have been drawn from Perry's plan for Chicago in 1929, with a list of primary school, doctor, corner shop, group of shops, public house, church and post office. Doubts could now be cast, just five years since its publication, of the likely viability for the post office and the pub. Both of these local facilities have been subject to market forces and the post office is likely to have been closed down in a drive towards rationalisation and the pub would also be vulnerable to takeover by one of the major corporate entertainment providers. The report attempts to bring together proposals for active, clearly delineated streets and pocket parks with the idea for a neighbourhood centre, thereby combining Jacobs with New-Town-style planning. The vitality to be ensured in its proposals is provided by 'mixed working areas', for the report argues that even in the suburbs, 'a more flexible approach to live-work units can be encouraged. Since a growing proportion of urban residents will work in the neighbourhood in which they live, their requirements for local facilities will also change and adapt.'[66]

This last statement appears to be aspirational rather than being based on any evidence of employment patterns or surveys of preferences. Indeed, proposals for live-work units as options for women who are housebound through caring responsibilities at first appear to be attractive. An expansion of ICT (information and communication technologies) assists this method of work organisation. The exploitation, however, that many unskilled women experience as homeworkers on piecework suggests that this may not be such a benign vision for the future. Haraway, in a dystopian review of the potentiality of ICTs, foresaw low-income women being trapped in 'electronic cages',[67] while the public realm became increasingly hostile.

The 'urban renaissance' envisaged by the Task Force report has much to commend it, in its championing of aspects of everyday urban civilies that could constitute the 'good city'. A more nuanced vision of the ideas set out in the report has been produced by three academics at the University of the West of England under the auspices of the European Region of the World Health Organisation.[68] This grapples with some of the problems glossed over by the taskforce, as for example the exact nature of the local facilities that might be provided within the 'sustainable neighbourhood'. In common with the Task Force report, it also proposes that the neighbourhood is connected directly to the wider transport networks of the city. Nevertheless the underlying emphasis of the guide is upon moving towards a local self-sufficiency. More clearly defined, safer streets, a more comfortable environment for walking and cycling and a better-supported public domain with more opportunities for chance encounters would be of benefit to all sections of the population. Nevertheless, a reversion to the 1940s' ideal of the desirability of self-containment gives cause for concern. There is a tension between reducing the need to make journeys by car and in the limiting of opportunity, for work and social contact. This tension is felt particularly by certain groupings of women, who historically have had less access to motorised transport and who are now, as the previous section demonstrated, gaining it.

As has been suggested previously, transportation scholars argue that women are more acutely affected by transport exclusion because, for example, single mothers and elderly women have lower incomes and less access to car use. Elderly people, female and male, may be physically unable to drive. An increased emphasis on the provision of locally based services and facilities would benefit both these groups. However if this provision were to be achieved at the cost of significant improvements in transport infrastructure, either in new developments or in retrofitting the suburbs, further progress towards social justice and equality would be limited. In case this seems too dramatic a statement, evidence emerging from the government's own Social Exclusion Unit has demonstrated that it is people living in the most deprived areas who are in greatest need of improved transport links out of them. The final report of their transport unit, *Making Connections*, highlighted the points made in Chapter 3, that it is frequently women who are most subject to environmental deprivation, in this case, poor access to public services, employment, shops and other facilities.[69] With regard to neighbourhoods, Biddulph, Franklin and Tait's study of urban villages in the UK concluded that the desire for self-sufficiency was unachievable and mistaken. They concluded: 'All in all, the goal of achieving greater self-sufficiency seems profoundly misplaced when such areas are embedded within wider urban networks and when confronted by contemporary aspirations and the specific circumstances of communities.'[70] The fear is that the gains made by women in achieving greater mobility, with its clear benefits of expanding opportunities and strengthening social bonds of friendship and activism, could be reversed by highlighting a concern for environmental sustainability in the form of the neighbourhood unit. In the swathes of suburbia and low-density development that characterise much of Britain, a refocus on an ideal 'neighbourhood' unit could be highly retrogressive for women, and would also adversely affect low-income and disabled men. The geographer Tim Hall's judgement that 'clearly, the benefits that the car has brought to some groups, such as women (particularly in terms of personal security) and the third of the lowest quintile of the UK population who own cars, cannot be ignored'[71] seems entirely fair.

While some feminist commentary in the 1980s and 1990s suggested that suburban life was disempowering for women, arguing that women were disadvantaged through lack of mobility and local employment and services, increases in car drivership, as previously discussed, have changed that observation. In a study of gender divisions and class, Bondi[72] comments on how a couple in her more affluent group of respondents enjoyed an egalitarian relationship within the context of a highly mobile lifestyle within a gentrified inner city neighbourhood. Moreover, they expected the structure of their relationship and its mobility to be continued when they started a family and moved to the suburbs. Similarly a single woman with an equivalent lifestyle in the same area also intended to move to the suburbs. By contrast, in a suburb of a completely different town, a couple from another group of low-income owner-occupiers who were struggling to make ends meet, had a relationship in which traditional gender divisions were more pronounced. Bondi considered this to be associated with their economic distress. This gender difference was compounded by the lack of spatial mobility that the woman in the couple experienced in contrast to her husband. Bondi concludes both that mobility is only remarked upon in its absence and that in contemporary Britain it is becoming a marker of re-stratification, that is the poor are less mobile and are also more likely to structure their gender relations in marriage on traditional lines. For these reasons, proposals to reduce mobility need to be scrutinised carefully in terms of their impact both on gender and class.

Women, networks and neighbourhoods in the twenty-first century

This chapter began its survey of the neighbourhood unit with an elaboration of the manner in which solidarities were built up through 'women's talk' in poorer urban communities of the nineteenth and early twentieth centuries. Such communities were the product of scarcity.[73] They are indeed 'lost' and their resurrection, as has been argued, would be undesirable as well as unfeasible. How then are urban designers and town planners to accommodate women's civic engagement and citizenship if the concept of the neighbourhood unit is to be discarded? One answer might lie in a pragmatic acceptance of what is known about socio-spatial relations. While claims for the 'ideal' size of neighbourhood unit range from 50 to 5,000 persons,[74] there is evidence to support Jacobs' contention that people identify with smaller areas around their home that are based on the street, section of the street or a small number of dwellings.[75] Talen,[76] in a review of the claims of physical designers to promote 'community', assesses that increased resident interaction in the public realm can be achieved through the types of layout proposed by Jacobs, the CNU and the mainstream of urban design thought. She is careful, however, to make the caveat that the meanings of these interactions to their participants cannot be produced by physical arrangements. The challenge for urban designers and planners is that the housing densities required to facilitate neighbourly encounters on these streets is higher than that to which the majority of the British population appears to aspire.

In a practical approach to designing for a reduction in car use, but recognising contemporary patterns of mobility, Clarke, a practising urban designer, proposes 'a walkable community' based around town centres. These centres are located on the linear routes that characterise many contemporary British cities, such as London, Birmingham or

Manchester. Each walkable community would have a catchment of 800 metres across, which is roughly the distance of a bus stop in either direction from the centre. Movement routes would be shared between pedestrians, cyclists, cars and buses and would go through the centre as well as residential neighbourhoods within the 'community'. Shops and commercial facilities would be located along the main routes, where there would also be a higher density of development, whereas community facilities, such as schools, parks and health centres would be distributed within the overall area.[77] This proposal answers the need for connectivity as well as allowing for local identity based around smaller units such as a street, a park or a group of streets. The provision of local facilities is possibly the most difficult aspect of making feasible design proposals for the neighbourhood. In a social democratic society, such facilities are beyond the remit of the planning system, however collaborative it may be. Increasingly provision is either determined by the market or by national or local politics.[78] For example, shops, cafes, banks and pubs are subject to the operation of the national and international economy. Facilities in which the public purse has an involvement are more subject to local political influence. These include post offices, doctors' surgeries, schools, libraries, community centres, youth clubs and nurseries. Activist citizenship is increasingly demanded to ensure that there is adequate local provision in the face of budget cuts and centralisation. Local papers frequently report petitions, marches, letter writing and small campaigns to retain facilities such as a local post office.

The first proponents for the 'neighbourhood unit' proposed that it was based around a primary school. In 1950s' New York, Jane Jacobs ridiculed this suggestion, asking 'which primary school', pointing out that there was a choice between public and private. The issue of choice, in public as well as commercial services, is coming to the fore in British public politics and cannot be wished away. There is a danger in urban designers or planners proposing any individual community facility, be it a school, a pub or a shop, as the focus for interaction in a neighbourhood because it could so rapidly change. The dry cleaner becomes a coffee shop, the local pub transmutes into a noisy nightclub and the local shop is put out of business by a nearby supermarket.

Contemporary urban designers have argued, following Jane Jacobs, that some traditional urban forms provide a better-supported public culture than the decentralised urban sprawl of the latter years of the twentieth century. Motorised transport has helped to produce this decentralisation alongside the phone and the internet. The more recent widespread diffusion of ICTs and an increase in car ownership has also facilitated the promotion and maintenance of social ties so that divisions between the spatially mobile and those who are not are becoming more apparent.

These are not the only consequences of these new forms of communication. Worpole comments that in his study of public parks, he found that his respondents were using them as places to get away from the intensity and intrusion of tele-communications into the home, in short, to use them as inti-mate, private places whereas the home had become public.[79] He muses that there are likely to be further reversals of this sort, with new fluidities and flexibilities between public and private. It is interesting that the home, which has previously been categorised as women's domain, is now connected to a wide variety of networks. These hold the possibility of being both intrusive and invasive, as video and photo phones become more diffused and computers can log how, when and between whom communications are occurring. There are now so many routes by which communication can enter a property, for example terrestrial phone, mobile phone, fax, internet, TV as well as the post and knocking at the door, that the nineteenth-century notion of the home constructed by women as a retreat from a male-dominated world seems hopelessly outdated. As Lievesley points out in Chapter 1, the media serve to promulgate 'norms' of consumerist beha-viour and the 'ideal' family directly into the home. Conversely, the public realm has been opened up to the private and the personal, not least through the use of mobile phones. This has already been commented on in the way the technology can be used to enhance feelings of safety and hence mobility, both of which are significant for women. The mobile phone also permits intensely personal exchanges to be continued in the most public of places.

Certainly the construction of the neighbourhood is as likely to be composed of virtual elements as physical. Personal networks of friends and family, activist networks and interest groups, geographically scattered, connected by phone and email, and maintained through periodic face-to-face contact, are becoming the norm.[80] Women play an important role in the construction of these networks within the household, and a study by Moyal of women's use of the telephone in Australia coined the phrase 'telephone neighbourhoods' as a descriptor.[81] Here Moyal found, in common with other studies, that women tended to use the phone more than men in constructing and maintaining their personal networks of family and friends. In her study, set in an Australian context where mobility was more difficult, she found that women were constructing a 'neighbourhood' of supportive social contact that was not physical, but virtual.

Other contacts are increasingly being assisted with the addition of virtual connections, for example, the major supermarket chains are marketing shopping online and the idea of the 'virtual town hall' and e-government has been a potent theme for over a decade. Subsidised dial-up bus services and taxi vouchers are being used by an increasing number of local authorities to provide tailored services for those who are suffering transport disadvantage.[82] More possibilities for practising citizenship are being provided, but more is being demanded of individual women in the construction of their own neighbourhood. For example, a component of the British government's policies towards its eighty-eight Neighbourhood Renewal Areas, which have a concentration of attributes of social exclusion, is the notion of 'capacity building'. This entails local residents being encouraged to take part in local enterprises and voluntary organisations and to learn the skills to do so. Reforms to the planning system, now enacted in legislation, require public authorities to consult local 'communities' as part of the statutory process to a greater extent than hitherto.

Conclusion

To conclude, active citizenship is a complex phenomenon. An underlying theme of this chapter has been that in order to exercise the most basic level of citizenship, that is participation in wider society outside the immediate family group, access to people, goods, services, organisations, activities, in short the public realm, needs to be assured. Without opportunities to meet and exchange views political processes cannot take place. Women's relationship to the physical public realm has been problematised, because historically particular groups of women have experienced and in some cases continue to experience constraints on their spatial mobility. In contemporary Britain, spatial mobility has become contentious, because planning and urban design policies have adopted goals of environmental sustainability that aim to reduce car use. It has been suggested that planning by neighbourhood raises important issues for women as citizens in that a reduction in spatial mobility further disadvantages those particular groups of women who experience the most limited access to the public realm.

This argument has been made because the neighbourhood unit superficially appears to answer many women's needs. Its incarnation in the 1950s was based around the needs of small children and the sociability of housewives. Its contemporary form, as proposed in the work of the New Urbanists and the Urban Village movement, is based on self-sufficiency and the use of local facilities. This formulation seems backward-looking and nostalgic for two reasons. The first is that control over local facilities, in a capitalist economy, does not lie with the planner or urban designer, but with large corporations and public agencies, which are required to behave as if they were market organisations. The second is that the diffusion of technologies such as motorised vehicles, the phone and the internet through the urban environment is blurring and shifting relationships between public and private, the global and the local, the neighbourhood and the city and the home and the urban area. The neighbourhood as a physical entity is reduced in its significance as a locus for social contact, while the ability to relate to contacts and organisations across a town or city region have become more important.

How then can urban designers respond to these challenges? On the one hand social justice would suggest that all women should be able to exercise citizenship within the public realm with ease and dignity. This means, for example, an older woman being able to go to a pensioners' group without having to rely on the kindliness of friends or family to transport her. It means that a young single mother might be able to join an environmental group without worrying about how she is going to get there and back at night. Contemporary urban design has a role to play at a strategic level in the creation of an accessible public realm through ensuring that links exist between the 'home area' and wider networks of public transport infrastructure. It means that issues of accessibility, for example moving between car parking places and the town centre, or changing between different modes of public transport are safe, comfortable and secure at all times of the day and late into the evening. In this way women, as a group, would have the capability of exercising citizenship at its most basic level.

Furthermore, the design of the physical layout within the neighbourhood can support citizenship in the sense of providing a safe space where strangers can be encountered. This recognises that while equalities should be achieved through mobility on a wider spatial scale, local areas are populated with individuals who are disadvantaged through physical impairment or social stratification. Women are disproportionately represented in that they live longer, have lower incomes and are more likely to have caring responsibilities. It is particularly crucial that the streets in an immediate locality are configured so that they are safe and attractive and that the pedestrian environment is made as comfortable and accessible as possible. This could provide a backdrop for a localised 'pavement politics' in which women can combine together to make political demands. This is not to suggest an environmental determinism that would enforce 'community' but to put forward a view, backed by evidence, that urban designers can facilitate contact through strangers literally passing each other on a street, superficial contact that promotes a springboard for deeper encounter.

The provision of safe, pedestrian-friendly streets and frequent, accessible transport systems might seem to be a modest demand by comparison to the housing cooperatives and other experiments with communality that have characterised a progressive built environment agenda. The difficulties of achieving such limited goals should not be underestimated. Making a public transport system viable economically means living at densities that are far higher than the norms of suburbia. It also means living in lower status styles and types of housing, such as flats and terraced housing. The tensions between personal freedom and social justice are not readily resolved in terms of the built environment. The ferocity of the (mainly) male-dominated response to the Chancellor of the Exchequer's modest rises in the price of petrol duty in 2000, the 'fuel blockade', illustrates the depth of feeling that surrounds the status quo.

Finally, the symbolism of neighbourhood, with its connotations of social solidarity needs interrogating. While nineteenth-century neighbourhoods may have been dominated by matriarchal figures, in the twenty-first century social solidarity is more diffuse, based on interest rather than propinquity. Spatial planners and designers need to search further for physical forms that celebrate and support difference between women as well as other groups. Rather than seeking locality-based definitions of identity, urban planners and designers need to recognise, define and articulate the hybrid networks that combine physical meeting with virtual communication, through which citizenship is practised.

Notes

1 F. Tibbalds, *Making People-Friendly Towns: Improving the Public Environment in Towns and Cities* (London: E & FN Spon, 2001, first published 1992), p. 101.

2 Department of the Environment (DOE), *Quality in Town and Country: A Discussion Document*, (London: DOE, 1994).

3 See for example: Department of the Environment, Transport and the Regions/Commission for Architecture and the Built Environment (DETR/CABE), *By Design: Urban Design in the Planning System: Towards Better Practice* (London: DETR, 2000). The Royal Fine Art Commission was restructured to become the Commission for Architecture and the Built Environment (CABE) funded by the Office of the Deputy Prime Minister and the Department of Culture, Media and Sport. CABE has taken up public space and public green space as an important area of work and has produced a number of research projects, guidance documents and set up training programmes to deliver improvements in public space of all kinds.

4 T. Lloyd-Jones, 'The scope of urban design' in C. Greed and M. Roberts (eds), *Introducing Urban Design: Interventions and Responses* (Harlow: Longman, 1998), pp. 15–35.

5 J. Gehl, *Life Between Buildings: Using Public Space* (Arkitektens Forlag: Skive, 3rd edn, 1996, first published 1971).

6 M. Carmona, T. Heath, T. Oc and S. Tiesdell, *Public Places-Urban Spaces: The Dimensions of Urban Design* (Oxford: Architectural Press, 2003), p. 57.

7 A. Holden and K. Iveson, 'Designs on the urban: New Labour's urban renaissance and the spaces of citizenship', *City*, 7:1 (April 2003), 57–72.

8 A much earlier version of this paper: 'Network versus neighbourhood: a critical view of current planning trends with particular regard to gender relations, neighbourhoods and social networks' was presented to the International Seminar: Social Sustainability of Technological Networks at New York University, organised by ISTC and LATTS, 14–17 April 2001. The author would like to thank the organisers of that seminar for their support and comments.

9 R. D. Puttnam, *Bowling Alone: The Collapse and Revival of American Community* (New York: Touchstone, 2000), p. 283.

10 R. Bromley, C. Thomas and A. Millie, 'Exploring safety concerns in the night-time city', *Town Planning Review*, 71:1 (2001), 71–96; R. Pain, 'Gender, race, age and fear in the city', *Urban Studies*, 38:5–6 (2001), 899–913, at p. 900.

11 J. P. Hine and F. Mitchell, 'Better for everyone? Travel experiences and transport exclusion' in R. Imrie (ed.), *Urban Studies, Special Issue on the Barrier-Free City: Possibilities and Prospects*, 38:2 (2001), 319–322, at 324.

12 B. Hillier and J. Hanson, *The Social Logic of Space* (Cambridge: Cambridge University Press, 1984), see pp. 126–127 for methodology.

13 R. Sennett, *The Uses of Disorder: Personal Identity and City Life* (Harmondsworth: Penguin, 1973).

14 D. Bell, 'Pleasure and danger: the paradoxical spaces of sexual citizenship', *Political Geography*, 14 (1995), 139–153.

15 M. Swenarton, *Homes for Heroes* (London: Heinemann Educational, 1981), pp. 67–87.

16 James Dahir, the compiler of a 1947 bibliography on the neighbourhood unit, argued that 'modern life has created a way of life hostile to neighbourliness', quoted in A. Homer, 'Creating new communities: the role of the neighbourhood unit in post-war British planning', *British History*, 14:1 (Spring 2000), 64.

17 See S. Muthesius, *The English Terraced House* (London: Yale University Press, 1982) for a full account of the development of the terraced house.

18 E. Gauldie, *Cruel Habitations: A History of Working-Class Housing 1780–1918* (London: Allen & Unwin, 1974): see Appendix 2.

19 B. MacFarlane, 'Homes fit for heroines: housing in the twenties' in Matrix, *Making Space: Women and the Man-Made Environment* (London: Pluto Press, 1984), pp. 26–36, at p. 32.

20 M. Tebutt, *Women's Talk? A Social History of "Gossip" in Working-Class Neighbourhoods 1880–1960* (Aldershot: Scolar Press, 1995).

21 *Ibid.*, p. 181.

22 *Ibid.*, p. 80.

23 M. Biddulph, 'Villages don't make a city', *Journal of Urban Design*, 5:1 (February 2000), 65–82.

24 Homer, 'Creating new communities'.

25 M. Roberts, *Living in a Man-Made World: Gender Assumptions in Modern Housing Design* (London: Routledge: 1991), pp. 63–77.

26 L. McDowell, 'City and home: urban housing and the sexual division of

space' in M. Evans and C. Ungerson (eds), *Sexual Divisions, Patterns and Processes* (Andover: Tavistock, 1982), pp. 142–163, at p. 150.

27 Homer, 'Creating new communities', 77–78.

28 M. Young and P. Wilmott, *Family and Kinship in East London* (Harmondsworth: Penguin, 1976, first published 1957).

29 See M. Stacey, *Tradition and Change: A Study of Banbury* (London: Oxford University Press, 1970, first published 1960).

30 M. Berman, *All That is Solid Melts into Air: The Experience of Modernity* (London: Verso, 1983), pp. 322–323.

31 J. Jacobs, *The Death and Life of Great American Cities* (New York: Vintage, 1961), p. 115.

32 *Ibid.*, p. 35.

33 *Ibid.*, p. 68.

34 L. Appleton, 'The gender regime of American cities' in J. Garber and R. Turner (eds), 'Gender in urban research', *Urban Affairs Annual Review* 42, (Thousand Oaks, CA, Sage, 1995), 44–59.

35 L. Bondi, 'Sexing the city' in R. Fincher and J. M. Jacobs (eds), *Cities of Difference* (London: Guildford Press, 1998), pp. 177–200.

36 K. Worpole, 'The social dynamic' in P. Neal (ed.), *Urban Villages and the Making of Communities* (London: Spon, 2003), pp. 119–131, at p. 30.

37 See S. Graham and S. Marvin, *Telecommunications and the City: Electronic Spaces, Urban Places* (London: Routledge, 1996) and S. Graham and S. Marvin, *Splintering Urbanism: Networked Infrastructure, Technological Mobilities and the Urban Condition* (London: Routledge, 2001).

38 *Transport Statistics Bulletin. National Travel Survey 1997/1999: Update August 2000* (London: Department of the Environment, Transport and the Regions, 2000).

39 A. Ellaway, S. Macintyre, R. Hiscock and A. Kearns, 'In the driving seat: psychosocial benefits from private motor vehicle transport compared to public transport', *Transport Research Part F: Traffic Psychology and Behaviour*, 6:3 (2003), 217–231.

40 London Planning Advisory Committee, *London's Environmental Quality* (London: LPAC, 1996).

41 The publication of this research was greeted by the London-wide evening newspaper, the *Evening Standard*, with the ironic headline 'Women like to drive cars' and a report attacking the so-called obviousness of its findings.

42 London Research Centre, *Women's Travel in London: Key Findings* (London: LRC, 1998).

43 A. Root, L. Schnitler and K. Button, 'Women, travel and the idea of "sustainable transport" ', *Transport Reviews*, 20:3 (2000), 374.

44 K. Hamilton, S. R. Hoyle and L. Jenkins, *The Public Transport Gender Audit*, www.uel.ac.uk/womenandtransport/gender.html, (Chapter 2, 2000), pp. 1–8.

45 See www.statistics.gov.uk/statbase/ssdataset/ Households with home telephones – source Family Expenditure Survey, Office for National Statistics.

46 Reported on BBC Radio 4 *The World Tonight* 12.2.2001 as part of a report

in which it was noted that British Telecom had received a 37 per cent drop in income from public call boxes in the last two years and Orange were discontinuing their pager service.

47 National Statistics, *Census 2001*, www.statistics.gov.uk/CCI/nugget. asp?ID=8&Pos=&ColTank+1&Rank=374

48 See for example L. Pickup, 'Hard to get around: a study of women's travel mobility' in J. Little, L. Peake and P. Richardson (eds), *Women in Cities: Gender in the Urban Environment* (Basingstoke: Macmillan Education, 1988), pp. 98–108.

49 J. Hine and M. Grieco, 'Scatters and clusters in time and space: implications for delivering integrated and inclusive transport', *Transport Policy*, 10 (2003), 299–306, at 300–301.

50 Hamilton *et al.*, *The Public Transport Gender Audit*, p. 5.

51 See W. Mitchell, 'The City of Bits hypothesis' in S. Graham (ed.), *The Cybercities Reader* (London: Routledge 2004), pp. 123–128.

52 W. T. Anderson, 'Communities in a world of open systems', *Futures*, 31 (1999), 457–463, argues that the growth of global communications systems and increased mobility have led to 'multi-community' identification for individuals.

53 A. M. Fernández-Maldonado, 'The diffusion and use of information and communications technologies in Lima, Peru', *Journal of Urban Technology*, 8:3 (2001), 21–43.

54 See Biddulph, 'Villages don't make a city', and E. Talen, 'The problem with community in planning', *Journal of Planning Literature*, 15:2 (2000), 171–183 for summaries.

55 M. M. Webber, 'The post-city age', *Daedalus*, 97:2 (1968), 1091–1110, wrote the classic text that argued that mere adjacency was insufficient for community in the modern world and that 'communities of interest' would become more important.

56 See, for example, H. Sherlock, *Cities are Good for Us* (London: Paladin, 1991) and Richard Sennett's recently republished works: *The Fall of Public Man* (London: Faber and Faber, 1977); *The Conscience of the Eye: The Design and Social Life of Cities* (London: Faber and Faber, 1990) and *Flesh and Stone: The Body and the City in Western Civilization* (London: Faber and Faber, 1994). Jane Jacobs' ideas formed the background to the influential urban design textbook, I. Bentley, A. Alcock, P. Murrain, S. McGlynn and G. Smith, *Responsive Environments: A Manual for Designers* (Oxford: Architectural Press, 1995).

57 A. Madanipour, 'How relevant is "planning by neighbourhoods" today?', *Town Planning Review*, 72:2 (2001), 171–191.

58 A. Madanipour, *Public and Private Spaces of the City* (London: Routledge, 2003).

59 M. Wallace, 'A new approach to neighbourhood renewal in England', *Urban Studies*, 38:12 (2001), 2163–2166.

60 The CNU hosts a website that sets out its history, principles and achievements: www.cnu.org/

61 There are some suggestions that the movement is split east coast/west coast, with a discernable ideological difference beween Duany's interests in Traditional Neighbourhood Developments and a west-coast focus on environmental sustainability.

62 A. Duany, 'Neighbourhood design in practice', in Neal (ed.), *Urban Villages*, pp. 85–102.

63 P. Hall, 'Smart growth' in Neal (ed.), *Urban Villages*, p. 44.

64 T. Aldous, *Urban Villages: A Concept for Creating Mixed-use Development on a Sustainable Scale* (London: Urban Villages Group, 1992).

65 Planning Policy Guidance Note 1: General Policy and Principles commended the Urban Village; this note has now been replaced by Planning Policy Statement 1 which sets out principles for sustainable development rather than prescribing particular forms.

66 Urban Taskforce, *Towards an Urban Renaissance: Final Report of the Urban Taskforce*, chaired by Lord Rogers of Riverside (London: E & FN Spon, 1999), p. 65.

67 D. Haraway, *Simians, Cyborgs and Women: the Reinvention of Nature* (London: Free Association Books, 1991), p. 166.

68 H. Barton, M. Grant and R. Guise, *Shaping Neighbourhoods: A Guide for Health, Sustainability and Vitality* (London: Spon, 2003).

69 Social Exclusion Unit, *Making Connections: Final Report on Transport and Social Exclusion* (London: Social Exclusion Unit, Office of the Deputy Prime Minister, February 2003).

70 M. Biddulph, B. Franklin, and M. Tait, 'From concept to completion: a critical analysis of the urban village', *Town Planning Review*, 74:2 (2003), 187.

71 T. Hall, 'Car-ceral cities: social geographies of everyday urban mobility' in M. Miles and T. Hall (eds), *Urban Futures* (London: Routledge, 2003), p. 105.

72 L. Bondi and H. Christie, 'The best of times for some and the worst of times for others? Gender and class divisions in urban Britain today', *Geoforum*, 31 (2000), 329–343.

73 E. Talen, 'Sense of community and neighbourhood form: an assessment of the social doctrine of new urbanism', *Urban Studies*, 36:8 (1999), 1361–1379.

74 K. Lynch, *Good City Form* (Cambridge, MA: MIT Press, 1981), p. 402.

75 A. Kearns and M. Parkinson, 'The significance of neighbourhood', *Urban Studies*, 38:12 (2001), 2103–2110.

76 Talen, 'Sense of community'.

77 P. Clarke, 'Urban planning and design' in R. Thomas and M. Fordham (eds), *Sustainable Urban Design: An Environmental Approach* (London: Spon, 2004).

78 Barton *et al.*, *Shaping Neighbourhoods*, pp. 96–105.

79 Worpole, 'The social dynamic', p. 130.

80 B. Wellman and D. Tindall, 'How telephone networks connect social networks', *Progress in Communication Sciences*, 12, (1993), 64–93.

81 A. Moyal, 'The gendered use of the telephone: an Australian case-study', *Media, Culture and Society*, 14 (1992), 51–72.

82 Hine and Grieco, 'Scatters and clusters in time and space'.

5

Identity, gender and citizenship: women in Latin and Central America and in Cuba

GERALDINE LIEVESLEY

Introduction

In the western, industrialised world, social and cultural developments in the 1960s and early 1970s, specifically the re-invigoration of feminism, the advocacy of black rights and the public emergence of the gay and lesbian movement, facilitated an interrogation of gender, ethnicity and sexuality and their consequences for citizenship rights. In the same decades, Latin and Central American societies were witnessing political authoritarianism, military dictatorship and mass repression and experiencing the incremental growth of what would become the debt crisis, while in Cuba a revolutionary government was wrestling with the difficult task of building socialism in an underdeveloped country which had long been subject to a neo-colonial relationship with the United States. The historical experience of poor women and women of colour within these Third World societies had been one of exclusion and oppression; this marginality was compounded by the political and economic circumstances of the late twentieth century.

This chapter is based on the premise that poor women mobilise (against dictatorship, against poverty and against patriarchy) and that their experiences and the knowledge gained from them are important. Academics, policy-makers and practitioners in the field need to listen to them. Women's activism should be understood as self-empowerment within the context of collective empowerment. Approaches which emphasise empowerment through external agency (be it the state, NGOs, political parties, feminist groups) miss the point. This is not to say, however, that such actors cannot offer support in these processes but that they should never seek to claim ownership over them. Women's resistance is undertaken through various traditional means such as social movements or unions and through survival strategies themselves. Such mobilisation must always be situated within the context of changes in the global economy, particularly in the Latin and Central American case in terms of the recession and the introduction of adjustment policies in the 1980s. These economic circumstances shaped women's roles. The unequal distribution of wealth and the manner in which economic disadvantage is transmitted from one generation to the next are givens in the history of the region. This absence of social justice was compounded by the debt crisis and the application of neo-liberal economic restructuring during that decade. Poor women, both in rural and urban areas, were forced to seek work in the formal and informal sectors, although much 'women's work' remained, and remains, unrecognised and many women and girls suffer super-exploitation at the workplace.

Implicit in my analysis is the contention that women's citizenship cannot be viewed as anything other than second rate until such persistent economic inequalities are addressed. Women are over-represented among the poor, so much so that the term 'the feminisation of poverty' has become a familiar allusion, as women assume ever greater burdens as they work for the physical survival of their families. Female-headed households are not, however, necessarily poorer. Women in male-headed households are dependent upon men (and this is the way that society expects them to be) but men may not spend their earned income on their families. Female-headed families may have less money but may spend it more wisely; there may also be women of different generations living together with children and, thus, more than one income coming in. However, this greater flexibility in their response to poverty will continue to result in an intensification of work given that it coincides with the state's abdication of service provision and skewing of social fund projects and employment programmes in favour of men. Indeed, government poverty alleviation programmes which do target women have focused upon small, temporary income-generating projects which emphasise 'feminine' tasks such as sewing and cooking. They have not addressed long-term poverty which has been compounded by structural adjustment.

Latin and Central American women have found that public legislation which has shaped family life has also determined their access to citizenship. Women were enfranchised over a long period (Ecuadorians being the first in 1929 and Paraguayans the last in 1961), although the right to vote was also beset by literacy clauses in many countries, a precondition which effectively disenfranchised many poor and indigenous women. *Potestad marital* (marital power) laws placed women under the legal control of their fathers and husbands and they enjoyed no distinct rights with respect to property ownership or the guardianship of their children (after the inception of the Argentinian Civil Code in 1871, women were not granted joint legal custody of their children until 1985). The huge influence of the Catholic Church conspired with other conservative forces in civil society and the media to ensure prohibitions on divorce and abortion. For Lucía Rayas, the Church 'has played a particularly insidious role in defining and enforcing ideologies of womanhood'.[1] There has been a countervailing trend within the Catholic community, that of liberation theology. Many priests, nuns and grassroots lay organisations have encouraged popular mobilisation and endorsed women's empowerment through education and self-help. However, women have often had to fight against hierarchies of power in their relations with the radical Church and many of the latter's representatives have wished to steer clear of difficult issues such as the right to abortion.

There have been further prohibitions on women from indigenous communities. In cultures where 'whiteness' was privileged and portrayed as defining beauty and womanhood – a perspective reinforced by the media and advertising – ethnic women did not receive the same reception or respect accorded those of paler skins. They were frequently the recipients of sexual violence with rape and murder regularly being used as weapons by landowners, factory employers, the police, the military and other state agencies. The contemporary abuse of indigenous communities in Chiapas in Mexico has been described by Lynn Stephen. The purpose behind the torture of men (and the emphasis upon public displays of their nakedness and attacks on their genitals) is to emphasise their powerlessness and inability to protect their wives and children. For women, rape and the threat of rape 'have been deployed as both physical and symbolic violence to discourage women from ongoing participation in community and regional forms of organisation.'[2] The horrific and ongoing catalogue of violence against women, such as the December 1997 massacre of thirty-two Tzotzil women in Acteal by paramilitaries, is thus used to silence defiant women. Women who challenge the state's authority are regarded as bad, fallen and whores and, thus, any treatment meted out to them is deemed appropriate. As in many societies, rape is a shaming experience, often explained in the discourse of traditional morality as the woman's fault. Women activists risk social opprobrium as well as leading their daily lives in an atmosphere of constant surveillance by military patrols and the always-present threat of sexual assault.

Historically, indigenous communities were perceived as conservative and resistant to progress. This legitimised both the state's neglect of them and its periodic attempts to integrate them into the development process on its terms. Thus since the 1930s, assimilation campaigns sought to impose a Mexican identity upon diverse indigenous cultures, forbidding certain practices (exemplified by language, dress, music and ritual) for being 'backward' and hindering modernisation. The danger of such attitudes of cultural imperialism remains within the context of those communities who have established strong links with the Zapatistas since their rebellion on 1 January 1994. The Ejercito Zapatista de Liberación Nacional (EZLN – the Zapatista Army of National Liberation) has proclaimed its vigilance against such fundamentalism and its commitment to political and cultural pluralism and the need for indigenous communities to lead the struggle and retain their identities. Women within these communities have challenged expectations concerning their status and freedoms. They face a double challenge – against the state, which has never respected them, and within their own cultures, where they seek to overturn traditional oppressions.

There was much anticipation surrounding the wave of transitions from military to civilian rule in Latin America in the 1980s (beginning with the end of military rule in Peru in 1980 and continuing with transitions in Argentina, Uruguay, Brazil and Chile), the apparent unravelling of authoritarian one-party states (Mexico) and 'partyarchies' (Venezuela, where two parties had dominated politics since the 1950s), and the peace settlements which ended civil war in Central America (although the latter failed to resolve the deep-seated political, social and economic problems which stimulated the insurgencies). With the electoral defeat of the Sandinistas in Nicaragua in 1990 and the widespread belief that the disintegration of the soviet bloc had sounded the death knell for the Castro government in Cuba, many commentators believed that Latin and Central America were entering a period of democratic consolidation. Women had been highly visible in the opposition movements which had attacked authoritarian regimes and demanded the introduction of representative, accountable and democratic governments which honoured the rule of law and respected human rights. However, optimism rapidly gave way to disillusionment as politically exclusive and predominantly male governments in Latin America adopted neo-liberal economic strategies.

The opening up of domestic economies to global competition, the deregulation of labour markets and the rolling back of state expenditure and social provision compounded female poverty and increased the precariousness of life in poor rural and urban communities. Civilian governments also failed to address human rights issues and treated women's policy agendas in highly cavalier fashion. During the struggles for democratic transition, aspiring political leaders had talked a great deal about the need for transparency in decision-making and democratic responsibility but these commitments were marred by continuing corruption and authoritarian political practices as well as seeming indifference to the structural causes of poverty and the continuing neglect of the rights of poor citizens. Women's issues and concerns, the demand for parity with men in employment and education, in opportunities and access, and the debate centred around sexual and reproductive freedoms were particularly targeted by a conservative counter-offensive. One example of the latter was the launching in 1997 by the Catholic Church in El Salvador of a 'Yes to Life' campaign which succeeded in modifying the law that for more than twenty years had allowed women the option of abortion for therapeutic reasons or following a rape. The Church also played a key role in blocking ratification of the Convention on the Elimination of all Forms of Discrimination Against Women, arguing that it would open the way for abortion on demand. The cross-party National Association of Salvadorian Women Councillors, Mayors and Alderwomen have campaigned against this trend and have introduced proposals to promote women's participation in politics, but the small number of women in elected posts prevents them exerting much influence.[3]

Women's identities

Although this chapter is primarily concerned with contemporary women, it permits itself the freedom to range between modern and historical examples of women's oppression and mobilisation. It does so in the spirit of the idea of the politics of cultural identity which was discussed in Chapter 1. It is remarkable how many similarities exist between old and new sources of the oppression and marginalisation of women and how women have responded to these. Women have experienced life under diverse political regimes and have had to create coping strategies in the face of extreme economic difficulty. They have had to contend with discriminatory behaviour on the grounds of their gender, their class, their ethnicity and their sexuality. They have also striven to project authentic identities in the face of the traditional iconography of 'womanhood' and the stereotypes it has imposed upon their lives. Machismo provided the cultural legitimation of the abuse of women and men's right to control them, while the Catholic Church linked public veneration of women, particularly through its construction of the cult of the Virgin Mary, to issues of fertility, domesticity and sacrifice. The idealisation of women as good and virtuous mothers and wives has always been systematically undermined by the treatment meted out to women who dare to transgress.

Nicki Craske has written about the role 'militant mothers' played in organisations such as the Argentinian Madres de la Plaza de Mayo, the Co-Madres of El Salvador and the CONVIGUA (Coordinadora Nacional de las Viudas Guatemaltecas – the National Coordinator of the Widows of Guatemala). Determined to prove the culpability of the military for the torture, murder and 'disappearance' of family members, the Madres contacted each other informally as they travelled between law courts, government offices and prisons. Their frustration at state indifference and obfuscation led them to stage impromptu events (such as chaining themselves to court gates) and symbolic demonstrations in other public spaces hitherto regarded as male preserves.[4] When the Argentinian mothers began their weekly silent demonstrations in Buenos Aires in 1977, they attracted growing press coverage and support from other opposition groups. They came to be regarded as posing a moral challenge to the national security state, which initially had no idea how to respond to them. However, as the mothers grew ever more militant, the military government responded in time-tested fashion, as the mothers were themselves tortured, murdered and 'disappeared'.[5]

Following transitions to civilian governments, mothers' groups continued to be thorns in the side of governments which wanted to draw a veil over the systematic state terrorism perpetrated by the military (fearful as they were that judicial inquiries might provoke a further wave of armed interventions). Thus, the government of Raul Alfonsín accused the Madres of endangering the new democracy by their refusal to forget the past. The more militant Madres continued to press for greater assertiveness but the opportunity for this was foreclosed by the Punto Final law which effectively prohibited further prosecution of military personnel. Over time and within these changed political circumstances, mothers' organisations were rent by internal divisions concerning agendas, tactics and strategies. Some women had previously regarded themselves as apolitical but their experiences politicised them, while others wished to distance themselves from politics and resolutely opposed embracing feminist ideas or developing links with other social and political movements. Nevertheless, it is clear that activism stimulated by the 'motherist' instinct to discover the circumstances of the deaths of children was a major element in movements against dictatorship. Sonia Alvarez has argued that 'motherhood, not citizenship, provided the principal *mobilizing referent* for women's participation in urban social movements'.[6]

During the 1980s in Nicaragua, women as mothers – particularly in relation to revolution and war – was a constant motif in both Sandinista and Contra discourse.[7] Both sides appropriated women's identities as mothers grieving for fallen sons or as fighters with babies at their breasts and guns slung over their backs. Women were expected to fulfil these roles as evidence of their loyalty to either side and, indeed, vied with other mothers in demonstrating their credentials. Thus, the Mothers of Heroes and Martyrs of Matagalpa (a Sandinista organisation located in a northern city close to the war zone) claimed to suffer more than the mothers of dead Contra soldiers. However, as the fighting intensified and the economic situation deteriorated and, particularly, when the government introduced the draft in 1984, the Mothers began to challenge the control imposed upon them by the Asociación de Mujeres Nicaragüenes Luisa Amanda Espinoza (AMNLAE – the Luisa Amanda Espinoza Association of Nicaraguan Women, the state's women's federation). Women's opposition to the draft and growing death rates was encouraged by Cardinal Obando y Bravo, the head of the Catholic Church, and in the anti-Sandinista press while the FSLN sought to convince mothers that it was an honour to have produced revolutionary martyrs. In the late 1980s, Sandinista mothers resisted a general amnesty for imprisoned Contra soldiers (which again the Church promoted, using the language of reconciliation), while Contra mothers questioned their manipulation by male politicians. The ending of the civil war following the 1990 elections found mothers and widows on both sides of the ideological divide in dire circumstances, which were compounded by their new government's enthusiastic embrace of neo-liberalism. Mothers' groups addressed themselves to creating mutual support networks but the debate as to who had been the 'real' mothers continued.[8]

Sexual politics

In addition to questioning traditional gender roles, women's long struggles for empowerment have also involved an investigation into the categories of feminine and masculine and of the physical ground upon which these contested definitions have been fought out – women's bodies. In Latin and Central America, the Catholic Church has played a major role in determining rules on sexual behaviour and in refusing women the right to control over their own bodies. Sex was only permissible within the confines of monogamous marriage and for the purposes of reproduction. Women, who were taught to regard motherhood as their destiny, were expected to be sexually compliant and passive and to submit to the will of their husbands. The hypocrisy of this approach is underscored by the fact that it has always been accepted that there are different kinds of women who can be treated differently. Thus, women as servants and as prostitutes do not command respect, women from ethnic and poor backgrounds are treated differently from more privileged women, and notions of female virtue go out the window when it comes to the commodification of women's bodies to sell goods or to promote tourism. To take just one example, before 1959 Cuban women, and particularly Afro-Cubans, were exoticised in the American imagination as being both sexually available and sexually voracious. For Lou Peréz, 'The idea that Cuba existed specifically for the pleasure of North Americans took hold early ... Havana was gendered as a seductive erotic landscape' where Americans could act out their fantasies.[9] Prostitution was banned after the Revolution but began to reappear in the 1990s as Cuba wooed foreign tourists and their dollars. Current practice may be very different from the institutionalised sex shows and brothels of the 1950s but it is a worrying development in a society which maintains a commitment to respect for women's rights.[10] Women's bodies have been subjected to objectification and fetishisation in a symbolic legitimisation of the subjugation of Latin and Central economies and governments to US power. A perfect historical example of this was United Fruit's appropriation of Carmen Miranda's body as the Chiquita logo for their bananas in the 1940s. Her image represented the super-exploitation of poor women on the plantations. Miranda would later be swallowed up by Hollywood, where she became emblematic of 'Latin Americanness' in a series of surreal and often humiliating roles.[11]

Over time and in response to economic exigencies and changing social mores, different kinds of households emerged and more flexible consensual unions between women and men became widespread, while increases in women's employment and the higher incidence of women working outside home or away from it combined to challenge the traditional approach towards marriage and the family and the stereotypical female identities they cultivated. The

1980s and 1990s witnessed a slow down in population growth mainly due to increases in women's use of contraception. Nevertheless, access to legal abortion remains very restricted and there are unacceptable costs for women's health in terms of the high incidence of back-street operations and subsequent problems of infertility. With the exception of Cuba, Guyana and Puerto Rico, where abortion is available on demand, abortion is legally penalised in Latin and Central America and the Caribbean. There are provisions for extenuating circumstances (such as a woman's life being in danger, for example) in most countries, although women have to go through long review processes, so they may be well advanced in their pregnancy before a decision is made and abortion will then be out of the question. In Chile during the Pinochet regime (1973–89), doctors and nurses were encouraged to denounce women who sought treatment after illegal, botched abortions. In practice, there are fewer legal cases against women in the contemporary period but, nevertheless, many women will be discouraged from seeking medical care for fear of the consequences.[12] In addition to their lack of control over their reproductive existence, women employees face problems of inadequate childcare provision, an unequal distribution of responsibilities within the home, domestic violence and the threat of dismissal should they become pregnant. If they work in the informal sector, there is, of course, no provision made for their well-being.

In the latter part of the twentieth century, movements for sexual and reproductive rights repudiated the hypocrisy of the old moral conservatism and sought to expose the gendered nature of political and economic power and of religious authority. Marta Lamas has demonstrated that as Mexican women enter the workforce in record numbers, the right to abortion becomes ever more pressing. She contends that: 'In Mexico, as elsewhere, sexual and reproductive rights, while occupying minimal space in the national debate over democracy, allow women to achieve self-determination, and are thus intimately linked to the meaning of modern citizenship.'[13] Yet progress has been extremely slow and many issues around sexuality and reproductive autonomy remain taboo subjects which are not deemed suitable for public debate. Women seeking control over their sexual lives also face a growing backlash in many countries. In the late 1990s,

Colombia and El Salvador joined Chile in prohibiting abortion completely. In 2000, the right-wing Partido de Acción Nacional (PAN – Party of National Action) won national elections in Mexico, defeating the long-incumbent Partido Revolucionaria Institucional (PRI – the Institutional Revolutionary Party). The new president, Vicente Fox, enjoyed close relations with the United States (he had been a Coca Cola executive) and the Catholic Church, particularly its fundamentalist, activist wings – Opus Dei, the Legions of Christ and PRO-VIDA (a pro-life lobby). There had been an official separation between church and state in Mexico since 1917 but in 1992 President Carlos Salinas de Gotari approved an amendment to the Constitution which strengthened the power of the Church.

It now has legal access to the media and, in line with privatisation practices elsewhere where religious organisations have brought schools out of the state system, it plays an increasingly important role in education. The Church has waged an effective campaign against the Secretariat of Public Education, which is responsible for sex education in schools, and has charged it with promoting sex outside marriage and abortion. In this, it has been assisted by the Parents' Association, and by Opus Dei, which has used its contacts with big business to influence the media. Campaigns have also been launched to close down family planning clinics in a number of states. The ascendancy of these organisations in public life was felt almost immediately after his victory when the legislature of Fox's home state of Guanajuato attempted to change the law on abortion by banning a woman's right to terminate a pregnancy after rape. The proposal was withdrawn following a wave of protests but it was clear that this was merely the first act of a determined effort to shift Mexican social life to the right. It is a worrying fact that there has been a noticeable absence of public figures willing to stand up against these bullying tactics. The main opposition party, the Partido de la Revolución Democratica (PRD – the Party of the Democratic Revolution), mindful of its chances of victory in the presidential race of 2006, has been relatively silent and it has been left to feminist and gay activist groups to protest. The EZLN, which is committed to respect for sexual diversity, believes that sexual relations do not need to be sanctioned by marriage and that divorce should be by mutual agreement, has also spoken up against the backlash.[14]

Similar and worrying developments have occurred elsewhere. In 2001 in Nicaragua, a draft of an Equal Opportunities and Rights Bill was criticised by the right-wing ruling Liberal Party for being too permissive and by women's organisations for being weak on reproductive and sexual rights and lacking any means to enforce its provisions. The following year, consultations about a revision of the draft bill were held with the private sector, the Church and other conservative interests. In 2003, the Episcopal Conference sent a letter to National Assembly delegates, arguing that the Equal Opportunities and Rights Bill represented a 'grave danger' because it referred to 'rights' which had traditionally not been regarded as human rights. Objecting to the use of the word 'gender' (which it argued was a term coined by foreign feminists), the letter voiced concerns about the recognition of women's sexual and reproductive rights and the threat this would pose to the continued existence of the family.[15] In 1995, President Alberto Fujimori of Peru announced the National Family Planning Programme, which legalised voluntary sterilisation despite the Church's opposition to it. Fujimori claimed that family planning should be used as a tool to fight poverty and aid development. However, its implementation was far from voluntary as thousands of rural indigenous women were sterilised without their consent (figures would reach 110,000 by 1997) by health workers who were threatened with dismissal if quotas were not achieved. It was not until 2002 that Fernando Carbone of the Health Ministry would offer a public apology but his remarks also made it clear that his government would be returning to a more traditional agenda on contraception.[16]

Women and food

One example of the parallels to be drawn between women's historical and contemporary experiences concerns their relationship with food. I consider the modern experience of food production in the following section but first explore a nineteenth-century situation. In his study of the dynamics of gender and Mexican cuisine, Jeffrey M. Pilcher explains how, following independence from Spain in the 1820s, liberal governments sought to eradicate the cultural differences between Europeans and Native Americans in order to construct a Mexican national identity. One strategy was to persuade Indians to jettison their traditional, 'primitive' lifestyles and adopt the trappings of European culture including its cuisine. The Mexican elite, which was naturally inclined to imitate the 'superior' European way of life, happily purchased thousands of cookbooks written by male professional chefs. These introduced them to highly standardised and cosmeticised versions of typical Mexican dishes such as mole, taking the food and its ingredients out of their cultural context and ignoring the rich diversity of regional cuisine. Such texts had little time for the cooking of the streets and of the poor which centred around corn, chiles rellenos (stuffed chillies) and frijoles (beans) and, therefore, made no mention of tamales, enchiladas or quesadillas. Mexico City grew rapidly as rural immigrants arrived in the hope of sharing economic growth. The contrast between elite and popular conceptions of the national cuisine became increasingly visible amidst this chaotic urbanisation. The municipal authority's attempts to curb street hawkers and regulate roadside cooking stalls particularly during major fiestas such as the Day of the Dead was, however, spectacularly unsuccessful.

Where does gender figure in this story? Elite and middle-class women supervised their kitchen staff in the creation of elaborate French meals which were dependent upon intensive labour and the use of imported specialities such as wines, hams, cheeses and olive oil. They did this in deference to their husbands' desires to be seen as civilised: the correct food (food which was as distinct from Indian fare as was humanly possible) was part of the vocabulary of modernisation and progress. However, their pretensions 'had little relevance for the majority of the people, particularly for women within the domestic sphere'.[17] In contrast to the cookbooks emanating from the pens of professional male chefs (often French imports themselves), there was an alternative network of more humble and authentic recipes produced by Mexican women. The former's purpose was to confine women to the kitchen but Pilcher speculates that the 'standards of domestic morality and national identity created by male authors did not necessarily reach a complaisant female audience. Indeed, community cookbooks ... imagined an alternative vision of the nation and of the female voice within it.'[18]

The weakness in this argument is that this female voice remained domesticated and its expression was tempered by class and ethnic divisions. Middle-class Mexican women might write recipes and supervise their own kitchens but they would not cook in them. This was the role allotted to young, indigenous women, who were often subject to brutal domestic regimes. Of course, the notion of a female vision of the nation contrasts sharply with the manner in which Benedict Anderson has discussed 'imagined communities', which he defines as states being created through nationalist struggles and nation-building. Historically, women have not been included as future citizens of these putative states, which are essentially imagined brotherhoods.[19] After the formation of new states, women have tended to find their political agendas sidelined as being peripheral to the national interest. I discuss this process within the context of political transitions in the 1980s and 1990s later in this chapter.

Women and food production

Historically, state policies, development theory and aid agency strategies ignored women's contribution to economic production, rendering invisible their participation in agriculture, industry and the informal economy. Agrarian reform legislation (most of which has been highly restricted in its reach and consequences) generally neglected the position of women, failing to include them as beneficiaries or grant them land titles. In rural Brazil, women were responsible for food production on family plots and, thus, for facilitating the commercialisation of the surplus which enabled families to accumulate funds towards buying land. Cheap foodstuffs supported capitalist expansion in urban areas. The military regime (1964–85) initiated a programme of agricultural modernisation under the aegis of 'the green revolution' which introduced 'superior' hybrid seeds, high-tech farm machinery, chemical fertilisers and pesticides to Third World countries.

The agricultural market was restructured in order to use the agrochemicals and machinery provided by the industrial sector, which was the recipient of vast state investment. Emphasis was placed upon export crops in order to reduce the balance of payments deficit, while other farmers supplied the export-oriented agro-industrial enterprises with raw materials. Credit was provided to rural households but in an uneven manner and income differentials increased. The majority of poor rural families did not have sufficient credit facilities to give them access to modern technology and many began the steady slide into pauperisation. Women's participation in agricultural wage labour increased, while they continued to assume responsibility for subsistence farming. Their plight was ignored by the Brazilian government, which, like others, did not recognise value in 'women's work'. Some women joined unions to mount campaigns around their grievances but many found militancy difficult to sustain under the double burden of out-work and domestic labour. A similar account could be given of women's experiences in all latino countries, in both rural and urban sectors and under the burden of debt.[20]

There is a gendered history of plantation agriculture and food processing in Central and Latin America. Women working in plantations are engaged in seasonal piecework, receive the lowest pay and are given the least prestigious jobs (primarily weeding and packing). Those employed in food processing plants endure the feminisation of hazardous tasks such as cleaning fruit or vegetables with chemicals and the tedium of sorting into size categories (the rationale here being that this is appropriate women's work because of their small, deft hands). Women's work encompasses other functions: 'women also provide a plantation's male workers with unpaid food production, childcare and sexual satisfaction. Women plantation workers and women farmers share a politics of invisibility.'[21]

Let me take the example of one food which is closely associated with female labour. Strawberries are a major Chilean export with the industry sending out-of-season fruit to the United States and Europe. The bulk of the workforce are women *temporeras* (temporary workers) but yet again their role is mainly ignored by employers, government and the media. Seasonal women workers come from the cities and rural areas where there are high levels of unemployment and poverty and work for between three and six months per year, engaged in highly flexible and insecure piecework which lacks both legal contracts and regulated conditions of labour. When they are discussed in official reports or by the press, the *temporeras* are presented as working for pin money (a typical ruse to devalue female employment), when in fact their earnings will be essential to household survival. There is an anomaly here. This highly exploitative work does offer women the opportunity to possess independent wages at least for part of the year and this may have a profound impact upon patriarchal relations within families. As wages are paid directly to the woman, she has more say in how the money will be spent. Young women who work in the strawberry fields enjoy time away from what can be the stultifying atmosphere of the home, and women with partners can escape from domestic and childcare responsibilities. Women, however, pay a high price for this relative degree of autonomy in terms of the working conditions they must endure.[22]

Communal kitchens and organic farming

The global commodification of food supply has transformed relations of work and also changed gender roles within the family. Male migration to work, which will take them away from home for long periods of time and results in a growing proportion of households headed by single women, and women's work in the casualised, informal sector have had significant and often highly negative consequences. Long working shifts dissolve the difference between day and night with the result that members of poor households will eat when and where they can. This trend has stimulated a growth in the demand for fast food (with its consequences for family health and the disappearance of traditional foodstuffs and ways of cooking). In contemporary Latin and Central America, these processes are challenged by many experiments in collective kitchens and dining rooms and by food banks and food share schemes. These projects – which are, of course, occasioned by necessity and not choice – improve the access of low-income communities to affordable and nutritious food. Women assume a high profile in such programmes, which can also foster a sense of collective identity and resistance in the face of the destructive urges of global capital. Women are seen as providers where men cannot or will not be and as challenging conventional food production processes and marketing and selling networks.

The imposition of foreign tastes upon the type of food grown by peasant farmers in export-driven economies and the strong pressures for such farmers to adopt the practices of globalised agri-business and particularly the use of genetically modified seeds have provoked movements of opposition in many Latin and Central American countries. Organic farming is especially important to the Cuban economy. It was first pursued on that island as a means of getting Cuba through the difficult period following the collapse of the Soviet Union and the Eastern Bloc in the early to mid- 1990s. The 1989 Plan Alimentario (Food Plan) aimed to reduce Cuban dependency upon imported food and to achieve as much self-sufficiency in feeding the nation as was possible. Over time, state farms were transformed into cooperatives, and urban *huertos* (patio gardens) and *organoponicos* (large state-owned allotments where the labour of women and older people is key) have become responsible for satisfying a large part of the food needs of Cuban citizens. Cuba's success in moving towards food sovereignty has been consolidated by its involvement in fair trade initiatives and, since the later 1990s, it has also exported its organic technologies to countries such as Brazil and popular movements such as the Movimento dos Trabalhadores Rurais Sem Terra (MST, the Landless Workers Movement).[23]

Another example of the importance of food sustainability and its relation to women's activities can be provided by the case of indigenous women in Zapatista communities in southern Mexico, who link their participation in agro-ecological cooperatives with a defence of Mother Earth from the encroachment of pesticides and genetically modified crops. The adoption of organic farming practices is seen as intrinsic to the re-configuration of traditional ethnic identities. The demand for land reform is a central element of the EZLN's political programme but this objective has extended into the need to take control of the production and selling processes. Women in these cooperatives have benefited from links with similar organisations in other regions and countries through their participation in information and communications structures. Trips abroad and the proximity which electronic technology provides have served to overcome their sense of isolation. Communities have established agro-ecological schools, where parents teach children in organic techniques.[24] The success of organic farming programmes is not always predictable, as Linkogle's study of the pursuit of food security in Nicaragua demonstrates. In the 1990s, the Soy Nica enterprise sought to promote consumption of soya as an alternative to the traditional reliance upon meat. Women cooking in the *ollas communes* were happy to accept free supplies, but only until they became the recipients of international food aid in the shape of tinned beef and pork. After this, soya was rarely served. When faced with free food, and the opportunity to escape the time-consuming preparation of soya-based meals, poor women made the obvious choice.[25]

Women and industry

Women working in manufacturing industry and in mining have always been subject to management attempts to control and direct their labour and their behaviour in line with patriarchal perspectives upon gender roles and relations. Company towns exercised paternalist control over the lifestyles of working-class men and women and sought to pre-empt any organised protests or strikes by incorporating them into social welfare programmes. The latter, as Miller Klubock's study of Chilean mining suggests, were particularly concerned to enforce a 'gender ideology of domesticity', to affirm masculinity and to police women's sexuality.[26] Such endeavours did not, however, prevent women's mobilisation and their involvement in major strikes and their support for the Unidad Popular government. After the 1973 coup and the advent of the neo-liberal economy, the corporatist welfare state was dismantled and organised labour was repressed. Mining communities lost their cohesiveness as men were compelled to travel large distances to find work and many families fell into debt. Wives and daughters sought employment in the growing service sector, introducing them to super-exploitation in terms of wages and conditions of labour but also giving them relatively more mobility and independence.

The hallmark of neo-liberalism has been the informalisation of labour and the expansion of 'feminised occupational niches'.[27] These niches are characterised by the precarious nature of employment conditions caused by the erosion of regulatory mechanisms and protective legislation. Many women escape from rural poverty and land scarcity to find work in the *maquiladoras* (assembly line factories), many others from Mexico and Central America cross the border to work in the US, often illegally, while others follow traditional patterns of rural to urban migration to work as domestic servants or in micro-businesses (such as selling food or handicrafts in street markets). Since the 1960s, the Dominican Republic has moved rapidly from an agricultural economy based upon sugar to a service economy dependent on tourism, export manufacturing and agri-business. Under the auspices of the Caribbean Basin Initiative (introduced by the Reagan Administration to protect Washington's strategic interests), the Dominican Republic became the leading garment manufacturer in the region with a large female labour force but with men retaining the better-paid technical and managerial posts. Appalling working conditions and constraints upon collective bargaining have forced many women to leave export processing zones and turn to international migration or sex tourism.[28] Women have been regarded as a favoured workforce because their temperaments are seen as docile and so better suited to the monotony of the assembly line. Increasing access to the labour market, which provides women with their 'own' money, may allow them to 'negotiate more decisively their relationship with men'.[29] However this 'empowerment' can be transitory given the difficult economic circumstances poor women inhabit and it will only have a permanent impact if it affects women collectively and not just as individuals.

The forces of modern neo-liberal capitalist production attempt to construct gender along the most profitable lines and will, therefore, be keen to maintain rigid controls over women's reproduction. The prohibition on pregnancy in many industrial zones has already been noted; women may be compelled to accept contraceptive pills as a condition of employment, while some firms oblige women to prove their employability by displaying sanitary towels during their menstruation. The humiliation of this procedure and the violation of these women's bodies does not need to be stressed. Women working in the *maquiladoras* of Mexico are generally very young (sixteen- and seventeen-year-olds are the norm but it is not unusual to see fourteen-year-olds) and they experience long hours (which curtail their access to education) and harassment by overseers. Their working lives tend to be short; as exhausted women in their twenties leave the assembly plants, there are always younger ones waiting to take their jobs. Many women *maquila* workers have resisted the gendering of their work – that is, the paradigm of 'femininity' which constructs them as malleable and deferential – and have pursued militant labour demands as well as establishing links with other centres of production in Mexico and forging links with women workers in the US. [30] However, such activities expose them to real danger as management fights back. Violence is never far away from the daily reality of such women's lives. This fact is graphically demonstrated by the serial murders and disappearances of young women and girls in the bleak Mexican border town of Ciudad Juárez . Many disappeared on their way to school or to assembly jobs and were raped or tortured before they were killed and their bodies dumped. It is estimated that 300 women have suffered such a fate since 1993; the figure may be much higher. Government officials and the police force have been castigated for their failure to mount a serious inquiry; many commentators regard the state police as totally inept, while some believe they may be complicit in the murders. The bottom line, of course, is that the lives of these young women are not deemed important enough for their deaths to be investigated.[31]

Women *maquila* workers on *la frontera* with the United States are judged as 'illegals' if they decide to seek better-paid work in *el norte*. One of the bases of the new global economy is the ease with which borders can be crossed as investors seek access to sharply differentiated labour markets in pursuit of ever greater profits. Transnational agreements such as the North American Free Trade Association (NAFTA) depend upon mobile capital and, since its inception in 1994, Mexican governments have sought to create an inviting environment for US and Canadian and other foreign companies.[32] However, easy border crossings for capital and commodities contrast sharply with the strict immigration controls Washington imposes on human traffic. If women do succeed in crossing the border, they are generally shunted into sweatshop apparel or servile house-cleaning jobs that offer the least opportunity for vertical or even horizontal mobility. The perils and insecurities of clandestine employment are compounded by racist attitudes and the fact that immigrant social networks are more typically committed to the enforcement of traditional gender roles.

The recognition of identity politics as a determining dynamic of contemporary political mobilisation suggests certain problems with respect to strategy and progress. Poor women in Latin and Central America comprehend their identity in both individual and collective ways and may acknowledge certain elements of that identity differentially at separate points in time and under changing conditions. Identities are cultural narratives which shift their boundaries depending upon an individual's age, experience, location and in response to events and processes which the individual may be involved in or may have no influence over. That women can be defined in a multitude of ways may attest to the complexity of citizenship but it creates obstacles for collective political activity. In her study of Peruvian women peasant unionists in the late 1980s, Sarah Radcliffe found that respondents regarded themselves as women, as mothers, as *campesinas* (peasants), as poor people, as defenders of the land, as Indians fighting racism and as producers responsible for the reproduction of life for the sake of both their families and their communities. For these women, there was a perception that men would have to be persuaded of the rectitude of women's interests at the same time as organising alongside them within a complex political environment where domestic and international institutions and organisations would not be supportive of their collective concerns.[33] I now turn to an examination of the different ways in which different women have attempted to assert their claims upon citizenship.

Women's strategies for political empowerment

The United Nations Decade for Women, launched in Mexico City in 1975, highlighted gender concerns and created an environment in which individuals and movements could organise on behalf of women. Various strategies emerged but they were beset by numerous problems. The starting point for evaluating progress made is the obvious but still crucial point that women are not expected to engage in politics. Historically, there has been tremendous cultural resistance – within government circles and from parties of the right and left – to women's political participation. In order to begin to challenge these false assumptions, one needs to return to three central debates which have already received considerable attention in this book. The first is that there is an intimate link between democratisation and the exercise of citizenship and women's empowerment and that democracy cannot be seen to exist if the latter is absent. The meanings of politics and citizenship must be broadened in order to encompass women's concerns and experiences. The second debate is the need to press for equality of opportunity between and within genders but also to acknowledge the differences between women. The final consideration is an examination of how the state deals with women and how they respond to neglect, co-optation and repression (often at the same time). Organised women and women living their daily lives without recourse to public activism have historically had to negotiate with different forms of state in Latin and Central America and Cuba.

Throughout the twentieth century, military rule was central to state-building in these societies and this had enormous consequences for the gendering of the public sphere. Nevertheless, and particularly in the most recent spate of military interventions beginning in 1964, women made strenuous efforts to oppose their exclusion and to promote their own agendas. They were aided in this by the very same masculine preconceptions of military regimes which they sought to resist. While the latter suspended and attacked the rights of citizens (construed as male), they did not attribute political importance to women and so were taken by surprise when the latter began to mobilise. The corporatist project, associated most closely with Peronism in the 1940s and 1950s, sanctioned a limited political space for women but with the aim of constraining their influence over policy-making. Revolutionary governments in Cuba and Nicaragua adopted similar strategies albeit, and particularly in the Cuban case, promoting far greater equality and opportunities for women.

Women and democratising governments

Following processes of liberalisation and democratisation, new constitutions and civil codes affirmed women's legal status and elected assemblies legislated on their rights. However, the implementation of such laws and their positive reception within power structures which remain predominantly male have been flawed. These deficiencies have disillusioned and alienated some women but have spurred others on to accomplish change through political lobbying. Those who choose this route tend to focus upon specific issues and concentrate upon key points of entry into official politics. Sonia Alvarez has described how during the first post-military government led by José Sarney in Brazil, the National Council for Women's Rights worked to influence sympathetic state officials. Its aim was to initiate an incremental process of the redefinition of concepts of equity in the justice system, particularly as they related to violence against women.[34] The downside of the revival of electoral politics was that it augured the remasculinisation of the political arena, implicit in which was the return of women to the private sphere where they were expected to address the social issues created by restructuring and privatisation.[35]

Women wishing to continue to engage with institutionalised political power face a dilemma. If they hope to influence policy-makers and bureaucrats, they may be compelled to moderate gender-specific agendas in order to make them more acceptable. However, such a course is likely to estrange them from feminist groups and popular women's movements. The Peruvian activist, Maruja Barrig, has given her appraisal of the possibilities of empowerment through institutional routes. Processes which might appear to have had positive outcomes, such as women occupying important executive and legislative positions, the creation of women's ministries, legislation against domestic violence and the establishment of electoral quotas for political parties, may, in reality, be far more ambiguous.[36] The relatively few women who achieve high executive and legislative office will not automatically advance women's issues and, indeed, may work against them. When Violeta Barrios de Chamorro won the Nicaraguan elections in 1990 (dressed in white; employing the iconography of widowhood and peacemaker; her victory a combination of the political legacy of her husband Pedro, the owner of *La Prensa* newspaper who was assassinated in 1979 for his opposition to the Somoza dictatorship, public exhaustion with the war and US backing), her government embarked upon a ferocious restructuring programme. A contemporary popular saying – 'First it was a war of the bullets. Now it is a war of the stomach' – provided a commentary upon the experience of poor women.[37] Under Chamorro, the Nicaraguan National Assembly also introduced legislation banning homosexuality as sodomy and recognising rapists as the legal fathers of children conceived during their attacks.

Many governments have responded to women's lobbying by creating women's departments and agencies. The objective has been to acknowledge women's demands (they are, after all, voters) but in a manner which seeks to sanitise them and confine them to particular areas of policy-making (soft issues such as health and education, for example). When the Servicio Nacional de la Mujer (SERNAM – the National Women's Agency) was created by the incoming centre-left Concertación government in Chile in 1990, it was largely as a result of lobbying by women activists. The agency's remit was to encourage women's programmes and to scrutinise the activities of other government departments. In practice, its effectiveness was hampered by inadequate funding, impotence with respect to intervention in the affairs of other state institutions, and reactive campaigns conducted from within government and by conservative political groups and the Catholic Church (which successfully blocked its agenda on abortion). Its achievements – including considerable progress upon domestic violence legislation – were overshadowed by internal divisions stimulated by these outside pressures and made problematic by the criticism aimed at it by Chilean feminists. The latter saw SERNAM as an instrument of the state which was intent on creating a corporatist relationship with poor women. Georgina Waylen has argued that its management of funding has created a hierarchy of women's groups, with the middle class – who know how to work the system – having the advantage over poor women who do not. Apparently unable to please anybody, SERNAM also risked jeopardising its own survival because it depended upon women's mobilisation outside the official system to enable it to continue to apply pressure within it.[38]

Women and revolutionary governments

Following the 1959 Revolution, the Cuban government committed itself to women's empowerment and created the Federación de Mujeres Cubanas (FMC) to pursue that end. The state introduced educational and health reforms, promoted female employment and legalised divorce and, over time, abortion; many women took full advantage of the new opportunities afforded them and a qualitative difference could be detected between their lives and those of other Latin and Central American women. However, a number of significant obstacles remained in the way of women's advancement. Party and governmental hierarchies were dominated by men; women continued to be mainly responsible for domestic work (despite the fact that the 1975 Family Code legislated for equality within the home) and, thus, had to contend with food rationing and the scarcity of consumer goods and, in times of economic difficulty, their position in the labour market was the first to be challenged. Gender stereotypes persisted in education and in the existence of double standards of morality in terms of what were deemed appropriate behaviours for women and men. As an arm of the state, the FMC's role was to act as a transmission belt rather than to represent women's interests in an independent and critical fashion. The institutionalisation of women's concerns 'meant that no organisational form existed through which a different practice might have been encouraged'.[39]

There have been changes in recent years as the FMC began to operate with a greater degree of autonomy and more diverse women's voices began to be heard as the state wrestled with the idea of political democratisation. During the Special Period, the initiative which aimed to weather the hostile economic environment created by the collapse of the soviet bloc, the state sought an opening to the market which included a vigorous courting of foreign tourism. The incursion of the dollar has had many consequences, not least of which has been the revival of prostitution (which the new revolutionary government had sworn to destroy in the heady days of the 1960s). Young women's bodies are used in the construction of Cuba as a tourist paradise, much as they were in the 1950s. Sadly this is not a phenomenon exclusive to Cuba, but it is profoundly depressing given the inroads made towards women's emancipation.[40]

A similar although briefer account of the consequences of state feminism can be given with respect to the experience of Nicaraguan women under the FSLN government (1979–90). AMNLAE, the official organisation, worked most closely with women as mothers of fallen sons, not with women organised as feminists. The tremendous problems of under-development which the FSLN inherited were compounded by the escalation of the war and the militarisation of civilian life. Sandinista mothers had to confront the loss of children and partners, forced migrations, the destruction of harvests and mounting economic crisis, and their discontent grew. The revolutionary government was unwilling to confront the Catholic Church over abortion and there was very little public examination of the concepts of male power and of gender oppression. Tension also arose due to AMNLAE's lack of autonomy from the Sandinista state and the latter's manipulation of its agenda. Following the 1990 elections, the women's organisation split and a number of feminist groups emerged which sought to project less traditional modes of representation for women. Maxine Molyneux has argued that women's specific needs were subsumed under the exigencies of the war effort and a broad, national agenda which was shaped by male sensibility and it was, therefore, unsurprising that women's support for the 'Revolution' diminished over time.[41]

Women in political parties

In common with other countries, in 1991 Argentina introduced a quota law with which all political parties had to comply. Women were to make up at least one-third of candidates and were to be placed no lower than third on electoral lists. Many provincial and local elected bodies subsequently adopted similar measures. The reality is that women remain heavily under-represented and those who are elected are often members of the political elite. Now, it is by no means inevitable that elected women should identify with a gendered perspective but they are the ones who propose 'gender legislation' which, even if its scope and degree of implementation may be wanting, can at least provide a constitutionally guaranteed structure for women's activities. Molyneux has observed that while state and government structures contribute to maintaining patriarchy, they may also underwrite change. Thus, 'as purveyors of new rights, states have acted in certain ways to equalise the gender order and to remove some of the more striking forms of injustice'.[42] The kinds of women elected to office – their class, their ethnicity, their educational attainments, their political experiences – will be crucial to the future changes made to the lives of all other women living in Latin and Central American societies. The predominance of privileged women in government and bureaucracy suggests that they will neither understand nor empathise with the lives led by the vast majority of their counterparts.

Women's organisations have found it difficult to create common agendas in the face of cleavages based upon class and ethnicity. Right-wing women, from the upper and middle classes, and poor women have been suspicious of feminist groups, though for different reasons. Conservative women might identify with some feminist demands (such as an end to domestic violence or support for pay equity) but would regard many others as undermining their class interests as well as pursuing a left-wing ideology. Right-wing women have been far less likely to seek independent organisation and have concentrated upon rising from subordinate positions in male-dominated parties and state agencies. Such women have been manipulated by authoritarian governments in order to underpin traditional views on womanhood and to consolidate social control. Thus, Nicaraguan women had campaigned for suffrage and educational rights since the 1880s and a dynamic movement existed by the 1920s. However, under the aegis of the Somoza dynastic dictatorship, this feminist history was hijacked as women mobilised in the Ala Feminista (the Feminist Wing) in support of the state. The Ala brought together elite and poor women, albeit in segregated sections. Women were encouraged to base their understanding of citizenship upon fulfilment of their domestic roles and through their unswerving loyalty to the regime. Participation in the Ala did, however, offer middle-class women a stake in the traditionally male enclave of politics.[43]

The centrality of the Catholic Church to such transactions between state and women cannot be discounted. During the first forty years of the twentieth century, upper- and middle-class women in Argentina, Brazil and Chile established social welfare and educational projects as an extension of their roles as parishioners. Their aim was to win over poor and immigrant populations to what were deemed acceptable understandings of morality and femininity as a means of pre-empting the appeal of anarchist and socialist ideas.[44] A similar account can be given of the mobilisation of privileged women grouped in Poder Femenino (Feminine Power) in opposition to Allende's Unidad Popular government although, once in power, the Pinochet junta was swift to order women out of the sphere of politics and back to the home.[45]

Historically, female activists in left-wing parties felt excluded from internal cultures which did not value their contribution and were unwilling to take their demands seriously. The left's ability to engage with the politics of poor women's and feminist movements was as problematic as its relationship with popular organisations. Female activists, tired of being relegated to mundane tasks (as cooks, couriers or keepers of safe houses) and frustrated by the machismo of their colleagues (Peruvian male militants talked disparagingly about *las locas*, the madwomen, who were pressing gender-specific demands), broke from left-wing parties and formed their own organisations. These initiatives were stimulated and facilitated by the UN Decade of Women.[46] The subsequent histories of feminist groups were mixed. Some chose to lobby governments in the hope of effecting policy change; the consequence of such interactions has often been the moderation of their demands. Others have maintained their links with left-wing and progressive parties in an attempt to influence their programmes and change their attitudes (the so-called double militancy). Yet others have eschewed contacts with male-dominated institutions and espoused an independent or autonomous strategy (which has led to the criticism that they are isolating themselves from mainstream politics and thus from playing any role in its transformation). Many have worked to develop links with popular women's organisations.

Women from poor communities have often felt that feminists treat them in a patronising manner, expecting them to be deferential and accepting of agendas imposed upon them. They have been anxious about dealing with government or party bureaucracies whose language, behaviour and rules are foreign to them and suspicious about entering into dependent relationships with the state, the Church, political parties, other groups from civil society and NGOs. However, the reality is that poor women must enter into such relationships because they can facilitate improvements in their lives and may contribute to an incremental empowerment. The result has been an obstacle course with some progress made but innumerable setbacks endured as women have experimented with a variety of organisational techniques, dealt with diverse actors and agencies and mobilised in a variety of political spaces.

Debates, divisions and new relationships

The differences between Latin and Central American women have accounted for ongoing political debates and divisions. These problems have been most publicly demonstrated in sites such as the Encuentros Feministas Latinoamericano y del Caribe (the Latin American and Caribbean Feminist Meetings) which have brought together representatives of diverse organisations and sectors (academic, intellectual, artistic, political, separatist, grassroots, human rights and indigenous activists, lesbians and women of colour) since the first meeting in Bogotá in 1981. Following accusations that these meetings had been hijacked by white, middle-class, heterosexual women, alternative initiatives followed. The first lesbian Encuentro was held in Cuernavaca in Mexico in 1987, while indigenous women have created their own national and transnational networks. The Encuentros have been preoccupied by discussions concerning how feminism should be defined, what strategies are most appropriate, whether women should work with men or rely upon themselves and by complaints that poor women and women of colour are accorded second-class citizenship within the women's movement. Participants have articulated concerns about the efficacy of feminist lobbying in influencing the introduction of gender-sensitive legislation and the co-optation of feminist programmes by the state in the name of modernisation but with little discernible progress being made in terms of the lives of ordinary women and the daily struggles they face.[47]

Another worry has been the interventions of international organisations (such as the various UN agencies and World Bank programmes), advocacy networks (such as those promoting human rights) and NGOs and INGOs (international non-governmental organisations) and the effect their presence has upon women searching for citizenship and a more equitable political economy. In some instances, such contacts may have a radicalising impact upon the policies and financing priorities of international bodies (for example, Keck and Sikkink's discussion of the evolution of the relationship between the Mothers and Grandmothers of Argentina and the Ford Foundation[48]) but the general picture is not so promising. Thus, not all NGOs and INGOs incorporate gender practices into their agendas and if they do, they may be regarded as excessively radical and will not find favour with governments. It is also the case, as Jasmine Gideon points out, that 'participation' by local communities in NGO programmes 'is merely a euphemism for unpaid work' and that much of the responsibility for the implementation of projects 'has fallen on women [which] has added to their already stretched productive and reproductive responsibilities'.[49]

There has been considerable speculation in recent years concerning a surge in the political influence of the Latin American left. The most significant event was the election of Luís Inácio Lula Da Silva as president of Brazil in October 2002.[50] Lula – a veteran trade unionist and a leader of the Partido dos Trabalhadores (PT) – was seen as being committed to implementing wide-ranging social justice programmes which would incorporate the poor and the hitherto excluded into the Brazilian political system. It has been argued that the PT shares with feminist discourse 'a vision of social transformation that goes beyond piecemeal legislative change or the demand for more opportunity in the existing social and political system' and that both 'strive to maintain their links to the popular base even as they work with elites in the existing political system'.[51] However, despite the PT's adoption of a more progressive gender agenda than other parties and a higher incidence of female candidates, its critics have feared that the quota requirement of 30% of women in leadership posts could be used as a glass ceiling and have complained of the prevailing sexist culture within the party as well as its reticence concerning abortion so as not to anger the Catholic Church. The PT's prospects in government will depend upon how effective its reform programme is and how the international community responds to a progressive government in Latin America's largest state. It will also be interesting to see how it acts to maintain its links with popular movements and particularly with the MST. The latter has been criticised for its conservative approach towards issues of gender and sexuality; very few women militants occupy leadership positions within its ranks, although they are prominent in occupations and the organisation of landless camps and settlements. It appears that women are achieving some measure of change in terms of their status and the respect accorded them within the MST.[52] If the PT government is to address gender issues, it is essential that it be lobbied by independent, critical voices both within and outside the official political arena.

The profile of Zapatista women in the southern states of Mexico is far more prominent than that of female *sem-terra* in Brazil. Women from the Mam, Tzotzil, Tzeltal and Tojolabal communities have been involved in the EZLN's peace talks panel, 'Indigenous Rights and Culture', since 1995 and have led discussions on discrimination in the workplace, state institutions and in the home. While determined to defend traditional cultural practices which define their identities, they have publicly rejected exclusionary practices which focus upon women, calling for the right to choose partners, to live free from domestic violence, to enjoy reproductive rights, to have access to education, to inherit land and to hold office. Women work in cooperatives, health projects and rural banks, have expanded their contacts with other women, for example Guatemalan refugees, and have learnt how to negotiate with authorities and, in so doing, have broadened their experience and confidence in themselves. Many men – and some women – have been resistant to overturning traditional attitudes and behaviour but have been convinced that the democratisation of rural life and a recognition of women's rights is essential if the Zapatista communities are going to survive. The EZLN itself (while mindful of its repudiation of a leadership role) has promoted negotiations between women and men concerning roles and responsibilities. Women militants control their own sexual activity (although given that they are not expected to become pregnant, a downside is that many are separated from their children, who live with grandparents outside the militarised zones). The possibility of the creation of new social arrangements in southern Mexico is, of course, imperilled by the military siege closing in on the communities and the efforts made by local landowners and paramilitaries to polarise internal divisions within them or, failing that, to terrorise them. As we have seen, women are particularly vulnerable to such aggression.

None of the political relationships Latin and Central American women experience in their pursuit of citizenship offer easy or straightforward trajectories. No one programme of activism should be privileged to the exclusion of others. The cumulative value of women's activities – be they political lobbying, feminism or popular mobilisation – can only be a constructive one if women respect each other's choices and are supportive of them. Short-term achievements are to be welcomed but only in the understanding that the movement toward women's empowerment as citizens remains a long and difficult struggle.

Notes

1 L. Rayas, 'Criminalizing abortion: a crime against women', *NACLA Report on the Americas*, 31:4 (Jan./Feb. 1998), 22.

2 L. Stephen, 'The construction of indigenous suspects: militarisation and the gendered and ethnic dynamics of human rights abuses in Southern Mexico' in M. S. Gutmann, F. V. Matos Rodríguez, L. Stephen and P. Zavela (eds), *Perspectives on Las Américas: A Reader in Culture, History, and Representation* (Oxford: Blackwell, 2002), p. 395.

3 M. Thomson, 'A step backwards for women's rights', *Central America Women's Network Newsletter*, 18 (Winter 2003).

4 N. Craske, *Women and Politics in Latin America* (Cambridge: Polity, 1999), p. 17.

5 There is a large literature on mothers' groups. Among many useful texts are P. M. Chuchryk, 'Feminist anti-authoritarian politics: the role of women's organisations in the Chilean transition to democracy' in J. S. Jaquette (ed.), *The Women's Movement in Latin America: Feminism and the Transition to Democracy* (Boston: Unwin Hyman, 1989); J. Schirmer, 'The seeking of the truth and the gendering of consciousness: the co-madres of El Salvador and the Convigua widows of Guatemala' in S. A. Radcliffe and S. Westwood (eds), *'Viva': Women and Popular Protest in Latin America* (London: Routledge, 1993) and J. Fisher, *Out of the Shadows: Women, Resistance and Politics in South America* (London: Latin American Bureau, 1993), ch. 4.

6 S. E. Alvarez, *Engendering Democracy in Brazil: Women's Movements in Transition Politics* (Princeton, NJ: Princeton University Press, 1990), p. 50.

7 The Frente Sandinista de Liberación Nacional (FSLN – the Sandinista Front for National Liberation) took state power in 1979 following a popular insurrection. The new revolutionary state's hegemony was challenged by Contra right-wing groups, financed by the USA, and the country, already devastated by decades of plunder by the Somoza dynasty, plunged into civil war.

8 See L. Bayard de Volo, *Mothers of Heroes and Martyrs: Gender Identity Politics in Nicaragua, 1979–1999* (Baltimore, MD: Johns Hopkins University Press, 2001).

9 L. A. Pérez Jnr, *On Becoming Cuban: Identity, Nationality and Culture* (Chapel Hill, NC: University of North Carolina Press, 1999), p. 141.

10 For an account of Cuban sex tourism before the Revolution see R. Schwartz, *Pleasure Island: Tourism and Temptation in Cuba* (Lincoln, NB: University of Nebraska Press, 1997).

11 Miranda's unhappy experiences in Hollywood are examined in A. M. López, 'Are all Latins from Manhattan? Hollywood, ethnography and cultural colonialism' in J. King, A. M. López and M. Alvarado, *Mediating Two Worlds: Cinematic Encounters in the Americas* (London: BFI, 1993). In her earlier incarnation as the public voice of samba in Brazil, Carmen Miranda has been credited with using her persona to convey social criticism and 'to defy gender roles that sought to confine women', although as a white Portuguese women she has also been criticised for acting as an acceptable interpreter – in a racist society – of what was essentially black music. See D. J. Davis, 'Racial purity and national humor: exploring Brazilian samba from Noel Rosa to Carmen Miranda, 1930–1939' in W. H. Beasley and L. A. Curcio-Nagy (eds), *Latin American Popular Culture: An Introduction* (Wilmington, DE: Scholarly Books, 2000), p. 189.

12 Rayas, 'Criminalizing abortion', 26. Cuba enjoys a very low rate of maternal mortality compared to its neighbours and women's health in abortion procedures is prioritised. However, it has markedly high abortion rates as abortion is used as de facto contraception. One of the reasons for this is that birth control devices are in short supply because of the US blockade.

13 M. Lamas, 'Standing fast in Mexico: protecting women's rights in a hostile climate', *NACLA Report on the Americas*, 34:5 (Mar./Apr. 2001), 37.

14 M. Lamas, 'Scenes from a Mexican battlefield', *NACLA Report on the Americas*, 31:4 (Jan./Feb. 1998).

15 Thomson, 'A step backwards'.

16 Susana Vicente, 'Democracy and reproductive rights: the right to decide', *Peru Update*, 98 (Mar./Apr. 2003), 5. Forced sterilisation is not new. One of the most infamous episodes is recorded in Jorge Sanjinés' 1969 film *Blood of the Condor* which depicts actual events which took place in a US-sponsored clinic in Bolivia. It has been estimated that 49% of Puerto Rican women between the ages of fifteen and forty-nine have been sterilised – a legacy of US-funded campaigns (Rayas, 'Criminalizing abortion', 26).

17 J. M. Pilcher, 'Many chefs in the national kitchen: cookbooks and identity

in nineteenth-century Mexico' in Beezley and Curcio-Nagy (eds), *Latin American popular culture*, p. 131.

18 *Ibid.*, p. 132.

19 See B. Anderson, *Imagined Communities: Reflections on the Origin and Spread of Nationalism* (London: Verso, 2nd edn, 1991).

20 See C. R. Spindel, 'The social invisibility of women's work in Brazilian agriculture' in C. D. Deere and M. Leon (eds), *Rural Women and State Policy: Feminist Perspectives on Latin American Agricultural Development* (Boulder, CO: Westview Press, 1987).

21 C. Enroe, *Bananas, Beaches and Bases: Making Feminist Sense of International Politics* (London: Pandora, 1989), p. 149.

22 See S. Barrientos, A. Bee, A. Matear and I. Vogel, *Women in Agribusiness: Working Miracles in the Chilean Fruit Export Sector* (Basingstoke: Macmillan, 2000).

23 The classic book on Cuban organic farming is P. Rosset and M. Benjamin, *The Greening of the Revolution* (Melbourne: Ocean Press, 1994).

24 The agro-ecological initiatives of indigenous women are discussed by A. Hernández-Castillo, *Histories and Stories from Chiapas: Border Identities in Southern Mexico* (Austin, TX: University of Texas Press, 2001).

25 S. Linkogle, 'Soya, culture and international food aid: the case of a Nicaraguan communal kitchen', *Bulletin of Latin American Research*, 17:1 (1998). Of course, while dependency upon aid is only storing up trouble for the future, it can be argued that reliance upon soya – a crop which is not native to Nicaragua – would not constitute a step in the right direction in terms of food sustainability.

26 T. Miller Klubock, 'From welfare capitalism to the free market in Chile: gender, culture, and politics in the copper mines' in G. M. Joseph, C. C. Legrand and R. D. Salvatore (eds), *Close Encounters of Empire: Writing the Cultural History of US–Latin American Relations* (Durham, NC: Duke University Press, 1998), p. 372.

27 S. Chant and N. Craske, *Gender in Latin America* (London: Latin American Bureau, 2003), p. 207.

28 H. I. Safa, 'Women and globalization: lessons from the Dominican Republic' in J. Chase (ed.), *The Spaces of Neoliberalism* (Hartford, CT: Kumarian Press, 2002).

29 Chant and Craske, *Gender in Latin America*, p. 225.

30 Useful accounts of the nature of *maquila* production are given in L. Sklair, *Assembling for Development: The Maquila Industry in Mexico and the USA* (Boston: Unwin Hyman, 1989) and A. Dwyer, *On the Line: Life on the US–Mexican Border* (London: Latin American Bureau, 1994).

31 D. Nathan, 'Work, sex and danger in Ciudad Juárez', *NACLA Report on the Americas*, 33:3 (Nov./Dec. 1999). She makes a direct connection between the fact that the city has the highest rate of domestic violence in Mexico with the institutionalised violence meted out to women in the *maquilas*.

32 The NAFTA agreement between Mexico, Canada and the United States was signed on 1 January 1994 and was hailed by its supporters as the first stage of a process of economic and political integration of the Americas.

Its detractors contend that NAFTA is just another stage in the dismantling of the economic sovereignty of latino economies and another expression of US hegemonic thrust.

33 S. A. Radcliffe, 'Multiple identities and negotiation over gender: female peasant union leaders in Peru', *Bulletin of Latin American Research*, 9:2 (1990).

34 S. E. Alvarez, 'Contradictions of women's space in a male-dominated state: the political role of the commissions on the status of women in post-authoritarian Brazil' in E. Staudt (ed.), *The Bureaucratic Mire: Women, International Development and Politics* (Philadelphia, PA: Temple University Press, 1997).

35 See N. Craske, 'Remasculinisation and the neoliberal state in Latin America' in V. Randall and G. Waylen (eds), *Gender, Politics and the State* (London: Routledge, 1998).

36 M. Barrig, 'Latin American feminism: gains, losses and hard times', *NACLA Report on the Americas*, 34:5 (Mar./April 2001).

37 Quoted in Bayard de Volo, *Mothers of Heroes and Martyrs*, p. 155.

38 G. Waylen, 'Democratization, feminism and the state in Chile: the establishment of SERNAM' in S. M. Rai and G. Lievesley (eds), *Women and the State: International Perspectives* (London: Taylor & Francis, 1996). See also A. Matear, 'Gender and the state in rural Chile', *Bulletin of Latin American Research*, 16:1 (1997).

39 M. Randall, *Gathering Rage: The Failure of Twentieth-Century Revolutions to Develop a Feminist Agenda* (New York: Monthly Review Press, 1992), p. 40.

40 For a discussion of contemporary prostitution, see C. Fusco, 'Hustling for dollars: *Jinterismo* in Cuba', in K. Kempadoo and J. Doezema (eds), *Global Sex Workers: Rights, Resistance, and Redefinition* (New York: Routledge, 1998).

41 M. Molyneux, 'Mobilisation without emancipation? Women's interests, state and revolution in Nicaragua' in D. Salter (ed.), *New Social Movements and the State in Latin America* (Amsterdam: CEDLA, 1985). See also A. Criquillon, 'The Nicaraguan women's movement: feminist reflections from within' in M. Sinclair (ed.), *The New Politics of Survival: Grassroots Movements in Central America* (New York: Monthly Review Press, 1995).

42 M. Molyneux, 'State formations in Latin America' in E. Dore and M. Molyneux (eds), *Hidden Histories of Gender and the State in Latin America* (Durham, NC: Duke University Press, 2000), p. 40.

43 V. González, 'Somocista women: right-wing politics and feminism in Nicaragua, 1936–1979' in V. González and K. Kampwirth (eds), *Radical Women in Latin America: Left and Right* (University Park, PA: Pennsylvania State University Press, 2001).

44 S. McGee Deutsch, 'Spreading right-wing patriotism, femininity, and morality: women in Argentina, Brazil, and Chile, 1900–1940' in González and Kampwirth (eds), *Radical Women*.

45 Allende's government had not addressed women's citizenship issues, nor had it improved their position within society. Indeed, UP discourse was disturbingly close to the traditional views espoused by the military. See G. Waylen, 'Rethinking women's political participation and protest: Chile 1970–1990', *Political Studies*, 40 (1992).

46 G. Lievesley, *Democracy in Latin America: Mobilization, Power and the Search for a New Politics* (Manchester: Manchester University Press, 1999), pp. 143–5. In her seminal study of Chilean feminism, Julieta Kirkwood contended that the left's failure to engage with the women's movement was instrumental in explaining why the right had been able to mobilise against Allende: *Ser política en Chile: Las feministas y los partidos* (Santiago: FLACSO, 1986).

47 F. Macaulay, 'Getting gender on the policy agenda: a study of a Brazilian feminist lobby group' in Dore and Molyneux (eds), *Hidden Histories*. For accounts of the Encuentros see N. Saporta Stembach, M. Navaro-Aanguren and S. E. Alvarez, 'Feminism in Latin America: from Bogotá to San Bernardo', in A. Escobar and S. E. Alvarez (eds), *The Making of Social Movements in Latin America* (Boulder, CO, Westview Press, 1992) and E. Beckman, 'The eighth Encuentro', *NACLA Report on the Americas*, 34:5 (Mar./April 2001).

48 M. Keck and K. Sikkink, *Activists Beyond Borders* (Ithaca, NY: Cornell University Press, 1998), ch. 3.

49 J. Gideon, 'The politics of social service provision through NGOs: a study of Latin America', *Bulletin of Latin American Research*, 17:3 (1998).

50 Other developments include the 1999 election of the left-centre Concertación coalition in Chile; the election of President Néstor Kirchner in Argentina in May 2003; the important role played by the Movimiento al Socialismo (Movement Towards Socialism) in Bolivian politics and innumerable electoral successes at state and municipal levels (including the capture of the mayoralties of Mexico City and Bogotá). It is difficult to judge whether this leftward trend can be sustained and, of course, whether such political actors will actually work on behalf of women's empowerment.

51 L. Haas, 'Changing the system from within? Feminist participation in the Brazilian Workers' Party' in González and Kampwirth (eds), *Radical Women*, p. 250.

52 The position of women in the MST is described in S. Branford and J. Rocha, *Cutting the Wire: The Story of the Landless Movement in Brazil* (London: Latin American Bureau, 2002), pp. 258–262.

6

Committees of Soldiers' Mothers: mothers challenging the Russian state

CATHERINE J. DANKS

Introduction: 'Democracy without women is not democracy!'

'Democracy without women is not democracy!' was a slogan of the Russian independent women's movement in the 1990s. The slogan captured the paradox that at the very time when democratisation appeared to offer all citizens the possibility of self-determined participation in political, economic and social life, barriers to women's participation were mounting. However, one of post-Communist Russia's enduring non-governmental organisations (NGOs) is the Union of Soldiers' Mothers Committees of Russia (UCSMR), which now has 300 committees throughout the country and draws thousands of women into their activities. The original Soldiers' Mothers Committee was founded in 1989 by a group of mothers who had lost their sons in the Afghan War (1979–89) and who wanted to ensure that Afghan war invalids received social security, qualified medical help, wheelchairs, artificial limbs, jobs and pensions.[1] They also had a broader goal 'to defend the rights of those due to be conscripted into the military, of military servicemen and members of their families'.[2] The activities of the Soldiers' Mothers are much broader than just protecting their sons. As Dr Ida Kuklina, a secretary of the UCSMR, Russian Academician and political scientist, explains: 'The mothers' love, the mothers' aspirations to defend their children, turned very soon into conscious human rights activity ... The soldiers' mothers understood that to defend their children they have to change the State and society. Their call for human rights in all military power structures meant a call for democracy.'[3]

This chapter analyses women and democratisation in post-Communist Russia and explains the strength and importance of the Soldiers' Mothers. The chapter first places democratisation in its historical context and explains the barriers to women's participation that have developed during democratisation. It then examines the political discourses available to women during democratisation, specifically feminism and women's rights, human rights and motherhood. It seeks to explain why motherhood has provided Russian women with a potent mobilising ideology through which they are able to challenge the Russian state. Finally it examines the activities of the Soldiers' Mothers and explains why their activities are important to women's exercise of citizenship and to the development of civil society in Russia's 'managed democracy'.

Women and democratisation

Post-Communist democratisation and the obstacles to women's political participation

Under soviet socialism the gatekeeper to public life was the Communist Party of the Soviet Union (CPSU) which had an ideological commitment to women's emancipation. While there was a good deal of rhetoric around this commitment and certainly before Reconstruction (1985–91) there was no tolerance of independent political activity or rival agendas, it did however mean that soviet women were well-educated, economically active outside the home and accustomed to social and political activism. During Reconstruction, people throughout the USSR took advantage of the freer political environment to organise themselves and to promote a wide range of political, social, cultural and nationality-based agendas. This was democratisation 'from below', as soviet women and men pushed at the restrictions of elite-sponsored democratisation. The late 1980s to mid-1990s witnessed a mushrooming of new NGOs and a cursory examination of website listings, handbooks and directories suggests that Russia now enjoys a vibrant NGO scene. However, research by the St Petersburg Open Society Organisation has found that only about 30 per cent of NGOs really exist.[4] The rest have fallen victim to a lack of resources or funds, exhaustion, inertia and frustration. This explains NGO websites that have not been updated for years and telephone and fax numbers that no longer work. In addition to these general problems experienced by all would-be activists, women are confronted by a range of very practical problems that act as obstacles, but not insuperable barriers, to political participation. For example, the end of soviet socialism saw women disproportionately hit by unemployment, social welfare spending has not kept pace with spiralling demand, childcare services have been reduced, and in the mid-1990s even government ministers began to speak of the 'feminisation of poverty'. The practical business of day-to-day living now takes up even more of women's time than before.

Women and elite recruitment: from USSR to Russia

In the USSR membership of the CPSU and the soviets (councils or representative bodies) was governed by an elaborate system of quotas to ensure the representation of women, workers, peasants, young people and different nationalities. Before Reconstruction the soviets at all levels were essentially rubber stamps for policies decided by the CPSU. Throughout the entire soviet period the closer one came to the CPSU's Politburo, the real apex of power in the USSR, the fewer women were to be found, a pattern discernible elsewhere, as Susan Buckingham has already identified in Chapter 3. The Politburo only ever had three women members: Ekaterina Furtseva (1957–60), Aleksandra Biryukova (1988–90) and Galina Semenova (1990–91). Women were allocated around 30 per cent of the seats in the USSR Supreme Soviet (parliament) and between 40 and 50 per cent of seats in the soviets at republican level and below. Reconstruction-era electoral reforms saw the introduction of multi-candidate elections for the soviets at all levels, although the CPSU remained the only legal political party until 1990. This rather modest electoral reform reduced the CPSU's ability to enforce its quota system and following the 1989 USSR Supreme Soviet elections the percentage of women deputies fell to 15.7 per cent, and the 1990 elections to the Russian Republic parliament saw the percentage of women deputies fall to only 5 per cent. Lievesley's discussion in Chapter 1 also points out the decline in opportunities for women in post-soviet Russia. Reforms to the electoral system begun in the late 1980s produced representative bodies from the parliament in Moscow to local soviets, in which the once substantial women's presence was dramatically reduced.

In post-Communist Russia the percentage of women's deputies briefly rose to 14 per cent in 1993 only to fall again to 10 per cent in 1995 and then to 8 per cent in 1999. Following the December 2003 Duma (the lower house of parliament) elections, that is over ten years after Russia declared its commitment to democracy, the percentage of women deputies stands at just 9 per cent. The significance of this low percentage is that according to the United Nations a critical mass of at least 30 per cent female membership is required to ensure that a parliament considers issues such as childcare and women's social problems as an integral part of its normal activities (see also Chapter 3 for a further discussion of critical mass).[5]

Obstacles to women's elite recruitment

Russian economic and political life is now dominated by informal male networks, which act as the gatekeepers to the formal economic and political structures. According to Maria Arbatova, a Russian feminist commentator, 'the new Russian political elite was born in a very specific way. [During perestroika], while women were waiting in line for food, men carved up the country into pieces.'[6] Writing before the 2003 elections Arbatova pointed out that men owned 92 per cent of Russia's private property and occupied a similar percentage of seats in the Duma. Russian women face a number of obstacles in standing for election and winning a seat in the Duma. According to the Russian political scientist Svetlana Aivazova there are plenty of competent, qualified women with an interest in taking part in politics.[7] Women are also well-represented among the educated and professional social groups from which many candidates are drawn, but they are under-represented in those groupings and networks that form the basis of the post-Communist political and economic elite. The main barrier to women's elite recruitment is created by the clientelist networks that dominate Russia's public sphere and the fact that 'the majority of women-candidates do not represent any influential groups of [the] political or business elite, which also significantly diminishes the chances of success, especially considering the manipulative nature of the contemporary Russian democracy.'[8] The continued importance of informal networks is in part a reflection of the weakness of civil society, which facilitates the dominance of the public sphere by existing elites.

Political parties in Russia today are not grassroots organisations but rather organisations created by members of the existing elite to harvest votes. Women are less likely to be selected to stand by a political party and will typically receive less funding for their campaigns than male candidates. For the December 2003 Duma election only the Union of Rightist Forces and the Russian Communist Party had any women in their top ten candidates on the federal party list, and the pro-Putin United Russia had no women candidates on its list.[9] When women candidates are included on a party's list of candidates, they tend not to be placed high enough to ensure election. In 1997 the Duma debated a proposal to establish a 30 per cent quota for women in parliament and government structures, but this was voted down on its second reading. In April 2002 the Duma again discussed a proposed amendment to a federal election law restricting a party to a maximum of 70 per cent of its candidates being of the same sex. The proposal was not passed. The use of quotas during the Communist period means that they have been devalued as part of anti-democratic manipulation of the electoral system, rather than a device to boost the number of women candidates from all political parties.

Women's political parties

The Soviet Women's Committee provided the structure and leadership for a new women's political party in the early 1990s. In 1990 under the leadership of Alevtina Fedulova, the Soviet Women's Committee became a NGO called the Union of Women of Russia, which quickly began to campaign for legislation on women's and children's issues and to prepare women to stand for political office. In 1993, the Union of Women of Russia united with the Association of Russian Business Women led by Tatyana Maliutina and the Union of Navy Women chaired by Marina Dobrovol'skaya to form a new political movement called Women of Russia. The Women of Russia movement recognised the unwillingness of other political parties to adopt women candidates and to promote women's issues. Women of Russia campaigned to promote women's involvement in the political and social life of the country at the federal, regional and local levels.[10] They selected women to stand in the December 1993 Duma elections and received 8 per cent of the vote and had twenty-five deputies. Women of Russia championed socially-oriented policies, and social and state support for the family. Their origins in the Soviet Women's Committee meant that its leaders were accustomed to working closely with government to promote women and family issues, a role they now continued in the reformed Duma. For example, Women of Russia deputy Galina Klimantova served as the chair of the Duma Committee on Women and the Family (1993–95). Klimantova played a leading role in the drafting of the new Family Code (1995) and legislation on domestic violence and on the protection of reproductive rights. In addition to these legislative initiatives, Women of Russia also lobbied executive, legislative and judicial bodies and the mass media on behalf of women's interests and to raise the status of women.

In subsequent elections the fortunes of Women of Russia plummeted and in the 1995 and 1999 Duma elections the party failed to reach the 5 per cent threshold for entry into the Duma by party list. Women of Russia had clear radical and conservative wings and this contributed to the break-up of the party as leading members left to join other political parties. Fedulova now supports the pro-Putin United Russia party. The 1999 election was contested by another women's political party called the Party for the Defence of Women headed by Tatyana Roshchina. The Party for the Defence of Women was committed to charitable programmes and social projects designed to help women, families and children but gained only 0.6 per cent of the vote. The absence of a specifically women's party has resulted in the loss of an important focus for women's activities within the Duma. While there are still women deputies their party allegiance runs across the political spectrum and they do not form a women's caucus.

The Russian transition to 'managed democracy'

When the Russian Federation (Russia) came into existence on 1 January 1992 it was described as being 'in transition' from soviet socialism to a liberal democracy with a market economy. While these were the stated goals of Boris Yeltsin, the first post-Communist president, their attainment is by no means inevitable. There is no automatic linear progression from soviet socialism to a democratic, capitalist Russia. There are no easy steps to follow and advances in some areas have been frustrated by difficulties and setbacks in others. The weakness of Russia's civil society, for example, has facilitated the development of a super-presidential system with a weak parliament. Yeltsin's successor President Vladimir Putin was first elected in 2000 committed to the concept of a strong Russian state (*gosudarstvennost'*) characterised by order, security and stability. Putin was elected following the renewal in 1999 of hostilities against Chechnia. Putin claims Chechnia as a constituent republic of the Russian Federation, but many Chechens assert their right to independence. The strengthening of the Russian state and the maintenance of its territorial integrity means that Putin has vigorously pursued a military campaign against the Chechen rebels.

Putin's strong Russian state has also been achieved by weakening all institutions apart from the presidency, the presidential administration and the security forces. Putin has brought the Federation Council (Parliament's upper house) and the once powerful regional leaders under increasing control. The judiciary, which was beginning to assert its independence, is once again coming under political domination. The mass media after a period of independence and pluralism in the 1990s have become more compliant and much less critical. In order to achieve this Putin has variously persuaded Russia's economic elite to either back him or stay out of politics and continue to enjoy their wealth, and subjected those who continue to challenge him to administrative and judicial attacks.

Putin advocates a 'managed democracy' for Russia. This entails using democratic means to solve problems that can be solved democratically, but adopting an authoritarian approach to problems that cannot be solved by democratic means. The arbiter of which approach is applicable is President Putin and his administration. Managed democracy means that elections are held and NGOs are allowed to exist, but that they must be 'managed' to achieve the appropriate results. So for example the 7 December 2003 Duma elections were 'managed' to ensure that the United Russia party won two-thirds of the seats and the remaining seats are held by parties which tend to vote with United Russia. The Organisation for Security Cooperation in Europe (OSCE) reported that the election was marked by 'serious shortcomings' and 'failed to meet OSCE and Council of Europe commitment for democratic elections'.[11] The OSCE also found that the March 2004 presidential election process that resulted in Putin's re-election with 70 per cent of the votes cast 'did not adequately reflect principles necessary for a healthy democratic process' such as 'a vibrant political discourse and meaningful pluralism'.[12]

Putin has also sought to co-opt and control civil society organisations by creating an administrative structure for them. In June and November 2001 he invited NGOs to a Civic Forum in order to open a dialogue between civil society and the Kremlin. The invitations were issued quite selectively, for example the human rights organisations Memorial[13] and the UCSMR were not invited to the June meeting. Memorial and the Soldiers' Mothers shine an unflattering light on aspects of Putin's Russia, which now stands accused by international and Russian human rights organisations of human rights abuses against Chechens and the deployment of young Russian conscripts in Chechnia against their will and in contravention of their constitutional rights.[14] As Putin's managed democracy has brought Russia's representative institutions, judiciary and mass media into line, Russia's NGOs play a vital role in maintaining a Russian civil society that can challenge the Russian state. The role of the Soldiers' Mothers, in encouraging women's participation and in holding the Russian state to account for its actions, is vital not just to the development of women's citizenship but also to Russia's broader democratisation.

Discourses as paths into politics

Feminism: from soviet dissent to Russian irrelevance?

As Chapter 1 has already discussed, 1970s feminism inspired a new generation of women in the West to social and political activism and underpinned new academic analyses of the concept of citizenship. In contrast in the USSR western-style feminism was a dissident activity undertaken by only a handful of women. Feminism and feminists if mentioned at all were depicted negatively in the soviet media. Feminist literature was not officially published and was only available in illegal, self-published (*samizdat*) copies. A *samizdat* feminist journal called *Almanach for Women about Women*, which circulated in Leningrad in the late 1970s was published in the West as *Women and Russia: First Feminist Samizdat*.[15] It was probably more widely read outside than inside the USSR. For most soviet women feminism was either unknown or an alien western ideology with little or nothing to offer them.

In 1991 before the collapse of the USSR the Russian feminist Ol'ga Lipovskaia explained that 'feminism is ... associated with the state exploitation of women in the labour force ... The total responsibility of women for childcare and domestic chores is never questioned.'[16] Many of the concerns of western feminism seemed irrelevant to soviet women, for whom paid employment was part of a double burden, which together with their responsibilities for the home and family led to exhaustion not liberation. Similarly, western feminism's focus on abortion rights rang hollow to soviet women who since 1955 had had the right to abortion, but who due to economic and housing constraints could rarely choose to have more than one child. Daša Duhaček writing about the hostility to western feminism in Eastern Europe explains that women in the state socialist countries and the West have very different understandings of the private sphere of the family. For women living in authoritarian regimes, the family, for all its possible problems, provided a space where women could express themselves freely, a residual civil society and a substitute public sphere and site of resistance.[17] Western feminism is not only seen as anti-men but also anti-family, which for women in state socialist countries was a sanctuary and source of strength against the world outside.

Feminist ideas have found a limited home in academic life: for example, in May 1990 the feminist economist Anastasia Posadskaya founded the Moscow Centre for Gender Studies. This followed a seminar organised by the Independent Women's Democratic Initiative, whose initials in Russian spells 'Ne Zhdi!' which means 'Don't Wait!' It was the manifesto of the Don't Wait! conference that provided the slogan

'Democracy without women is no democracy!', which was adopted by the first Independent Women's Forum in 1991 and later by the Women of Russia movement. In 1991 the First Independent Women's Forum, the Moscow Centre for Gender Studies and the Free Association of Feminist Organisations (SAFO) established the Women's Information Network (Zhenset). This is an on-line database designed to keep women's organisations in contact, disseminate information and to build a women's community. Zhenset's work has been supported by the Eurasia Foundation, USAID, the Global Fund for Women, NIS-US Women's NGO Consortium, and the Embassy of The Netherlands.[18] The Consortium of Women's Non-Government Associations [19] and the Information Centre of the Independent Women's Forum [20] similarly maintain regularly updated websites to disseminate feminist ideas and information about women's NGOs. While feminist ideas have not provided a significant mobilising ideology for Russian women, the soviet tradition of women's activism focusing on children, the family and women's concerns has continued. This tradition combined with the impact Russia's transition, has created a situation in which women's NGOs are the most vigorous and dynamic part of Russian civil society. In addition to the Soldiers' Mothers, there are also NGOs of Russian businesswomen, entrepreneurs and professionals, crisis centres and charitable organisations.

Human rights: from soviet dissent to Russian democratisation?

The UCSMR describes itself as a human rights NGO, which aims to defend the rights of conscripts and recruits. This self-description is quite remarkable in a country that lacks a human rights discourse. The USSR was a signatory to the United Nations Universal Declaration of Human Rights (1948) but did not inform its citizens of the Declaration's contents. The USSR was also a signatory to the Helsinki Accords (1975), which committed its participants to respect human rights, and successive soviet constitutions enshrined various rights but they also imposed corresponding duties. The whole tenor of the soviet period was that the state and the collective had precedence over individual rights. From the 1960s onwards dissidents called on the soviet state to observe the rights enshrined in its own constitutions and laws and in response they were subjected to harassment and imprisonment. Ella Polyakova,[21] a leading member of the St Petersburg Soldiers' Mothers Organisation, cited these soviet-era dissidents, specifically Vladimir Bukovsky and Alexander Yesenin-Volpin, and the dissident slogan 'Observe the existing laws' as inspirations for the St Petersburg Soldiers' Mothers. Chapter 2 of the 1993 Russian Federation Constitution[22] is entitled 'The Rights and Liberties of Man and Citizen' and was supposed to signal Russia's commitment to human and civic rights. In 1996 Russia was admitted to the Council of Europe[23] despite the Council's concerns over Russia's actions in Chechnia. President Yeltsin established a Presidential Commission on Human Rights, whose first chair was Sergei Kovalyov, a former dissident who had been imprisoned in a labour camp (1975–87) for publicising the cases of the USSR's human rights prisoners. Kovalyov denounced the 1994 invasion of Chechnia and resigned in 1996 accusing Yeltsin of authoritarianism.

In July 2002 Putin appointed Ella Pamfilova, who in 2000 had been the first woman to ever stand in a Russian presidential election, to chair the Commission. Ella Pamfilova had served as the Minister for Social Security (1991–94), but resigned over Yeltsin's policies and the Chechen war. She later went on to found the For Civic Dignity (Za grazhdanskoe dostoinstvo) political movement, which unsuccessfully contested the 1999 Duma election. The UCSMR worked with Pamfilova and For Civic Dignity and so in 2002 Ida Kuklina also joined the President's Commission for Human Rights. The Commission provides a forum for the UCSMR to demand increased pensions for disabled war veterans, the identification of missing persons and the dead, information about prisoners of war and the interned, accurate data on all war casualties and for an end to the practice of returning soldiers who have gone AWOL, to avoid abuse, to their units. In September 2004 Putin, who seems to have abandoned his 2002 Civic Forum initiative, transformed the Human Rights Commission into the Presidential Council for the development of civil society and human rights institutions, with the stated goal of 'strengthening social institutions'.[24] Although welcomed by Ella Pamfilova as a timely development, this new body could also be interpreted as a further attempt to co-opt and control civil society organisations and activities.

Lyudmila Alekseyeva, the chair of the Moscow Helsinki Group human rights NGO, while valuing the work that her own and other NGOs were able to do with the support of the Commission, believes that it is the day-to-day routine work supporting human rights groups and their activities out in the regions that is important. She argues that what Russians call a vertical, that is a top-down organisation, is vulnerable as it can easily be destroyed by removing its head. In contrast networks comprising independent organisations are more difficult to destroy[25] and are therefore a firmer foundation for civil society.

Human rights in Russia are in danger when their observation conflicts with the state's priorities. They are also endangered by a general lack of information among the population at large. International NGOs such as Amnesty International[26] and Human Rights Watch[27] have Russian branches, and the liberal political parties such as Yabloko[28] and the Radical Party[29] are committed to human rights. Russia also has its own NGOs, such as the human rights and historical organisation Memorial,[30] which was founded during Reconstruction, and the Andrei Sakharov Foundation,[31] which is dedicated to continuing the work of the eponymous former soviet dissident and human rights campaigner. There is also a very extensive and constantly updated website called Human Rights of Russia (Prava Cheloveka Rossii).[32] Nonetheless, outside the Russia intelligentsia there is a widespread lack of knowledge about human rights. For example in summer 2003, lawyers from the Russian Movement for Human Rights organised an event called 'Travelling from Ekaterinburg to Moscow to study the human rights situation in Russia's regions'.[33] They found that up to 90 per cent of Russians did not know how to defend their rights and that they did not even have a precise idea of what their rights were.

This does not mean that Russians submit willingly or unthinkingly to human rights abuses, but rather that they have been denied the necessary information and skills to defend their rights. This is where the Soldiers' Mothers are playing a vital role. Everyone in Russia comes into contact with conscription through a son, a grandson, a nephew, a cousin or a friend; this is the point at which human rights cease to be an abstract intellectual concept and become a tool to protect a loved one. A leaflet produced by the St

Petersburg Mothers' Organisation in 2002, for example, stresses the importance of knowing one's rights and using the law, not just for conscripts to resolve their individual problems but for the good of society as a whole. It declares that the only way 'to liberty and civil society in Russia' is by eradicating the totalitarian consciousness. It continues: 'Every single Russian citizen, every Russian family has to know about their rights and has to become an active member of society. Only pressure from below can guarantee a democratic development in Russia.'[34] The UCSMR and its sister organisation the Mother's Right Fund (Fond 'Pravo Materi') are therefore seeking to create a human rights discourse in Russia rather than basing their activities on an already existing and widely accepted ideological foundation.

From soviet women's emancipation to mother heroines

The Bolsheviks were committed to women's emancipation and their enjoyment of the same civic rights and access to education as men; women were also encouraged to enter the labour force. Abortion was legalised, divorce was made easier, marriage became a civil rather than a religious contract and cohabitation was recognised. In the early 1920s the Bolsheviks were generally hostile to the family; women were to be defined not 'as wives, but by their work and activity outside the home'.[35] In 1919 the Bolsheviks set up a Women's Department (Zhenotdel), of the Central Committee Secretariat which stood at the apex of a network of women's departments throughout the country. The purpose of the Zhenotdel was to educate women, encourage them to participate in the public sphere and to protect women's interests. The Zhenotdel was headed by Russian feminists, first Inessa Armand and on her death in 1920 by Aleksandra Kollontai, who challenged the essentialist assumption that underpinned the prevailing gender stereotypes. In fact at no point were these assumptions questioned by the Bolshevik and then CPSU leadership. In 1930 Stalin closed the women's departments, declaring the 'Woman Question' to be solved, meaning that as women now enjoyed freedom and equality with men they no longer needed their own organisations.

Through the 1920s there was an increasing moral panic about growing social instability. Many soviet women had good reason to believe that the Bolsheviks' marriage and family reforms had made it easier for men to evade their responsibilities and had merely added to women's burdens. By the mid-1930s many of the early Bolshevik initiatives were reversed, the traditional family was exalted and pro-natalist policies were adopted. Divorce was made more difficult, legal marriage rather than cohabitation was championed, and abortion was outlawed again. A new system of medals was introduced to recognise the achievements of the mothers of large families. Motherhood medals were awarded to mothers of five or six children, Motherhood Glory medals to mothers of seven or eight children and Mother Heroine medals to mothers of ten or more children. The new stress was on the strong soviet family as the nucleus of soviet society and women were depicted as inherently nobler than men, capable of great self-sacrifice and as the pillar of the family.[36] In the 1930s the CPSU began to organise new bodies called women's soviets or councils (*zhensovety*), which were designed to draw women into gender-stereotypical social welfare activities such as work with children and vulnerable families, and mass political work and the mobilisation of women to fulfil the party's economic plans. The rapid economic developments of the 1930s and the demands of the war drew even more women into the labour force and public activities. The huge losses of the war meant that post-war women were expected to replenish the population, maintain the family and be economically, politically and socially active.

Democratisation, motherhood and the 'womanly mission'

The women's soviets developed rapidly under Khrushchev's leadership (1953–64) but were reduced to a merely formal existence under Brezhnev (1964–82).[37] At the 27th Party Congress in 1987, Gorbachev called for the reactivation of the women's councils in order to help women fulfil their 'womanly mission'. Just as the 1930s had witnessed a conservative reaction to the instability of the 1920s, during the disruption of Reconstruction and in post-Communist Russia the high divorce rate, growing juvenile delinquency and alcoholism are all attributed to 'women's absence from the family'.[38] Gorbachev, for example, noted that in the quest to make women equal to men in everything, 'we failed to pay attention to women's specific rights and needs arising from their role as mother and home-maker, and indispensable educational function as regards children'.[39] and that 'we have discovered that many of our problems – in children's and young people's behaviour, in our morals, culture and in production – are partially caused by the weakening of family ties and slack attitude to family responsibilities'.[40] He noted that the country was now debating what should be done 'to make it possible for women to return to their purely womanly mission'.[41] The combination of a tradition of gender stereotyping, panic over social crises, economic dislocation during marketisation and a demographic crisis threatening Russian genocide, have all contributed to calls for women to concentrate on their natural role as wives and mothers for the good of Mother Russia. The positive image of mothers and motherhood combined with a tradition of women's social and political activism has provided Russian women with a maternal path into politics. The Soldiers' Mothers have exploited this path in order to promote a human rights agenda and women's citizenship, and in so doing they are challenging the Russian state in the traditionally non-women's areas of war and military reform, and helping to preserve Russia's civil society during Putin's 'managed democracy'.

Soldiers' Mothers, the development of women's citizenship and democratisation

Reconstruction and the beginning of independent maternal politics

The Red Army was always depicted as one of the great prides and strengths of the USSR. Twice a year the latest groups of conscripts would be treated to a festive send-off from their home towns and villages before they embarked on their two-year compulsory service. During Reconstruction, the armed forces were subjected to the unflattering scrutiny of glasnost (openness), which revealed that the reality of service life was far from the propaganda ideal. Conscripts were routinely subjected to a form of institutionalised bullying known as *dedovshchina. Dedovshchina* derives from the word *ded* or grandfather, because it is the grandfathers or conscripts in their second year of service who were and still are the main perpetrators of this abuse, although officers may also be involved. *Dedovshchina* includes a wide range of practices such as beatings, rape, murder, extortion of cigarettes and alcohol, and the use of new recruits as 'serf' labour.[42] *Dedovshchina* leads to deaths and conscripts committing suicide to avoid further abuse.

In 1989 the journalist Veronika Marchenko began a series of articles in the newspaper *Yunost* (Youth) about the deaths of soldiers during peacetime and mothers responded by sending Marchenko stories about the deaths of their sons. This led in June 1990 to the establishment of a charitable organisation called the Mother's Right Fund (Fond 'Pravo Materi') to defend the rights and interests of parents whose sons died in the army during peacetime.[43] The Moscow Group of the Soldiers' Mothers Committee organised a demonstration outside the Kremlin and demanded protection for their sons. Gorbachev met their representatives and issued a presidential decree in 1990 on 'Measures to Implement Proposals from the Committee of Soldiers' Mothers', which stressed the need to investigate injuries and deaths among service personnel, ordered the partial disbandment of the army's notoriously brutal military-construction battalions and stressed the use of law to protect soldiers' rights.[44] A commission was set up to investigate these problems and the UCSMR obtained the right to be present at the post-mortems of soldiers killed through *dedovshchina* and to investigate living conditions in twenty-two military units.[45] These inspections marked a tentative step in the opening up of the armed forces to civilian scrutiny. In 1992, the first year of the new Russian Federation's existence, the Mothers held hunger strikes and demonstrations outside government buildings to support their demand for the abolition of conscription, for the armed forces to be held judicially accountable for their actions and for the unit commander of any soldier or sailor who died to be discharged.

From co-option to reclaiming motherhood

In the late 1980s the Soldiers' Mothers initially worked closely with military committees and officials at the local level and sometimes the Mothers' offices were even located in the local military headquarters.[46] This can be seen as an attempt to co-opt and channel the Mothers' activities into the social welfare functions that soviet women's organisations had traditionally performed. While championing the family and motherhood, the leadership had also hijacked this imagery to serve its own propaganda aims. For example, mothers of soldiers killed during the Afghan War were encouraged to deliver speeches on international solidarity rather than to show their personal pain.[47] The imagery was of mothers making the ultimate maternal sacrifice, the loss of a child, in the interest of international solidarity. Ella Polyakova of the St Petersburg Soldiers' Mothers Organisation argues that far from strengthening the family, in reality the CPSU used military service to try to destroy it and so consolidate its own power.[48] This is an analysis of the soviet system which stresses the attempt to destroy or control institutions between the individual and the Communist party-state. The development of maternal politics therefore involves the liberation of the concept of motherhood from the one promoted by the CPSU, to build upon the soviet tradition of stressing the family and mother-love, but to use these sentiments to promote a human rights and democratisation agenda.

The Mothers' organisations use essentialist arguments about the nature of women and their role, namely that women are responsible for life. For example, the slogans of the 'Black Kerchief, Day of Children's Protection' collective action, which was held in 1992 to find out why soldiers were dying in peacetime, included 'To save her son is the mother's duty' and 'Let's protect our sons'. The St Petersburg Soldiers' Mothers also use very strong religious symbolism, including the Icon of God's Mother of Kazan and the Mother's Prayer. Similarly, the Mother's Right Fund uses the imagery of a Madonna-like woman cradling a child on the front cover of its books of remembrance of dead soldiers entitled 'One Hundred from a Thousand'.[49] The Soldiers' Mothers use the symbolism of sacred, incorruptible mothers with the sole motivation of protecting their sons. In this way the traditional private sphere role of motherhood has provided an opening into the public, political arena. The championing of motherhood by both the soviet and now the Russian states, has provided women with a powerful tool with which to challenge the state and its armed forces.

Overcoming totalitarianism: you are a citizen

The Soldiers' Mothers Committees are organised into the Union of the Committees of Soldiers' Mothers of Russia.[50]

The St Petersburg Soldiers' Mothers Organisation, however, specifically rejects the name 'committee' as being too reminiscent of the party committees that formed the backbone of soviet totalitarianism. According to Ella Polyakova, the practice of people going to party committees to have their problems solved for them was part of the development of a slave mentality and the soviet system of control.[51] The St Petersburg Mothers, therefore, stress that they do not want to be a committee to which people come to have their problems solved, as this would just perpetuate the slave mentality and the power relations that form the basis of totalitarian control. This belief is also reflected in the St Petersburg Mothers' horizontal rather than vertical organisation.

The St Petersburg Mothers hold a twice-weekly School for Human Rights on Wednesday evenings and Saturday mornings, in addition to their thrice-weekly reception hours. A banner in the organisation's main meeting room declares 'School for Human Rights – We protect our sons'. Each school is attended by over 100 people and lasts several hours. (When I attended on 5 June 2002 there were an estimated 150 people present; over 95 per cent were mothers, with only a handful of fathers and a few young men.) The school takes the participants through their constitutional rights and the relevant laws. The participants were asked to share their knowledge and relevant experiences and to take turns in reading aloud the laws that were being discussed. The style was participatory rather than a lecture. There were certain repeated key refrains such as 'You are a citizen', 'You have rights', 'You pay taxes', 'Officials are supposed to serve the citizens' and 'Knowing your rights and the law makes you powerful'.

The St Petersburg Mothers also teach mothers how to conduct and present themselves as citizens in a democracy rather than as subjects of an authoritarian state. Mothers attending the human rights seminar were advised to make it clear that they know their rights, such as the legal requirement for an official to respond in writing within a given period to an approach from a citizen. Mothers were advised not to cry or to be emotional, not to plead for their sons, but to behave like well-informed citizens. The immediate motivation of the women attending the human rights school or contacting the various Mothers' committees and organisations is the looming threat of their son's conscription, or the need to find out how to help a son who has gone AWOL, or who is being abused. In so doing they are taking an important personal step in the development of Russian civil society and their own education as citizens. Only a handful of mothers go on to be volunteers or activists, but mothers have reported that the lessons learnt from the Soldiers' Mothers organisations have held them in good stead when dealing with bureaucrats, on for example, a housing issue.[52] The St Petersburg Mothers' Human Rights School in addition to providing practical information also feels like a consciousness-raising session.

The Soldiers' Mothers also train activists throughout the country. In 1999 the Moscow Research Centre on Human Rights, Committee of Soldiers' Mothers of Russia (CSMR) and the Mother's Right Fund published a book entitled *To Help the Regional Soldiers' Parents Organisations*.[53] The first part of the book, prepared by the CSMR, dealt with defending the rights of conscripts, service personnel and their parents; the second part, prepared by the Mother's Right Fund, concentrated on parents' rights; and the third part, written by Aleksei Bodungan, the Director of the Golubka (Dove) Training Centre, explained possible sources of funding and how to apply for them. Regional activists have also been brought to Moscow for training and seminars are held in the regions.

Overcoming totalitarianism: know your rights

The UCSMR and the Mother's Right Fund stress the empowering role of knowledge about citizens' rights, Russian law and the military and civil court systems. The Mother's Right Fund's publication *To the Parents of Dead Soldiers*,[54] for example, includes sample letters to the Procuracy and gives information about parents' pension and compensation rights, tax requirements and general entitlements. The Mother's Right Fund also provide free legal advice, financial assistance and psychological counselling to the families of dead soldiers.[55]

Similarly, a St Petersburg Mothers' leaflet states that its aim is 'to help people (and especially conscripts and recruits and their relatives) to protect their human rights to life and health by informing them on their constitutional rights and showing them how to make use of the laws that protect them, to get rid of the totalitarian consciousness and totalitarian slavery'.[56] Since 1997 the St Petersburg Mothers have published a regularly updated paperback handbook, *The Defence of the Rights of Draftees and Conscripted Service Personnel*,[57] which includes information about the legal framework of conscription, liability to conscription, alternative service, the court system and how to defend one's rights, sample letters, lists of useful acronyms, and explanations of the health and social grounds for exemption from conscription. They also published a small pamphlet, *Your Rights, Soldier*.[58] The Soldiers' Mothers played a leading role in the campaign for a law on alternative civilian service, so that young men can exercise their constitutional right to conscientious objection to military service. In 2002 the Duma passed a law and in 2003 Putin issued a presidential decree on alternative civilian service. However, under counter-pressure from the military, civilian service lasts three and a half years (rather than two years of military service) and may even take place on a military base. In 2004 the St Petersburg Mothers were awarded the Aachen Peace Prize for their 'courageous actions and efforts for more than 100,000 Russian conscientious objectors and deserters, as well as resistance against the dirty war in Chechnia'.[59] Approximately one thousand people ask the St Petersburg Mothers for legal advice each month. In the period 1991–2004 they provided legal advice to over 150,000 people, helped 100,000 conscripts to assert their legal right not serve in the armed forces, and helped more than 5,000 deserters to leave the army.[60]

The Soldiers' Mothers and the Chechen wars

In November 1994 Moscow sent troops to force Chechnia back into the Russian Federation. For the Soldiers' Mothers this meant that their peacetime campaigns against human rights abuses within the armed forces and for the democratisation of the armed forces, now had the added concern of the deployment of conscripts in a war zone. The UCSMR immediately took an anti-war stance, both because they opposed the war itself but also because they saw the war as a threat to Russian democracy. During the first Chechen war (1994–96) they encouraged mothers to support their sons' right to refuse military service and petitioned the government for the observance of the constitutional right to conscientious objection to military service. The UCSMR ran a weekly School for Conscripts, and during the first six months of the war received up to 200 letters a day and nearly 10,000 people came in person seeking information and support. The UCSMR also supervised a special military unit for the rehabilitation of deserters. One of the most high-profile activities of the UCSMR was the March of Mothers' Compassion in March 1995; this was a peace march to Chechnia by hundreds of mothers to bring their sons home. While in Chechnia the mothers also worked with the local Russian government and Chechen military officials to organise prisoner of war exchanges.

When the second Chechen war broke out in 1999 the UCSMR again took an anti-war stance and has worked with Russian and Chechen peace and human rights NGOs to call for an end to the war. Some mothers also travelled to the war zone to monitor the human rights situation and thereby challenge the Russian government's attempts to control information about the conflict. The UCSMR opposed the deployment of conscripts in the war zone and challenged the official war casualty figures using data provided by its regional committees. According to the Ministry of Defence, by 25 January 2000, 1,173 Russian soldiers were dead and 3,487 wounded in the 'anti-terrorist operation in Chechnia'. The UCSMR immediately countered that 3,500 servicemen had been killed and that if the military actions in neighbouring Dagestan were included the figure rose to 6,000. The UCSMR also revealed that soldiers missing in action were routinely being defined as deserters to keep the casualty figures artificially low.[61] The Soldiers' Mothers have moved a long way from their earlier welfare activities to revealing human rights abuses within the armed forces, challenging the official accounts of the war, calling for the constitutional right to conscientious objection to be honoured, for military reform to end conscription, and for the creation of a professional army.

'Whoever pays for a girl's dinner dances with her'

The Russian state cannot openly condemn women for doing what it has told them to do, which is to look after their children. However, 'administrative measures' are increasingly employed to harass and frustrate the work of NGOs, including Soldiers' Mothers. The St Petersburg Mothers had a

Chechen War Veterans organisation housed in the same building for a while and the police actively check the papers of young men in the vicinity of their offices. The St Petersburg Mothers have also been threatened with legal action: for example, in January 2003 Igor Lebed, the military prosecutor for the Leningrad Military district, accused the St Petersburg Mothers of spreading lies and promoting desertion from the armed forces and therefore encouraging crime. Also in 2003 the St Petersburg Prosecutor's Office sent a letter to the St Petersburg Soldiers' Mothers, stating that their use of religious posters and icons did not correspond to the group's charter and gave them one month to comply or change their charter.[62] The St Petersburg Mothers have also been told that they must vacate their rented premises as the building is going to be turned into a hotel; however, none of the other tenants have received similar notifications. These are all attempts to frustrate the Mothers' work and to tie them up in red tape and bureaucracy, while not actually challenging their right to exist and function.

In his 26 May 2004 State of the Nation Speech, Putin attacked the integrity and motivation of particular organisations by distinguishing between constructive organisations working to defend the real interests of the people, and those concerned with gaining funding from 'foreign foundations' and 'dubious groups and commercial interests'.[63] Soldiers' Mothers committees have received foreign funding for their work; in 2003 one regional committee received 40,000 euros from the European Commission, and another regional committee received the same sum in 2004.[64] The Soldiers' Mothers are open about their sources of finance but it does leave them vulnerable to attack. In October 2004, Viktor Alksnis, a Duma deputy for the nationalist Rodina (Homeland) party and a retired Air Force officer, accused the UCSMR of being an agent of its foreign financial backers. He is reported to have told the independent radio station Ekho Moskvy (Moscow Echo) that 'Whoever pays for a girl's dinner dances with her.'[65] He accused them of seeking to undermine the armed forces' defence capability by encouraging desertion and conscription dodging.

In a 2004 survey of women's opinions conducted by Yuri Levada's Analytical Centre, 72 per cent of respondents stated that the Committee of Soldiers' Mothers is good for

Russia and only 5 per cent believe that the Committee is serving western interests and weakening the country's defensive capability. It is the belief of 9 per cent that the Soldiers' Mothers' work does 'neither good nor harm' and 14 per cent found it difficult to answer. In response to the question: 'How would you regard the Committee of Soldiers' Mothers acting as a mediator in negotiations between Federal forces and Chechen militants?', 65 per cent responded positively, and 15 per cent gave a strong or a rather negative response.[66] These results suggest that the Soldiers' Mothers continue to be viewed positively by the majority of Russians, despite attacks on their integrity by politicians and armed forces chiefs.

Conclusion: Soldiers' Mothers – a social movement and a political party?

The soviet tradition of women's activism particularly in social and welfare issues, combined with the dominance of essentialist arguments about women's natural role as mothers, has provided Russian women with a path into politics. The Russian state by continuing conscription has also unwittingly provided an issue which has mobilised thousands of women who might otherwise have not become involved in challenging the Russian state. Women who contact the Soldiers' Mothers are typically those who lack the skills or the personal contacts and networks to be able to solve their problems without advice and support. The motivation of protecting a son propels these women into seeking what is in effect a crash course in democratic citizenship. The strength of the Soldiers' Mothers is their network of committees, which provide Russian mothers with the information, skills and an organisation through which they can seek to protect their sons.

The activities of the Soldiers' Mothers are part of a broader democratisation and constitute an important part of the development of Russia's civil society. The Soldiers' Mothers have managed to work with and within bodies such as the Presidential Commission on Human Rights to achieve their aims, while simultaneously preserving their independent activities. The vote for Russia's main liberal parties collapsed in the December 2003 elections, resulting in a Duma dominated by pro-Putin political parties. In response to this in January 2004, Ida Kuklina announced that the Soldiers' Mothers intend to set up a new pro-democracy political party called the United People's Party of Soldiers' Mothers. The stated purpose of the new party is to defend the rights of children and women, promote progressive social and economic programmes, and according to UCSMR Executive Director Valentina Melnikova, it will fight to ensure that 'the authorities respect their obligations towards citizens'.[67] The Soldiers' Mothers began as essentially a welfare organisation, and then also became a human rights organisation campaigning to end the Chechen wars, for conscripts' rights and for military reform. The foundation of a political party provides another organisation through which Soldiers' Mothers, as well as liberals and democrats, may enter politics and challenge Putin's ability to manage democracy.

Notes

1 O. Lipovskaia, 'New women's organisations' in M. Buckley (ed.), *Perestroika and Soviet Women* (Cambridge: Cambridge University Press, 1992), p. 76.

2 Statute of Soldiers' Mothers Organisation quoted by E. Zdravomyslova, 'Peaceful initiatives: Soldiers' Mothers movement in Russia', *Centre for Independent Social Research, St Petersburg*, www.indepsocres.spb.ru/zdrav2.htm

3 The Right Livelihood Award, 'Roll of honour: the Committee of Soldiers' Mothers of Russia (CSMR), 1996', *Right Livelihood Award* website, www.rightlivelihood.se/recip/csmr.htm

4 Personal communication to the author from a representative of the Open Society Organisation St Petersburg, 16 June 2002.

5 Cited by F. Mereu, 'What women want: a seat in the Duma', *The Moscow Times*, 17 September 2003, www.themoscowtimes.com

6 M. Arbatova quoted by Mereu, 'What women want'.

7 Cited by S. Salmenniemu, 'Democracy without women? The Russian parliamentary elections and gender equality', *Baltic Database for Business and Public Administration* website, 7 November 2003, www.balticdata.info/russia/elections/russia_elections_suvi.htm

8 Moskovskaia Khel'sinskaia Gruppa, 'Discrimination against women in the sphere of electoral rights', Moscow Helsinki Group website, www.mhg.ru/english/1EBF2E5

9 Salmenniemu, 'Democracy without women?'.

10 'Women's Movement of Russia', *Open Women Line Information Portal*, www.owl.ru/win/women/wmr/indexe.htm

11 OSCE, 'Russian Federation Election to State Duma 7 December 2003, Preliminary Report', 8 December 2003, *OSCE* website, www.osce.org/documents/odihr/2003/12/1629_en.pdf

12 OSCE, 'Russian Federation Presidential Election 14 March 2002, Preliminary Conclusions', Moscow, 15 March 2004, *OSCE* website, www.osce.org/documents/odihr/2004/03/2283_en.pdf

13 Memorial Society website, www.memo.ru/eng/index.htm

14 Amnesty International, 'Justice for everybody: human rights in the Russian Federation', www.amnesty.org/russia/russia.html and ' "Dedovshchina": the violent and cruel treatment of young recruits in the Russian army', www.amnesty.org/russia/soldiers_feature.html

15 Women and Eastern Europe Group, *Women and Russia: First Feminist Samizdat*, (London: Sheba Feminist Publishers, 1980).

16 Lipovskaia, 'New women's organisations', p. 72.

17 D. Duhaček, 'Eastern Europe' in A. M. Jaggar and I. M. Young (eds), *A Companion to Feminist Philosophy* (Oxford: Blackwell, 1998), pp. 131–132.

18 Women's Information Network (Zhenset), www.owl.ru/eng/women/aiwo/zhenset.htm

19 Consortium of Women's Non-Government Associations, www.wcons.org.ru/eng/main.php

20 Information Centre of the Independent Women's Forum (ICIWF), www.owl.ru/eng/women/org001/index.htm

21 Personal communication to the author from Ella Polyakova of the St Petersburg Soldiers' Mothers Organisation, 11 June 2002.

22 The Constitution of the Russian Federation is available on-line at the Bucknell University website, www.departments.bucknell.edu/russian/const/constit.html

23 The Council of Europe website includes information about the observance of human rights in Russia, www.coe.int/DefaultEN.asp

24 'Putin orders funding for international HR center', *MosNews*, 27 September 2004, www.mosnews.com/news/2004/09/27/hrfunding. shtml

25 L. Alekseyeva, 'Networks are better than Verticals', *Moscow News*, 12 November 2004, www.mosnews.com/commentary/2004/11/12/human rights.shtml

26 Amnesty International's Russian website, www.amnesty.org.ru/rus/index-rus

27 Human Rights Watch website, http://hrw.org/doc?t=europe&c=russia

28 Yabloko party website includes statements about their human rights policies, www.eng.yabloko.ru/

29 The (Transnational) Radical Party is organised in a number of countries including Russia, where it has taken a strong anti-Chechen war stance, www.radikaly.ru.org/

30 Memorial Human Rights Organisation website, www.memo.ru/

31 A. Sakharov Foundation website, http://asf.wdn.com/

32 Human Rights of Russia website, www.hro.org/actions/index.php

33 V. Melnick, 'Russians do not think about their rights. The majority of Russians do not even think about defending their rights', *Pravda.Ru*, 3

June 2003, available through *Johnson's Russia List*, 2:4, June 2003, www.cdi.org/russia/johnson/7208-2.cfm

34 St Petersburg Soldiers' Mothers Organisation, Leaflet, Geneva, May 2002.

35 S. Fitzpatrick, *Everyday Stalinism* (Oxford: Oxford University Press, 1999), p. 156.

36 *Ibid.*, p. 143.

37 Genia Browning, 'The zhensovety revisited' in Mary Buckley (ed.), *Perestroika and Soviet Women* (Cambridge: Cambridge University Press, 1992), p. 98.

38 Lipovskaia, 'New women's organisations', p. 72.

39 Mikhail Gorbachev, *Perestroika* (London: Collins, 1988), p. 117.

40 *Ibid.*, p. 117.

41 *Ibid.*

42 Human Rights Watch, 'The wrongs of passage: inhuman and degrading treatment of new recruits in the Russian Armed Forces', *Human Rights Watch Report*, 2004, www.hrw.org/reports/2004/russia1004/index.htm. See also A. Politkovskaya, *Putin's Russia*, (London: The Harvill Press, 2004), trans. Arch Tait.

43 V. Marchenko, *Takaia armiia … Narusheniia prav cheloveka v vooruzhennykh silakh* (St Petersburg: Norma, 1995), p. 1.

44 Lipovskaia, 'New women's organisations', p. 77.

45 B. J. Vallance, 'Russia's Mothers: voices of change (Committee of Soldiers' Mothers of Russia)', *Minerva: Quarterly Report on Women and the Military* (Fall–Winter 2000), p. 17.

46 E. Zdravomyslova, 'Peaceful initiatives: Soldiers' Mothers Movement in Russia', www.indepsocres.spb.ru/zdrav2.htm

47 M. Liborakina, 'Women fight to be heard in Chechen war dialogue', *ISAR: Initiative for Social Action and Renewal in Eurasia*, www.isar.org/isar/archive/ST/Chechwomen44.html

48 Personal communication to the author from Ella Polyakova of the St Petersburg Soldiers' Mothers Organisation, 11 June 2002.

49 V. Marchenko has produced several books of remembrance for the Mother's Right Fund including *Kniga Pamiati: Sto iz tysch*, vol.1 (Moscow: Fond 'Pravo Materi', Izvestiia, 1992); collected vols 2–3 in 1994; collected vols 4–7 published by the Fond 'Pravo Materi', Pravo Cheloveka, 2000.

50 The Union of the Committees of Soldiers' Mothers of Russia website, www.ucsmr.ru/english/ucsmr/hra.htm

51 Personal communication to the author from Ella Polyakova of the St Petersburg Soldiers' Mother Organisation, 11 June 2002.

52 *Ibid.*

53 *V pomoshch' regional'nym organizatsiiam soldatskikh roditelei* (Moscow: Prava Cheloveka, 1999).

54 Veronika A. Marchenko (ed.) *Roditeliam pogibshikh soldat* (Moscow: Fond 'Pravo Materi', Sovety Iurista, prava cheloveka, 1997).

55 The Mother's Right Fund, *Civil Society International* website, www.civilsoc.org/nisorgs/russwest/moscow/mright.htm. Marchenko, *Takaia armiia*.

56 St Petersburg Soldiers' Mothers Organisation, Leaflet (Geneva, May 2002).

57 Human Rights Organisation 'Soldiers' Mothers of St Petersburg', *Zashchita prav Prizyvnika i voennosluzhhashhchego po prizyvu* (St Petersburg: Tuskarora, 10th edn, 2003).

58 Human Rights Organisation 'Soldiers' Mothers of St Petersburg', *Tvoi prava, soldat* (St Petersburg: Tuskarora, 2001).

59 Aachen Peace Prize, 'The Aachen Peace Prize 2004 is awarded to Eren Kekskin (Turkey) and the Soldiers' Mothers of St Petersburg (Russia)', 1 September 2004, www.aachener-friedenspreis.de/english/english.html

60 *Ibid.*

61 These figures are taken from an interview with Valentina Melnikova, an executive secretary of the Union of Committees of Soldiers' Mothers by Zoya Svetova, 'Do we still not know how much is too much?', *Noviye Izvestiia*, 29 January 2000, pp. 1 and 4.

62 'Soldiers' Mothers under pressure in Putin's home town', RFE/RL Newsline, vol. 70, no 140, Part 1, 25 July 2003, www.hrvc.net/news6-03/26d-7-2003.htm

63 'Vladimir Putin discredits NGOs', Federation Internationale des Ligues des Droits de L'Homme, 31 May 2004, www.fidh.org/article.php3?id_article=1177

64 S. Saradzhyan, 'Inquiry urged into Soldiers' Mothers', *The St Petersburg Times*, 22 October 2004, www.sptimesrussia.com/archive/times/1014/news/n_13978.htm

65 MosNews, 'Duma to investigate Soldiers' Mothers for undermining Russian Army', 20 October 2004, www.mosnews.com/news/2004/10/20/soldiers.shtml

66 Prima-News Agency, 'Russian women support Soldiers' Mothers', 10 November 2004, www.prima-news.ru/eng/news/news/2004/11/10/30147.html

67 AFP (Moscow), 'Russian anti-war NGO to set up new pro-Democracy party', 4 February 2004, available in RFE/RL's *(Un)Civil Societies*, vol. 5, no. 4, 5 February 2004, www.hrvc.net/news2004/5-2-04.html

7

Conclusions

SUSAN BUCKINGHAM, KAREN MORROW,
CATHERINE DANKS, GERALDINE LIEVESLEY
AND MARION ROBERTS

Although only two of the authors are professionally involved in spatial analyses (as a geographer and an urban designer), two spatial nexus have spontaneously informed much of this book's arguments: the relationship between public and private space, and that between the local, national and global. Contemporarily, both concepts are less spatially well-defined and are affected by diverse ideologies, processes and technologies. This chapter will explore each nexus in turn to attempt to summarise how women's citizenship finds expression.

As Chapter 1 demonstrated, the original western concept of citizenship was very much grounded in the public and the national and those who habituated these activity spaces were both the architects and the beneficiaries of citizenship. The burdens of domestic life have historically excluded the vast majority of women from officially sanctioned 'legitimate' activity, thus appearing to confirm citizenship as a male prerogative. At the same time, the intrusion of public affairs into apparently private spaces created and continues to create circumstances which impel women to make claims upon citizenship, that is to seek to appropriate it as their own and to fashion it to their demands. The chapters in this book discuss a wide range of situations where women's citizenship is contested. Although the authors sometimes employ different terminologies and nuances, what emerges is a remarkable commonality of issues. We are all concerned with citizenship as offering an opportunity to have control over our environments whether they be our physical surroundings (natural and built), what happens within our families and local communities, and what occurs at the national and global levels of life. Some situations open up opportunities for women to rework the terrain of citizenship, adapting or transforming known templates in order to suit them to their needs. In other situations, women are impeded from obtaining such outcomes by a variety of structural restraints – physical, political, cultural, legal, socio-economic and spatial.

Public/private spaces

Any discussion of the concept of citizenship will typically initially focus on legal definitions of who is a citizen, then broadening this out to link citizenship with issues of suffrage (basic voting rights), of political efficacy, access to welfare provisions and social and environmental justice. It is increasingly recognised, as the foregoing chapters have shown, that the effective exercise of citizenship requires not only political commitment but also full social, economic, environmental and cultural underpinning. The elasticity of the term and its significance in all areas of life brings to mind the 1970s feminist slogan 'the personal is the political', which signalled a broader understanding of what is political citizenship. What is understood by 'the personal' is also highly variable. In North America and Western European countries, it tended to be interpreted as to do with such issues as contraception, sexuality and the impact of pornography. Studies of women outside these geographical areas (or of minority religious and ethnic groups within them) have alerted us to how culturally specific these definitions of 'personal' are. Increasingly, also, we can recognise that such personal issues are remarkably permeable to penetration by the public and the commercial (think, for example, of abortion legislation, or the trialling of the contraceptive pill on poor Third World women).

This raises questions about the nature of women, particularly contrasting ideas about their essential nature with concepts of the social construction of womanhood and femininity. To argue that women are doing something 'as women' or 'as mothers' can give these women's activities some kind of 'legitimacy' and an issue around which they can organise and mobilise in the public arena, as Catherine Danks' chapter on Soldiers' Mothers in Russia illustrates. Motherhood forms a bridge between public and private worlds. Essentialist arguments about the nature of women seem at odds with legal-liberal concepts of citizenship which stress individual rights of citizens and argue that differences that might exist (religious, ethnic, gender, sexual) are irrelevant to acquisition of citizenship. Clearly, the exercise of citizenship is profoundly affected by such differences, and women may find it useful to explore them. The danger is that essentialist arguments about women (and men) could (and have been) hijacked to restrict, rather than promote, women's citizenship.

As with all dualisms, the public has always been defined by its opposite and has been characterised by its domination by customarily defined 'heads of household' in paid work: adults, politicians, waged or salaried workers, men. As women have entered paid work in increasing numbers, they have laid claim to public space. Working-class women in low-income households have, of course, consistently undertaken paid work, often within the home space, and usually in poor environmental and health and safety conditions, during eras in which it was considered unseemly for women from middle-class and wealthy households to do so. It could be argued that it is the incursion of middle-class and educated women into the paid workforce that has forced the pace of these claims. (Although see Marion Roberts' identification of working-class women's role in the Glasgow rent strike in Chapter 4.) Sometimes these claims have been a by-product of their economic activities and the changed life-styles these produce and sometimes this claim has been a deliberate political action such as the 'Reclaim the Night' marches in the UK and North America in the 1980s. Arguably these activities, though highly visible and public, were organised to protect that most private of spaces, the body, which, in itself, emphasises the overlap between the public and private.

That most intimate space, the body, is also the site of some of the most rehearsed claims for women's rights and exercise of women's citizenship. In Chapter 5, Geraldine Lievesley vividly examines the ways in which women's bodies are used: through rape and mutilation by the military to establish power over women and indigenous communities in Mexico; by the prohibitions on women's rights to contraception and abortion in Catholic-dominated countries such as El

Salvador; and by the contradictory idealisation of women as bearers of children alongside the objectification of their bodies to sell commodities. Women have frequently used these violations and stereotypes to challenge authority and campaign for economic and representative parity, reproductive freedom and protection from violence, both domestic and state. Indeed, as both Lievesley and Danks respectively demonstrate, the position of mothers of 'the disappeared' has been a powerful mobilising force for some women in Latin America and Russia. Thus the locality of the body represents a primal organising space for women's citizenship status and an umbilical link into the collective spaces of the neighbourhood, community, workplace, civil society, the state and the globalised political economy.

Women have taken their grievances into a range of locations, the diversity of which is important if these are to be successfully addressed. While it is important for women to capture state politics, it is not sufficient: women's mobilisation through social movements of varying degrees of formality raises issues that a gender-sensitive state can take up, but rarely initiates. Moreover, the very process of community mobilisation, as both Susan Buckingham and Lievesley demonstrate in their chapters, is empowering as a mechanism for constructing citizenship. It is exactly the multiplicity of women's lives – as mothers, carers, domestic workers, neighbourhood activists, and paid workers – that provides the platform for an equal variety of social action. Women have been adept at taking (or subverting) stereotypical home-based activities and turning them into political protest. In addition to the 'mothers' movements already referred to, there are many other examples which infuse this book, including women's role as household cook (see Chapter 5) and shopper/food provisioner (see Buckingham's use of activities by the Women's Environmental Network in Chapter 3). A recent book published by the editor of a New York based self-styled 'Third Wave feminist' magazine has even pressed knitting into service as a 'good as any way' to illustrate gender inequities.[1]

Just as there has been an intrusion of the private into the public arena, conversely, there has been considerable infiltration of the public into the private, so that it is increasingly difficult to consider each as a discrete space, with its own bounded activity. Feminists have long critiqued the public/ private boundary as artificial, citing a history of women in paid work, and therefore presence in the public realm, and the power of men in the private realm underscored by often neglected and, until very recently, unpoliced, domestic violence. This is violence which increases in times of economic, environmental and political turmoil. An early twenty-first-century manifestation, however, takes the public/private imbrication a stage further. As Roberts writes in Chapter 4, the private space of the home is now the site of many 'public' activities, mostly made possible by information and communications technology, such as working from home, internet shopping and electronic voting. At the same time, she describes people escaping these new demands of the home space to find peace in public space, and non-work discussions on the street. However, for women, 'the street' and the community have been powerful crucibles in which citizenship battles have been fought, although as Roberts points out, the early twentieth-century street as a positive 'women's space' was contradictorily a space for both support and for censure.

Local/national/global

Another spatial theme that has emerged through this book is the relationship between local, national and global spaces, although not necessarily in a linear fashion. Just as Roberts' investigation of the use of ICT reveals the porosity of the public/private boundary, so does it reveal its power to enable women to make global connections. It is through IC technology that women have been able to make contact across national boundaries through such organisational processes as the Latin American and Caribbean Feminist meetings (Lievesley) and the UN, particularly the preparatory committees that underpin UN conferences (Lievesley and Karen Morrow).

Global economic processes have significant impact on local areas and national legislation and therefore on the lives of women. This is through both the geographical mobility of multinational companies (particularly those involved in the assembly of consumer products in the *maquiladoras* of Latin

America and other export processing and enterprise zones in the world), and structural adjustment programmes which have been introduced to 'rescue' national, indebted, economies and which inevitably transfer a significant amount of 'care work' back into the home and to the responsibility of women. Much of the social action that women have engaged with in the Third World has involved challenging this reliance on their unpaid work and has served to politicise women.

The dominant paradigm of neo-liberalism has changed the relationship between state and civil society and introduced a minimalist definition of the public sphere involving a diminution of the role of the state and an increase of market intrusion into social life. As state involvement has decreased, civil society has been expected to move into the gap. Arguably, civil society could be said to be redefining citizenship, again emphasising its collective and communitarian aspects as a reaction to the rampant individualism of the currently dominant market-based neo-liberal paradigm. Citizenship rights have been interpreted in an increasingly individualist manner with citizens defined as market participants rather than social beings, and national governments withdrawing their obligations to provide for them. The privatisation of social provision (under the aegis of neo-liberal structural adjustment) in Third World and many other societies means that women's endeavours must be focused upon the substitution of that provision at the local level, itself a stressful and precarious activity and one which will affect their perceptions of what citizenship and the democratic experience means to them.

The official locations of political activity – principally at the level of the nation state – may never have been best suited to address women's interests and, furthermore, women act as citizens in ways quite diverse from conventionally identified ones. Women mobilising within social movements at the local level are expected to learn how to operate in the institutional arena, using the appropriate channels and acting out what are seen as acceptable behaviours. If they fail to have an effect (such as, for example, changing policy and legislative agendas), they are seen as failures. However, social movements also create their own networks and distinct public spaces, which are not based in and do not share the aspirations of the official arena. Women engaged in these forms of activity are rewriting the boundaries between the public and private and are engaged in redefining the concept of democratic citizenship. For women, dealing with the state has always been particularly difficult because its institutions continue to be generally masculine preserves and its representatives often do not even recognise the validity of women's demands (the same could be said of the state's response to indigenous, disabled, gay and lesbian struggles). Thanks to the revolution in communications technology, women in grassroots social movements are also able to transcend national borders and construct global solidarity networks. For women dealing with global institutions, the obstacles of the latter's power and influence and their abdication of social responsibility are enormous but these mobilised poor women demonstrate remarkable resilience and fortitude.

Locating women's citizenship

Liberal citizenship theory should be regarded as problematic with respect to all groups, including women, who historically have been excluded from its purview and its practice. If citizenship is viewed as static and one-dimensional (that is tending to ignore the broad socio-economic and cultural in favour of the narrowly political and legalistic), it will not aim to facilitate civic activity and social progress. There is a need for an active meaning of citizenship based upon the notion of the common good not selfish individualism, and of acceptance and celebration of difference as vitalising democracy rather than inhibiting it. The issue of women's relationship to men with respect to the pursuit of rights needs to be considered here. Men are interested in many of the issues around which women mobilise: for example, fair trade, human rights, poverty and debt, environmental justice and sustainability, improved working conditions, peace and anti-racism. Can there be a shift to the withering of distinctions between the genders in the pursuit of common agendas or is the notion of people collectively mobilising for social justice inherently utopian? Taking a negative stance on this possibility, it must be admitted that there are restrictions upon the development of commonalities between women themselves. Social movements are not intrinsically egalitarian, stratified as they are by hierarchies of wealth, gender, race, age and sexuality. Women do not inherently agree what their interests are or how they should go about realising them. The divisions between women pose difficult questions. As Buckingham points out, women suffer the impacts of poor environmental quality disproportionately and the lowest-income women suffer it the most. Affluent women create degraded environmental conditions for poorer women through their use of cars. A similar contradiction applies to the issues of food production and consumption; western women expect to choose from a wide variety of fruit and vegetables in their supermarkets, produce which poor Third World women grow in arduous and often dangerous conditions and for which they receive meagre payment. In Chapter 5, Lievesley discusses the issue of the cultural imperialism of Western feminism which has impaired joint understandings and initiatives with poor latinas, and western women have been criticised for being insulated from the everyday concerns of the latter. Women's mobilisation is also vulnerable to the interventions of governments, NGOs, INGOs and global capital. The latter groups are in a position to shape the political, socio-economic, legal and cultural environment within which women have to act. It is also difficult to see how women's political organisation can move from the effective community or lobbying groups that have been potently described in these chapters to a mass movement. It is similarly true that a huge amount of energy goes into activist politics and creating a new climate for women's empowerment, but the achievements are incremental and results often disappointing. On the other hand, it could be argued that women are taking a more discriminating approach to citizenship in modern times, picking and choosing those issues with which they want to engage, the forums with which they deem working worthwhile and the levels of participation that they view as appropriate. This pragmatic approach to citizenship, far from being criticised for not fitting into traditional models, is to be praised as a practical response to the overwhelming levels of social complexity with which women are required to engage in the modern world. In addition, this act of self-definition with respect to citizenship, featuring selective and targeted engagement with issues of particular concern to women, could be seen to represent a form of empowerment as it promotes a view of citizenship founded in personal self-determination.

The authors of these chapters, in different ways, have combined their intellectual and academic interest in women and citizenship issues with activist roles in the broad field of social, political and environmental movements. Our academic and intellectual concerns are informed by this activism, as they are by our family circumstances, professional experiences and social networks. To conclude this conclusion, we each reflect on the personal and community dimensions which inflect our public academic work – both to acknowledge those influences, and as an illustration of the discussions we have had through the production of this book, and which have consequently helped to shape it. These discussions have helped us understand each other, and each other's disciplines, from which the ideas we communicate are drawn.

Personal reflections

Catherine Danks

I first went to the USSR in 1971 while still at school; I then studied politics and modern history as an undergraduate and soviet government and politics as a postgraduate. From 1971 to 1985, things in the Soviet Union were pretty stable, with no major political changes. From 1985 with the advent of perestroika, changes rapidly gained momentum and the USSR itself collapsed. For academics these changes have presented seemingly endless new research possibilities as archives have been opened and many of the former restrictions on research have been considerably eased. A more stimulating environment for researchers has, however, coincided with increased physical hardship and vulnerability for many Russian citizens.

It is one thing to examine concepts of democratisation, citizenship and civil society as intellectual concerns, it is quite another to sit in rooms with women who are not there as detached observers of democratisation in practice; they are there because they want to save their sons. It would be inhuman not to recognise their pain and not to question one's own motivations for being there. As a British academic,

I am subjected to the pressures of the Research Assessment Exercise (RAE) and as the next deadline approaches, I have to be concerned to have the requisite number of publications. I have to fulfil my research plan and I am very aware of how soviet that sounds. Interesting topics for which materials are available are the basis of a publishing and academic career. However, there is an ethical problem with conducting research into and building a career upon other women's misery. There is no simple answer to this question and I can only relate how Soldiers' Mothers reacted to me and no one condemned me. Instead all the women were keen that the 'world should know' about what they are doing and why they are doing it. My responsibility is to record what I observed and to honestly and openly interpret what is happening.

Karen Morrow

My participation in this project has been as the result of both personal and professional motives. I encountered Susan Buckingham at two conferences; one academic, the other community sector based and we found shared interests in crosscutting concerns between the very different disciplines of geography and law. The potential for developing a constructive dialogue taking environment and gender issues beyond subject disciplines into a cross-disciplinary context proved to be even more rewarding in practice than in principle. Discovering the breadth of shared concerns that we encountered and the links between issues raised in our separate disciplines and engaging in dialogue have served to make this book more than a mere sum of it parts.

On a personal level, I have a long experience of working with community groups and NGOs in the environment and planning sectors, helping in capacity building. My chief aim has been to facilitate their engagement with decision-making procedures that are ostensibly carried out in the public interest, but in which the public is often ill-equipped to participate. In these situations, women are most often marginalised. It has been my personal experience that, despite the advantages that education and familiarity with the law have given me, my voice is often (though not always) either drowned out by men, despite supposed equality of opportunity to participate, or simply not heard by overwhelmingly male decision-makers. These experiences have led me to recognise that, even in a western democratic context, our ability to effectively promote women's voices in respect of the environment is compromised by the implicitly gendered approaches to decision-making. The opportunity to participate is plainly not enough – women's participation must also be effective. It is my hope that this book, and others like it, will go some way to promoting discussion about how to meet that challenge.

Marion Roberts

I have never really recovered from the shock of moving from a middle-of-the-road straight-laced girls' grammar school in the 1960s to a male-dominated architecture course in an elite university in the 1970s. The transition from a culture of demure conformity to that of flamboyant egoism was abrupt and disruptive. Participating in this book forms part of a journey away from those two extremes of English education. Happily times have changed and the impact of feminism has made some impression on secondary education and on the built environment professions. Architectural education may still be focused on iconic buildings, but at least now there are (some) women designing them. The postgraduate planning students in my department are overwhelmingly female. Oh yes, and we have rediscovered urban design, the art of relationships between buildings.

Writing a chapter for this book enabled me to explore some of the contradictions I felt as a woman about the current politically correct agenda that is emerging for cities. Many men feel this too, but for me and I suspect for other women, it is particularly poignant. I love the freedom and security that driving a car gives me, but am aware that I am polluting others. I regret not being a mother and absolutely do not want to be tied to my neighbourhood, but hear my friends who are single parents and indeed, my mother, talk about the solidarities of their personal neighbourhoods.

Participating in this book has made me see urban design from another perspective. It provides support to what, from inside the professions, can still feel like a lonely position. It has been interesting also to find overlaps between my experiences as a political activist in a mainstream political party and the research of other feminists. It has reinforced my view that all women should walk free of violence and the threat of violence, whether within their homes or outside them and that is an essential prerequisite of citizenship.

Geraldine Lievesley

I participated in the writing of this book for a number of reasons. The first reason was born out of a long friendship with Susan Buckingham and I am glad we have finally managed to give life to this project rather than just talking about it in the late hours of the night. I was also attracted by the prospect of working with women from other academic disciplines. It is exciting to cross boundaries. While acknowledging the importance of each discipline's history and creation of knowledge, it is good to appreciate that, in terms of the creation of practical and inclusive feminism, such boundaries are intrinsically unnecessary. I write as a woman, a partner, a mother and an academic. I think it is vital to bring all these identities together in my writing. I am acutely aware of the different opportunities accorded my mother (growing up in rural Catholic Ireland), myself and my two daughters. I am also mindful of the privileged position I enjoy as a reasonably affluent, educated western woman in comparison with millions of women throughout the world. In my academic life, I have long been committed to research-ing on and lecturing about Latin America. When I first went to Peru to undertake my doctoral studies, I entered the hot-house and extremely masculine world of left-wing politics and, indeed, for many years I believed that 'the revolution' would solve the problems of both men and women. With age comes greater understanding. I do still believe, however, that the empowerment of women can only come about through collective struggles with women acting for themselves rather being acted upon by governments, political parties and the like.

Susan Buckingham

I like working collaboratively. I enjoy the camaraderie and the reassurance that comes with working with colleagues who share, and constructively challenge, my ideas of social and environmental justice. Some of my friends, Geraldine Lievesley high among them, have become valued colleagues; some of my colleagues have become good friends. The private–public divide in such conditions dissolves. Most of these friend-colleagues are women, but some are men. I come from a warm and supportive family dominated by women, which probably explains my gravitational pull towards working with women. The department in which I work is unusual in that the majority of its staff, including its senior staff, are women (60 per cent of staff, 80 per cent of senior staff), and I am strongly of the view that this makes a difference. The Women's Environmental Network, with whom I volunteer,[2] is another female space which benefits from a more cooperative and sensitive atmosphere than most more male-dominant environmental groups.

From time to time my undergraduate students give me pause to wonder whether, indeed, gender equality has been won (at eighteen fresh out of school where female students are outperforming male, or at twenty-one where female undergraduates are overtaking male in degree achievement, this is understandable[3]). As Geraldine Lievesley has already pointed out, our lives are qualitatively different to our mothers' and grandmothers', by orders of magnitude: politically, economically and socially. And yet, the most cursory readings of basic earnings data from the world's most economically 'advanced' countries reveal continued gross gendered inequalities.

Contrary to my own experience, the research I am currently engaged in examines the problems that women with dependent children face in accessing and progressing through training.[4] What has struck me most forcibly in this research is that, while UK government programmes encouraging women (particularly single mothers) into paid work, through training, are demanding wide-ranging accommodations that women need to make to juggle child-rearing, family care, domestic work and other paid work around training, their male partners (where they exist) make few such accommodations and expect to carry on their domestically supported lives as usual. These issues, and the inequalities discussed in this book, reinforce the fact that gender inequality is alive and well and shows little sign of abating. What inspires me, however, is the energy and commitment women apply in trying to overcome these personal, institutional and structural inequalities. While their gains may be small, they accrue. My life and work experience persuade me that, as Lipietz[5] has raised in the context of environmental change, there is a possibility that these 'micro-ruptures' in the structural edifice perpetuating inequalities can accumulate to create meaningful social change.

Notes

1 D. Stoller, *Stitch 'N Bitch Handbook* (New York: Workman Publishing, 2000). This information is taken from a *Guardian* magazine interview of Stoller by Zoe Williams (8 January 2004) in which Stoller and Williams agree that women's activities such as knitting have been downgraded and patronised while women have used them, usually intuitively, as a way of building links between women family members, friends and neighbours.

2 As this book is published, Susan Buckingham is Chair of the Board of Trustees of the Women's Environmental Network.

3 For research into the extent to which female students are outperforming male, see F. Smith, ' "It's not all about grades": accounting for gendered degree results in geography at Brunel University', *Journal of Geography in Higher Education*, 28:2 (2004), 167–178.

4 S. Buckingham, E. Marandet, F. Smith and E. Wainwright, *The Training Needs of Women with Children Under Five* (London: London West Learning and Skills Council, 2004). S. Buckingham, M. Diosi, E. Marandet, F. Smith and E. Wainwright, *Women's Progression through Training: From Socialisation to Qualification*, (London: London West Learning and Skills Council, 2005).

5 See A. Lipietz, 'Political ecology and the future of Marxism', *Capitalism, Nature, Socialism*, 11:1 (2000).

Index